AND THEY
WITNESS
LIGHT ACROSS THE SKY:
Belief in the age of UFOs

KEVIN
STORRAR

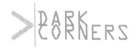

And They Witness Light Across the Sky: Belief in the Age of UFOs

Text and images © 2017 Kevin Storrar

First published 2017 by
Dark Corners Publishing, United Kingdom (This edition 2017)
Printed in San Francisco, California, USA

ISBN: 978-0-9894462-3-5

Typeset in Optima, courtesy of Hermann Zapf and the D Stempel AG
Foundry. Frankfurt, Germany

Contents

Acknowledgements

Many thanks to all those who have helped, supported and contributed toward the research and production of this book. In particular I would like to thank my wife Alaina for putting up with me spending numerous evenings working on research and artworks, and all other socially reclusive things that come with a project like this. I would also like to thank the TELAH Foundation for their insightful information, and willingness to discuss sensitive issues with someone who may not share their point of view about many a thing. A big thanks also to Steve Gronert Ellerhoff for not only proof-reading this document, but for years of stimulating conversations that have, in various ways, informed many aspects of the project.Thanks also to the numerous researchers, skeptics, UFOlogists, and believers who keep the subject alive, and who have provided much of the information that this book draws upon. For the boys, A & T.

KS 2017

I Might Be Wrong....
(An Introduction)

On the afternoon of Wednesday 26th March 1997, Deputy Sheriff Robert Brunk went over to investigate what he thought was probably a prank tip-off regarding a UFO cult known as Heaven's Gate. He arrived at 18241 Colina Norte, Rancho Santa Fe, a 9,200-square-foot mansion in an affluent area of San Diego, and found a side entrance unlocked. He and another officer entered to find thirty-nine dead bodies, each lying on beds in an orderly fashion. In the heat of the Californian spring many bodies had already started to decompose.

They were all dressed in identical black jumpsuits, most with a purple shroud over their heads, and each with an embroidered badge on their shoulder that read 'Heaven's Gate Away Team'. Under the shrouds it was found that each individual had a plastic bag over his or her head. They all had the same Nike shoes on, and all had the same short-cropped haircut. In each of their pockets were five dollars and three quarters and a 'Heaven's Gate' ID badge. Personal artifacts were neatly packed in bags beside each bed. Throughout the mansion were images of alien-human hybrids, and on one computer was flashing the text 'Red Alert'.

On further inspection police officers found hundreds of audiotapes and a dozen videos of the deceased cult members speaking to people they had left behind. The group had committed suicide in shifts between 22nd and 24th March, by consumption of applesauce laced with barbiturate washed down with vodka. Members had helped each other get into bed and position their bags and shrouds. Medical examiner Brian Blackbourne identified twenty-one women and eighteen men amongst the dead, with the cause of death confirmed as ingestion of phenobarbital. He also found that seven of the men had been castrated. As well as the 'Away Team' and 'Red Alert' references to *Star Trek*, it was found that one of the dead was Thomas Nichols, brother of the actress Nichelle Nichols, best known for her role as Uhura in the original *Star Trek* TV series.

The group was led by Marshall Applewhite, who had been among the dead. Through examination of video footage it became apparent that the aim of the group was to transfer to 'the next evolutionary level' and exit their bodies (or 'vehicles' as they called them) in order to join with a space ship, believed to be travelling behind the comet Hale-Bopp, which at the time was in close proximity to Earth. Applewhite encouraged obedience to the cause through a strong belief system, cultivated over years of sermonizing. His followers were not forced to stay physically with the cult, but mentally their perception of reality was molded to fit with the established beliefs developed by its leader. Members wore uniforms, had unified haircuts, changed their names, and were encouraged by Applewhite to begin every sentence with the phrase 'I could be wrong, but...' A subtle piece of enforced self-deprecation, allegedly to show modesty and humbleness, really served to erode any questioning of the dominant belief system. The Heaven's Gate incident remains the largest mass suicide to occur within the United States.

On 28th March that same year, Robert Nichols (no relation to Nichelle) committed suicide in the same way as the Heaven's Gate group members. He was not a member of the cult, but had left a suicide note stating, 'I am going on the spaceship with Hale-Bopp to be with those who have gone before me.'

Five weeks later, on 6th May, former Heaven's Gate members Wayne Cooke and Chuck Humphrey dressed in dark clothes, packed a bag each, placed five dollars and three quarters in their pocket and attempted suicide by ingesting phenobarbital. Cooke succeeded. Humphrey, who did not, decided he had been saved so he could proselytize, and soon after created his own website to dispense the Heaven's Gate theology. In February 1998 he drove into the Arizona desert, placed a plastic bag over his head and used his car's exhaust to fill his vehicle with carbon monoxide. He was dressed in black, with his 'fare' in his pocket and a purple shroud on the seat next to him.

Mark and Sarah King had left the Heaven's Gate group in 1987. However under the guise of TELAH (The Evolutionary Level Above Human) they act as a clearinghouse for the group's public image. TELAH replies to e-mails and maintains the group's archived material, teachings and intellectual property. Such continued devotion has involved lawsuits and legal appeals in an attempt to safeguard items belonging to the group, at a cost of around $375,000 to protect, archive and disseminate such a legacy over the last 20 years. Thanks to TELAH, www.heavensgate.com is still active, with the same 'Red Alert' message on its home page. The website includes hours of video footage recorded at various points between 1993 and 1997, mostly lectures by Applewhite, with copies of videos and collective writings still available to buy. The website acts as Applewhite's legacy, an archive to his belief system. It is there to guide other lost souls towards the evolutionary level above human, and today a small handful of Heaven's Gate believers still exist.

I have been in contact with TELAH, exchanging a number of messages and in turn gaining a fascinating insight into both the belief system, and the final events of the Heaven's Gate group. According to TELAH, interest in the group has grown in recent years from around a dozen daily emails to spikes of over 100 messages a day. But where do such ideas come from? What is the broader cultural context that allows individuals to adopt beliefs so beyond what many would consider rational? I am fascinated by the development of the cultural environment required for such groups to exist.

The Heaven's Gate group is without question an extreme manifestation of delusion, but variations of 'questionable belief' filter into the everyday, and everyone is susceptible to this to some degree. Whether it is a simple difference of opinion, misunderstanding of information, an unquestioning acknowledgement that some speak 'the truth'—religion, the media, marketing, political views, hearsay, gossip or folklore—we all no doubt 'believe' things that are inaccurate or outright wrong. Plus who is to say that some people who are considered delusional are not in fact correct? Perhaps the Heaven's Gate group really did join 'the next level' on a spaceship following Hale-Bopp. Rational thinking, dubious scientific plausibility and lack of any actual evidence seem to suggest that this is pretty unlikely, however on some level you can never really *really* know for absolute certainty. You cannot prove or disprove a negative—this is the zone they call 'belief'.

The belief in UFOs and aliens is a fringe belief, but it is a widely accepted fringe belief. In 2014 a National Geographic survey suggested that 77% of Americans believe that there are signs that aliens have visited Earth. 36% believe aliens had actually landed, and as many as 80% believe the Government was hiding evidence relating to UFO activity. If this study is only half right, then this still suggests that over 40 million American adults have a level of open mindedness toward a belief in UFOs.

In the United Kingdom a recent survey conducted by Opinion Matters, an independent research and consultancy agency, concluded that 10% of adults had reported a UFO sighting, 20% believed aliens had landed on Earth and that 52% believed UFO evidence had been covered-up. Another survey of 1000 people conducted by YouGov found 32% of those surveyed believed that they had experienced something they would class as 'paranormal', and 48% believed that some people had witnessed UFOs of extraterrestrial origin.

This book attempts to look at some of the reasons why such beliefs in the fantastical take hold, by examining the root cause of significant UFO cases that have captured the wider cultural imagination. Exploring this belief in the fantastical should also act as a reminder that people are susceptible to misinformation, and that if many can believe this, then what else could people believe?

I'm not wholly against the idea that other life exists somewhere out there in the vast almost infinite expanse of the known universe. In many ways it seems a somewhat grander claim that it doesn't. Considering the scale of just what we can observe, the idea that this tiny floating rock we live on is the only place where life exists would make us extraordinarily unique. Perhaps we are, perhaps we are not. In a sense this book isn't really about UFOs or flying saucers or aliens themselves. What I find fascinating is not the 'evidence' or imagery of any alleged UFO or alien, but the researchers, contactees, abductees, witnesses, hoaxers and investigative journalists who contribute to the concept of UFOs. It is within the minds, perceived experiences, statements and reports of these individuals that the UFO phenomenon exists, and within the belief of others who want, or need, to believe in such claims.

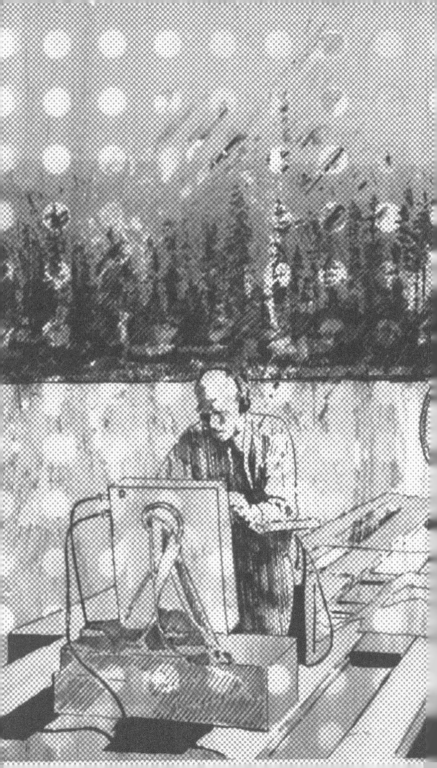

PART ONE
Flying Saucers Have Landed

A UFO claim now becoming known as The High Bentham Incident occurred in January 2005, when a family from Lancaster, England, was driving home from a restaurant. Rachel Devereux, her mother Anne, and her two young boys claimed they saw a bright light overhead whilst in the car. Anne later contacted local radio stations, making claims about the amazing bright light in the sky, and implying an extraterrestrial explanation for what they had seen. After hearing of the account UFO researchers Janet Walkey, and later Joe McGonagle, took interest in the story. The family was interviewed, and an initially skeptical Rachel Devereux was eventually convinced she'd seen something otherworldly after undergoing a hypnosis session, which itself featured as part of a TV documentary on UFOs. The Devereuxs claimed that the journey from the restaurant took one hour and twenty minutes longer than it should, and that the light gave them all 'positive feelings'. It is no surprise that Rachel's young boys have later claimed to spot UFOs from their back garden.

The main support for the UFO claim comes from Rachel's mother, Anne Devereux. Since gaining some attention from their UFO tale Anne has since remembered seeing triangular UFOs during her childhood. Amongst other things she has also attributed a faulty kettle and a worn out coil in the family car to 'aliens'. It seems probable that Anne has had an interest in UFOs for quite some time. Further still it seems likely that her account was based, consciously or subconsciously, on something she'd heard before. A UFO sighting from 1976 describes the account of three women, Mona Stafford, Louise Smith and Elaine Thomas, driving home from a restaurant to their home in Lancaster, Kentucky. They claimed they witnessed a bright light in the sky and that they could not account for one hour and twenty minutes of the home trip. The return journey from a restaurant, the same town name, witness to a bright light, and also the exact same amount of missing time, all seems a bit too much of a coincidence. Anne's memory of an old UFO story was likely triggered when events in her own life seemed to match something she half-remembered, or perhaps when she was looking to revise her own experiences to fit in with any alien hypothesis. Interestingly Anne's namesake, Paul Devereux, is a British researcher interested in, amongst other things, UFOs being exotic natural entities he calls 'Earthlights'. Devereux has suggested such lights have intelligence, and are associated with the energies of the Earth. He has written books such as *Earth Lights Revelation* and also featured in a Channel 4 documentary about these anomalous light phenomena, first broadcast in the UK in 1996. Perhaps Anne saw it.

Driving home down what they admitted was an unfamiliar winding road in the early winter evening, chances are Rachel, who was driving, was just dazzled by the evening sun, and the journey took slightly longer than they thought it should. The event occurred around 5pm, about sunset; in their statement the family noted the stark contrast between the shaded buildings and the sky and a deeply yellow Moon that had just appeared. The bright UFO light appeared to their left as they drove home, to the West of the A65, towards were you would expect to have seen the setting Sun. Such a mundane event, whatever the exact details were, is now growing to become a recognized UFO yarn, due to the belief systems of a number of people, and the willingness of enough to accept the account as filtered through such a belief structure. Such claims need time to gestate before they become accepted into UFO circles, and the High Bentham incident, now more than ten years old, is slowly maturing as a folk tale assisted by a bit of luck, some media promotion and a lot of perseverance from the claimants to develop the myth. Half remembered or reinvented stories based on past traditions and tales are a common ingredient to the UFO myth as a whole, and such a process can be used not only to create new accounts, but also create or revise the entire history of the phenomenon itself.

The fact that humans have seen things that they can't immediately account for is not new and neither is the fact that those things are often seen in the sky. People will rationalize unexplainable sightings based on their own beliefs, own culture and own worldly understanding. The way in which current cases (and retrospective re-interpretations of past events) are commonly attributed to alien UFO craft is however a more recent phenomenon emerging slowly during the industrial revolution and growing during the atomic age of the mid to late twentieth century.

The term Unidentified Flying Object emerged during the mid-1950s, a military term that means exactly what is says, just a thing in the air that is not currently identifiable. It is now synonymous with alien spacecraft and is just part of an ongoing tradition of attributing a name to any observed or perceived unknown aerial phenomenon. Sky Gods, Mystery Airships, Foo Fighters, Flying Saucers, UFOs or what some now call AFOs, UAPs, or EFOs are all historic variations of the same thing. Accounts of strange sightings take on new meanings with revisionist thinking, and often 'historical UFO sightings' are classified as such retrospectively, as age old reports are re-imagined or even flat out invented.

The earliest claimed event I can find concerns a supposed UFO crash in Bayan-Kara-Ula, on the Sino-Tibetan border, which is alleged to date back to 10,000 BCE. The archeological site supporting such claims contained cave drawings, circular stones and remains, all suggesting an ancient extraterrestrial sighting. The site was apparently discovered in 1938, though records of the case first surfaced in a 1960 article from Russian magazine, *Literaturnaya Gazeta*, regarding such evidence of ancient aliens as discovered by Chinese archeologist Chi Pu Tei. In 1962 the story was apparently re-invented by a Professor Tsum Um Nui of the Beijing Academy of Ancient Studies as evidence of a crashed UFO. Details of the case, commonly referred to as the Dropa Stones (named after the circular stones allegedly discovered at the site), were first published that same year in German Vegetarian magazine *Das Vegetarische Universum*. It was then re-published word for word in the German UFO magazine *UFO-Nachrichten* in 1964, with both articles written by a Reinhardt Wegemann. The same story was then re-written by Vyacheslav Zaitsev in 1967 for *Sputnik* magazine.

The case of the Dropa Stones has since gained some following, but is certainly a hoax. How are we sure? No archeologist by the name of Chi Pu Tei seems to have existed, and in some accounts he or she is listed as the equally non-existent Qi Futai. Neither Professor Tsum Um Nui nor Reinhardt Wegemann exists, there has never been a Beijing Academy of Ancient Studies, and the remains of any supposed archaeological evidence have never been seen, beyond some bad quality photographs. The Dropka are a genuine Tibetan tribe of nomads, but the **Bayan-Kara-Ula** region may well be fictitious, as no references to it are made beyond those concerning apparent alien artifacts. The only documentation of the case is a magazine short story. The tale was again re-imagined as the 1978 fictional novel *Sungods in Exile* written by David Gamon, which replaced Tsum Um Nui with the equally fictitious Dr Karyl Robin-Evans. For some however the case still has merit as more than just a fun story; it is a piece of a puzzle that aims to make the world a more fantastical place. The interweaving of fiction and deception are to some irrelevancies that do not cloud their belief in the account supporting genuine evidence of visitors from other worlds. If a general belief is strong enough, having a piece of text supporting some aspect of that belief, whatever its origins, is evidence enough.

Possibly the first suggested written account of a UFO comes from Ancient Rome in 214 BCE. Titus Livius Patavinus was a Roman historian who wrote the *Ab Urbe Condita Libri*, a grand history of Rome and its people. He recorded within it one account of 'ships that had shone forth from the sky'. It is most probable that he was describing some sort of natural phenomenon observed in the sky, possibly unusual cloud formations or mirages. The use of the term 'ships' also refers to the current cutting edge military and transportation craft of the day, a recurring theme in UFO accounts, and the concern over 'seeing ships' may have had more to do in this case with a wider social anxiety over a growing Carthaginian threat, rather than invading space aliens. Titus Livy records such public sightings in a skeptical way, and the revision of such accounts as extraterrestrials dates to writings of the early 1950s by people such as Harold Wilkins.

The popular press is a common source of UFO cases, but such traditions go back a long way. Another example of a celestial phenomenon attributed to UFOs was recorded as happening over Nuremberg during the sixteenth century. A contemporary broadsheet paper, complete with woodcut illustration, described certain events in the sky as observed on 14th April 1561. The case became better known after being published in Carl Jung's book on flying saucers, where he analysed the archetypal meanings behind such UFO sightings. Despite the argument put forward by Jung that it was a good example of a natural phenomenon that had just been reported with a degree of religious and military interpretation, UFO enthusiasts have subsequently adopted the event as a historic example of people witnessing alien spacecraft. It seems most likely the event was an observation of sun dogs, a type of halo caused by light refraction through certain types of clouds. It was however reported in such a way that reflected contemporary concerns relating to ongoing wars between the Catholics and Protestants during the Reformation; hence an optical illusion becomes a heavenly symbol of crosses. Creative journalism and spin is not it seems a modern phenomenon.

Historical texts are not the only things open to re-interpretation by those searching for historical evidence. Misunderstandings of the semiotics and symbolism of Byzantine art have also provided 'examples' of UFOs in several medieval paintings. Symbolism in Byzantine and Medieval period art, in particular those concerning religious narratives, are often cited by UFO enthusiasts as 'documentation' of alien craft. Common examples of such imagery include a fourteenth century fresco in the Visoki Decani monastery in Kosovo, a depiction of the Crucifixion in the Svetitskhoveli Cathedral of Mtskheta, Georgia, and *The Baptism of Christ*, a painting by Aert de Gelder.

When taken out of context and with little understanding of the conventions and traditions of such period artwork, it is easy to see from a contemporary perspective why what looks on the surface like little men in space ships is taken as such. In many cases such painted objects technically are 'otherworldly', but they do not represent visiting aliens. A common motif of Byzantine representations of the Crucifixion includes both the Sun and the Moon on either side of the Christ figure. The Sun and the Moon represent the darkening of the heavens at the moment of Christ's death; such things also represent Ecclesia and Synagoga, a pair of figures personifying the Church. These figures often appear aside the crucifixion in Romanesque art, or aside entrances to church buildings.

In some depictions they take on more abstract forms, such as trees, animals or more commonly the Sun and the Moon, and generally represent the Christian Church and the Jewish Synagogue. As a result such circular sky objects are often depicted with human characteristics, faces or even full bodies. Such images are not men in spacecraft, but symbolic of Judaism witnessing the birth of Christianity as the *true* religion. Other 'UFOs' in medieval art are either depictions of the Sun, angels or some other very common form of celestial symbolism. The idea that such things are UFOs ignores centuries of religious semiotics, and the concept that they are anything other than this has its roots in the same 1967 *Sputnik* article describing the cave paintings found by Professor Tsum Um Nui.

The blending of religious beliefs, visions and visitations

provide a number of examples later adapted into UFO culture. The 'Miracle of the Sun' was an event that occurred on 13th October 1917, and apparently witnessed by over 30,000 people, close to the town of Fatima, Portugal. Three young children, Lucia Dos Santos, Jacinta Marto and Fransico Marto, who had previously claimed to have seen Our Lady of Fatima, as well as Our Lady of Sorrows, Our Lady of St Carmel, Saint Joseph, Jesus, an angel and also a vision of Hell, announced that one such visitation would occur in a field just outside the town, and that a great miracle would be performed. A large crowd gathered and after a period of rain, the Sun appeared as an opaque spinning disc in the sky. It is then said to have cast multi-coloured lights upon the crowd, before moving toward them in a zig-zag pattern. The Roman Catholic Church later accepted the event as an official miracle.

Such descriptions are almost entirely based on the writings of the Catholic Priest John DeMarchi, who recorded the accounts of apparent members of the crowd during the late 1940s, thirty years after the alleged event, eventually going on to write the 1952 book *The Immaculate Heart: The True Story of Fatima*. The relatively small numbers of witness statements are vague, scant in detail, often in contradiction to each other and made mostly by devoted Catholics who had been determined to witness *something* that day. UFO revisionists have also since appropriated the description of such an event. Former Astronomer and computer scientist turned UFOlogist Jacques Vallée studied the phenomenon for years, working towards his Fatima UFO hypothesis. Vallée has also speculated that other religious apparitions, such as the visitations at Lourdes, may have been the result of UFO activity. Joaquim Fernandes built on these ideas, writing a series of books around the topic, including, *Fatima Revisited: The Apparition Phenomenon in UFOlogy, Psychology and Science*.

Critical assessments of the 'Miracle of the Sun' suggest that such miracles cannot be taken at face value, and that the claims of the Sun performing apparent acts of marvel are numerous throughout history and cultures. Sun worship is not exactly a new thing, and reported observations may simply have been a result of the optical effect on the retina caused by prolonged staring at the Sun. Most likely the event at Fatima is an example of religious groupthink, a psychological phenomenon where a group of people with a shared desire for conformity or a specific experience, create their own, often irrational, decisions or interpretations concerning any such occasion.

The belief in such celestial phenomenon can be based on cultural superstitions, but also on misidentifications of actual things: both real celestial objects like the Sun or stars, but also man-made devices. The early accounts of otherworldly aerial craft tend to parallel the development of flying machines manufactured on Earth. Although assisted human flight may have its roots in kites developed in China around fifth century BCE, it was not until the nineteenth century that things emerged to allow for the advances in modern aircraft technology around today. The first powered, controlled and sustained flight is believed to have taken place on 24th September 1852 when Henri Giffard flew an airship around fifteen miles over part of France. The development of the air balloon as a method of transport continued over the remainder of the nineteenth century; in turn a spate of UFO-type sightings and even attempted abductions were reported over the US between 1896 and '97. Often described as 'mystery airships', many reports were in fact suggested to be simple hoaxes, sensationalist journalism or sightings of these early airships, many of which were privately owned and had been freely operating over the US since 1863. The observation of such craft was a completely new experience for many people, and it is no great surprise that many of the 'large cigar' shaped mystery airships spotted around this time are simply sightings of such dirigible style aircraft. Accounts of such unusual observations during the time of the Wild West have fueled popular culture, more recently, for example, the 2011 movie *Cowboys & Aliens*, which is (very) loosely based on these accounts. The Wild West mystery airship reports only received further attention in the second half of the twentieth century, as UFO researchers suggested they were earlier sightings of alien craft.

Another Wild West case occurred in April 1897, when

a UFO is reported to have crashed at a farm near Aurora, Texas. Reported in the *Dallas Morning News* by local resident S E Haydon, the article describes a craft that is alleged to have hit a windmill before impacting, and a mysterious body, 'clearly not of this world', which was subsequently recovered and then buried. The details of the case also act as a template for later tales involving UFOs crashing into remote areas, sometimes with recovered bodies. Indeed the Aurora account may be the root of recurring stories concerning alien corpses found in parts of rural America. It has been suggested that Haydon was not adverse to practical jokes and foolery, and the story was invented in an attempt to revive the local fortunes of the town, which had recently suffered a spate of fires, infestations and fevers. Beyond his initial report there are no further follow up articles on the case, and no physical evidence has ever been found. The closest thing to evidence is the claim by Brawley Oates, (who purchased the same land in the 1930s); after hearing the story of the UFO crash he developed arthritis and blamed his medical condition on alien debris contaminating his water.

Accounts like the mystery airships provided a template for the UFO phenomenon that developed in the second half of the twentieth century. Such sightings mixed with folklore, fiction, media reports and speculation about aliens visiting Earth began to form within the popular consciousness.

Another event to have a significant impact on the emergence of the UFO myth is the apparent hysteria caused by Orson Welles and his radio production of *War of the Worlds*. On 30th October 1938, the Mercury Theatre on the Air enacted a version of the HG Wells science-fiction fable concerning invaders from Mars. Common folklore has you believe that there was mass panic, as audiences perceived the opening (fictional) news broadcast concerning alien invaders to be genuine. There was mass hysteria across America, many fled in panic, there were near riots on the streets and some people even resorted to suicide in fear. Apparently.

The reality was far less dramatic, but newspapers, such as *The New York Times*, sensationalized a few minor claims, describing 'Terror by Radio!' Really it was more of a chance for traditional print media to take a jab at the relatively new medium of radio, describing it as something that the public doesn't need, doesn't understand, and certainly one that cannot be trusted as a source of news reporting. Welles himself encouraged the stories, as he understood the marketing potential of such media attention. Despite the fact that there was very little if any evidence of such hysteria the tale of 'mass panic' only grew through numerous retellings. In 1940 Hadley Cantril wrote an article, 'The Invasion from Mars', claiming 1 million people had been frightened by the *War of the Worlds* broadcast. Despite being based on a number of flawed and unverifiable pieces of data, it further encouraged the story to stick within the popular consciousness. *The War of the Worlds* episode is a good example of both a developing folk myth and how revisionist groupthink can influence widespread beliefs. It also demonstrates the willingness, perhaps the need even, for such myths to exist within Western society of the time.

The early twentieth century saw a great shift in society. As Europe was ravaged by war in the trenches so, too, America was shaken by a huge growth in wealth punctuated by periods of depression and economic crash. The rise of Nazi Germany and the events that resulted in the Second World War unleashed the truly worldwide horrors that modern technology could deliver. The Western world was changing and so, too, were its folktales. Reports of UFOs gathered pace during World War II, as fears of very earthly alien invaders were high on many people's minds. Radar operator Donald J. Meiers of the 415th Night Fighter Squadron came up with the phrase 'Foo Fighters' after describing being chased in his plane by a red ball of fire. The term stuck and soon became a way to describe many strange observations made by pilots during the war. Most foo fighter accounts were probably reflections or sightings of natural phenomenon, and accounts of floating black objects and fireballs are likely to be debris from exploded shell casings or damaged airplane fragments. Wartime reports of such sightings have since been exaggerated and possibly even invented following the end of the conflict. A classic foo fighters account in Martin Caidin's book *Black Thursday*, published in 1960, is based on a supposed secret document he somehow got hold of. The book details a 'historic account' of a bombing raid over Germany, and other than this writing no further evidence of claims involving flying discs as spotted by a B-17 bomber in October 1943 has ever been produced. Unsurprisingly Caidin was best known as a fiction writer, producing novels such as *Cyborg* and the Bermuda triangle-based *Three Corners to Nowhere*. A creative individual, by the mid-1980s he also began making claims that he had powers of telekinesis.

The period during the Second World War offered a fertile breeding ground for escapism, and the myth of the UFO would emerge from this time with confidence. The war has also provided a good number of UFO cases of its own, though most are retrospective interpretations. In 1941 a UFO is reported to have crashed near Cape Girardeau, Missouri, with reports of an alien body being recovered from the wreckage. The case however was not brought to wider attention until 1991 by investigator Leonard Stringfield in his book *UFO Crash Retrievals: The Inner Sanctum*. The details of the case are based entirely on accounts from one person, Charlette Mann, who related her grandfather's (the Rev. William Huffman) alleged deathbed confession about witnessing a UFO crash and alien body. Charlette even managed to present a drawing as 'evidence'. Not produced until 1999 it was based on her memory of a photograph from 1941 that she apparently saw once. The drawing depicts a classic 1980s style 'grey alien' and is so generic that the case can't even be considered as an example of interesting fantasy.

Often described in dramatic fashion as 'The Battle of Los Angeles', an incident that occurred in February 1942 is attributed by many UFO enthusiasts as another classic alien encounter. Less than three months after the attack on Pearl Harbor, and only one day after the bombardment of Ellwood (a Japanese attack on the coastal area near Santa Barbara), the LA incident is really a case of WWII nerves. A west coast aerial attack was thought to be imminent and the US Military was on high alert when a false alarm triggered a somewhat 'enthusiastic' response from a nervous US defence force. Several hundred rounds of surface to air ammunition were fired into the sky as

LA was lit up with explosions and aerial searchlights. It turned out to be nothing, but a later re-touched photograph printed in various newspapers at least made it look like there might be 'something' in the sky, more to preserve National pride than to allow the thought the military was at war with clouds, especially as fallout from the shells had killed a number of civilians on the ground. The case was largely forgotten, however in 1979 filmmaker Steven Spielberg became interested in making a comedy loosely based on the reports of the LA 'raid'. The script was worked on while Spielberg was in the middle of filming *Close Encounters of the Third Kind*, and the combination of themes may be the origin of the UFO connection.

The modern UFO phenomenon really started during World War II and the period following its immediate aftermath, as a society traumatised by years of war and the horrors of nuclear destruction invented new imaginative specters fueled by a mix of escapism and paranoia. The first real signs of this were the Swedish 'Ghost Rockets' or 'Spokraketer', sighted mostly over Sweden, but also some other Scandinavian countries throughout 1946. The sightings often consisted of fast-flying rocket shaped objects in the sky, with many reported to have crashed, often into lakes, but no debris was reportedly ever recovered. The first report was actually made in Finland in February 1946, but by December that year around 2,000 sightings had been logged. Swedish Air Force Officer Karl-Gosta Bartoll conducted a three-week search after one rocket apparently crashed into Lake Kolmjarv, but ultimately he turned up nothing.

By August the US Army had begun to take interest. Investigations concluded that meteors probably caused many of these sightings, specifically from the Perseid meteor shower. US Army Gen. Hoyt Vandenberg later informed President Truman that the weight of evidence suggested rockets had also been launched from a nearby base. At the end of the war the former German rocket facility at Peenemunde was under the control of the Russians, who were likely testing captured V2 rockets. There is also the issue that the mid-1940s were the dawn of jet propulsion, and many people would have found the sight of engine contrails an unusual aerial observation. Stories such as the Swedish 'Ghost Rockets' were reported worldwide, and some had begun to speculate that the sightings might have an extraterrestrial origin. This may have played a large part in the 'flying saucer' excitement that broke out across America the following year. There was growing fear around the possibility of enemy Soviet aircraft invading US airspace, worldwide nuclear annihilation seemed feasible, and the exploration of space was quickly becoming a reality. The end of the War, the start of the Cold War and the development of the atomic bomb all had a massive cultural impact on the world, and in particular on popular culture in America.

There were a number of 'flying object' stories published earlier in 1947, but a key moment occurred on 25th June that year when journalist Bill Bequette wrote an article for the *East Oregonian* newspaper. The report concerned an account by Kenneth Arnold, a businessman from Idaho, who had seen some strange objects in the sky while flying his own aircraft near Mount Rainier. A description by Arnold concerning the objects' movements as 'saucers skipping across water' was then condensed into the more newspaper savvy term 'Flying Saucers' by editor Nolan Skiff. A journalist named Ted Smith interviewed Arnold the next day on KWRC radio and the story soon gained wide attention. The flying saucer term stuck and the modern UFO myth had begun.

For Ken Arnold the story begins on 24th June as he was flying home from a business meeting. He had spent about an hour searching for a lost C-46 Marine Transport Plane for which there was a $5,000 reward. At around 3pm and about twelve miles from the peak of Mount Rainier he observed a group of 'very bright lights'. They were viewed by Arnold from several miles away, and in his own witness report he states, 'they flew like many times I have observed Geese to fly, in a rather diagonal chain-like line'. On returning to Yakima, Washington, Arnold told the airport general manager Al Baxter about his sighting. Arnold was convinced he'd seen something strange, perhaps secret military craft, perhaps something stranger. The next people Arnold spoke to that day about it were members of the press and the story soon developed. Exactly what it was that

Arnold saw that day we'll never know for certain. However, the likelihood of it being alien spacecraft—though not outside the realms of any absolute impossibility—seems unlikely.

There have been many possible explanations put forward for what Arnold saw, though the most plausible, as suggested by Marty Kottmeyer and James Easton, is alluded to in his own statement—he probably did see a flock of geese, or possibly swans or some other waterfowl. Unusually high from sea level, but not any higher than such birds would normally fly over mountainous terrain, as geese keep a relatively steady distance from whatever ground they are passing over. They fit all his descriptions of 'crescent shaped' objects, as well as the pattern the group flew in and the characteristics of their movement. Canadian snow geese follow a number of migration patterns; one of the main ones, the Pacific flyway migration path, follows the mountain range from the North Cascades to Willamette National Forest. Mount Rainier is roughly in the middle of this stretch, and small flocks of geese are often seen in the area around May and June looking for nesting grounds.

The combination of some Cold War paranoia, tiredness after a business trip, the excitement of a $5,000 reward and the glare of the Sun probably just meant he misidentified some birds reflecting light from their backs. The chance of an experienced pilot, as Arnold was, misidentifying birds as spacecraft seems questionable, but he went on to make a habit of it. About a month after his famous sighting, while on the way to Tacoma, Arnold witnessed '25 brass coloured objects' with 'the same flight characteristics of the large objects I had observed June 24th'. He also went on to say they 'looked like ducks'. By sheer coincidence, local farmers in the vicinity of the sighting had reported seeing clusters of peculiar birds, probably ducks, flying high up that morning.

Some researchers too have expressed reservations about Arnold's psychology. His public statements often show signs of a delusion of observation, and the possible presence of paranoia. Arnold went on to have ten apparent UFO sightings over the twenty years following 1947, gradually going on to make speculations about UFOs being space animals with the ability to change their density. In 1952 he reported seeing two living transparent UFOs, and in the same year he wrote *The Coming of the Saucers* with pulp writer Raymond Palmer. Palmer was an influential editor of *Amazing Stories* magazine from 1938-1949. He also published the magazines *Mystic*, *Search*, *Flying Saucers* and *Fate*, and was himself a prolific author of science fiction and fantasy stories. Palmer published Arnold's flying saucer story in the first issue of *Fate* magazine, which further helped raise the national recognition for the story.

Kenneth Arnold's first contact with Raymond Palmer was shortly after the initial flying saucer story broke. Arnold received a letter from Palmer, offering him $200 to help investigate another strange aerial sighting that had been reported at Maury Island in Puget Sound, Washington. The sighting of several donut shaped objects flying over Harold Dahl's boat reportedly happened on 21st June, just a few days before Arnold's own experience. However it wasn't actually reported until 22nd July, suspiciously after Arnold's story had gathered national press interest.

The account of the strange craft in Maury Island comes only from Harold Dahl and his friend and co-worker Fred Crisman. They claim not only seeing the craft, but that it was shedding material, a piece of which even hit Harold's son Charles on the arm—and they had the debris to prove it! Arnold was taken in by the story and rushed to get the air force involved. They eventually investigated, but very quickly the story began to unravel. Arnold it seemed was gullible as well as bad at identifying birds.

The 'flying saucer debris' turned out to be common volcanic slag, and Charles Dahl, who was apparently hit by it, later stated he was never even there. Fred Crisman however was a hobbyist fantasy writer, conman, hustler and pathological deceiver; he was also deluded, and had a habit of picking up government stationary to write 'official' letters. As well as this he was an avid reader of Palmer's *Amazing Stories* magazine, having written several letters to the editor previously. Harold Dahl went on to admit the whole thing was made up, but that the domineering Crisman pushed him into it. Fred Crisman had seen the Kenneth Arnold story as a route to gaining personal attention; Crisman pops up several times in conspiracy theory circles, most notably claiming to be a key witness in the assassination of JFK.

Coincidentally what would become one of the most culturally influential UFO incidents actually happened a few weeks before the Ken Arnold case, though, like the Maury Island incident, it was only reported after the Arnold story had gained wide attention. In early July 1947 ranch foreman William Ware 'Mack' Brazel informed the County sheriff about some strange material found on the Foster ranch, which he looked after near the town of Roswell, New Mexico. Referring to recent news stories, Brazel described the material as 'one of those flying disks'. The Sheriff passed on details to the nearby Army Air Force Base, who dispatched officers to investigate. The material was recovered, and a botched press release was sent out confirming recovery of a 'flying saucer'. The story was big news for a day or so before the US Army released a second statement confirming the debris was simply a weather balloon.

The Roswell case is in many ways the archetypal UFO story, and one of the key moments for the development of modern day folklore concerning extraterrestrial sightings or activity. Interestingly the incident itself didn't cause a huge stir at the time; though it received some national press attention it was just part of the flying saucer flap during 1947-48. The case itself was largely forgotten after a year or so, but the half-remembered accounts and hearsay allowed the story to slowly develop over time. Rumour and folklore slowly began to develop and over the next forty years the story expanded to include government cover-ups, alien bodies, multiple crash sites and a whole cottage industry of UFO exponents.

The story of the Roswell 'Crash' actually begins in New York. In November 1946, the New York University Constant Level Balloon Group was founded, with the objective to develop suitable balloons capable of carrying Army Air Force instruments at high altitude for long-range detection of nuclear explosions and rockets. It was part of a top-secret surveillance programme known as Project Mogul. The project was such a closely guarded secret that head of the New York group, Charles Moore, didn't even know what Project Mogul was, or even that it existed. Dr Maurice Ewing created Project Mogul with the aim of using balloon technology to carry microphones and radio transmitters over foreign areas, principally the USSR. Mogul was the forerunner to the Skyhook balloon programme, as well as similar balloon surveillance initiatives like Project Grandson and Project Genetrix. The testing of these projects may have accounted for several notable UFO sightings during the late 1940s. The use of experimental balloons was soon abandoned in favour of more conventional high altitude aircraft, such as the Lockheed U2 spy-plane, a version of which is still commonly used today.

Several of the early Mogul test balloons were launched from Alamogordo Army Air Field in New Mexico throughout June and July 1947. Flight Number 4 was released on 4th June, and disappeared somewhere over Arabela. Flight Number 5, released the day after, was recovered twenty-five miles east of the town of Roswell. Such was the nature of these early balloons that neither the Army nor the New York Group was particularly desperate to locate missing test flights. The early prototypes, although large, were just rubber and string with very basic structures, and sometimes just held together with tape. Mack Brazel's description of the debris found on his ranch matches the components of the missing Flight Number 4: strange tinfoil-like material, sticks, patterned tape and rubber. The Mogul projects were imposingly big, made up of clusters of meteorological balloons and instruments like radar reflectors; they reached as tall as several hundred feet when inflated and would be a unique looking object in the air. Crashed and in tattered bits, their identification by a casual observer would have been difficult.

The wreckage had probably been lying in part of the large ranch grounds for around two weeks, getting blown around by wind, and trodden on by sheep and cattle before Brazel found it. After a loud thunderstorm he conducted a thorough search of the ranch, principally to check that the livestock was okay, and upon finding debris in the way of a sheep pasture, eventually gathered up parts of it. Several weeks later he visited the nearby town of Corona where he may have become aware of Ken Arnold's flying saucer story, which was in the press at the time. Depending on accounts he may also have taken parts of the wreckage over to his neighbor, Loretta Proctor, who lived around eight miles away. Proctor has later shown herself to be an eccentric attention-seeking UFO enthusiast, and one who has changed and embellished her account of the alleged meeting a number of times. If she ever saw the debris or even discussed it with Brazel is unclear.

On 7th July, Brazel went into Roswell, mainly with the aim of selling some wool, but also to have a chat with the County Sherriff about the debris on his ranch. The subsequent discussion was more likely an attempt to get someone to clear up the mess than any concern about alien spacecraft. Sheriff George Wilcox later notified the local Army Air base due to Brazel's claims that the debris was probably the result of some military project. Apparently it wasn't the first time bits of failed military test flights had crashed into the land around the Foster Ranch and he had previously found two weather balloons on the grounds.

Major Jesse Marcell and Captain Sheridan Cavitt from Roswell Army Air Base were later sent over to investigate the debris. Portions of the wreckage were collected, but there was not an overt concern about any security issues as Marcell took the bundled fragments home with him before taking them back to the base the next day. At home he showed his twelve-year-old son, Jesse Marcell, Jr, telling him it was a 'crashed flying saucer'. Upon returning the material to the base the next day, 1st Lt. Walter Haut put out a press release, which stated the Army had recovered a 'flying saucer'. The press quickly picked up on the information, and papers such as the *Roswell Daily Record* and *The Sacramento Bee* ran stories concerning the capture of a flying saucer.

Haut was a twenty-five-year-old Public Information Officer for the Army base at Roswell. Despite being involved in some campaigns towards the end of World War II, Haut's time at Roswell was relatively uneventful and he was eager to latch on to any potential excitement. Haut hadn't seen any of the wreckage, and his press release was based on one phone call from base commander Col. William Blanchard, who may have used the phrase 'flying saucer' to describe some aspect of the initial report from Mack Brazel. The press release wasn't authorized, and senior officers soon reacted; according to reports Haut was severely reprimanded, and his military career ended soon after. Blanchard, too, was instructed to take a period of leave and on return was re-assigned, with control of the Air base being passed to someone else.

After hearing the Haut press report, journalist Walt E Whitman interviewed Brazel who then described the debris found at the Foster Ranch. Whitman was no doubt more interested in a paper-selling UFO yarn than reporting the collection of a damaged balloon. A general recluse, Brazel was not enthused by the media attention, and refused to give any further interviews regarding the incident. The next day General Roger M Ramey quickly produced a second press release, stating that the debris was nothing more than a weather balloon, and interest in the story died down soon after. The fact that this was in essence a cover-up of the Project Mogul programme does not mean there was anything more sinister than the army not wanting to admit to trying to spy on Russia. The US government finally released the details of Project Mogul in 1994. The genesis of the UFO aspect of the Roswell crash seems largely to come from a few throwaway comments, which were likely influenced by the Ken Arnold saucer story. It is an almost certainty that Roswell would not be associated with aliens, UFOs or government conspiracies without the career destroying press release from Walter Haut.

There were several other notable UFO encounters not long after the Ken Arnold and Roswell incidents that captured the public imagination. One involved Captain Thomas Mantell, a twenty-five-year-old Kentucky Air National Guard pilot who crashed his aircraft, allegedly in pursuit of a UFO. On 7th January 1948, Godman Air Field, near Fort Knox, received a report from the Kentucky Highway Patrol concerning an unusual aerial object near Maysville. Several witnesses observed it through binoculars as a large, white, round, object. Several

P-51 Mustangs already airborne were told to investigate. One was piloted by Mantell, who ignored suggestions that he should level his altitude and try and assess the object. He passed 25,000 feet without an oxygen mask and blacked out from hypoxia; unconscious, his plane began to spiral toward the ground. A number of sensational rumours spread regarding the crash, and the story received significant news media attention. Claims of a UFO and a rather dramatic transcript of Mantell's last communications were all just media invention, and the craft Mantell was pursuing was very likely a balloon from the Skyhook programme, but the story stuck. Public concern about UFOs dramatically increased following the Mantell case. It now seemed UFOs were not just potentially extraterrestrial, but also potentially hostile.

Another case occurred on 1st October 1948 over Fargo, North Dakota, when George F Gorman a pilot with the North Dakota National Guard, observed a UFO, and then claimed to have engaged in a dogfight with it. The encounter happened in the dark, just after 9pm, and Gorman had been flying all day long. After the sighting Gorman was interviewed by military agents, and the report jumped to a dramatic UFO conclusion. It later transpired that Gorman had initiated a 'dogfight' with a lighted weather balloon, released by the air weather service ten minutes prior to Gorman's confrontation. Both the Thomas Mantell encounter and the Gorman 'dogfight' received wide national publicity, aided like other UFO stories with a good dash of overly creative journalism. Whatever the reality, the public appetite for such accounts was strong. As UFO encounters became more frequent it was surely only a matter of time before someone came face to face with an actual extraterrestrial.

George Adamski was born in Poland in 1891. A self-styled 'Professor' (though he held no graduate or undergraduate degree from any institution), his background involved working in a flourmill and a concrete factory. He soon became interested in the occult and select elements of Eastern religions, going on to create his own version of Universal Progressive Christianity. Adamski founded the 'Royal Order of Tibet' in the early 1930s, which was given a government licence to make wine for 'religious purposes' during prohibition. Adamski had admitted to making a fortune trading wine to anyone he could get away with selling it to. The end of prohibition marked the decline of his profitable winemaking, telling friends he was then going to try 'this flying saucer crap'. By 1949 he was giving talks describing government knowledge of giant spacecraft that existed on the far side of the Moon.

Adamski made his first real step towards a UFO career when the 1953 book *Flying Saucers have Landed* by Desmond Leslie included accounts provided by Adamski, claiming that Nordic aliens from Venus routinely visited earth. He claims to have witnessed, with friends, a large cigar shaped 'Mother Ship' near Palomar Mountain, California, in 1946, of course pre-dating both the Roswell and the Ken Arnold accounts. In 1952 he apparently made contact with an alien called 'Orthon'. He would soon be taken on trips around the solar system, and visit civilizations on Venus, Mars and the Moon. To support his writings he produced a series of photographs supposedly taken from 1947 onward (though not released until 1953) that showed close up images of alien craft.

Adamski claimed he had been selected by the Nordic aliens to bring their message of peace to the humans, becoming the latest in a line of apparent historic 'contactees'. The aliens warned of nuclear destruction and the damage that could result, obviously concerned that no one on Earth had noticed the damage caused by the nuclear bomb detonated over Hiroshima. Adamski went on to regularly meet with aliens, often in the bars and restaurants of Southern California. He principally claimed that his aliens came from Venus, though sometimes Mars and other planets in the Solar system, and described a trip to the Moon were he saw cities, forests and snow capped mountains.

At a 1954 UFO conference at Mount Palomar, which featured some other emerging 'contactees' like Truman Bethurum and Daniel Fry, Adamski talked about his experiences and made the most of selling autographed books. Discussions soon circulated about Venusians who were living on Earth, and Adamski was likely involved in starting a rumour that two men and one woman among the crowd were in fact disguised aliens from the planet Venus. The men were Donald Morand and Bill Jackmart, while the woman was Dolores Barrios. Don and Bill were music students, and Dolores was a dressmaker. All three lived in Manhattan Beach in California.

In 1959 the Soviet probe Lunar 3 photographed the Moon, revealing it as a barren, lifeless surface. Soon after Venus was proven to be totally inhospitable, with an atmosphere made almost entirely of carbon dioxide, rain made of sulfuric acid, and surface temperatures of 464°C, as well as an atmospheric pressure on the planet's surface 92 times that of Earth's. Questions began to emerge from Adamski's followers. Under closer inspection, Adamski's UFO photographs appeared to be close up pictures of streetlights or models made from chicken brooders and 100w General Electric lightbulbs. Several 'witnesses' to Adamski's encounters, such as George Hunt Williamson, have since come forward to state that they were staged events. His 1955 book *Inside the Spaceships* is now commonly considered to be a 're-make' of the 1949 novel *Pioneers of Space* by Lucy McGinnis. Adamski was a talented con artist, whose UFO stories were designed to make money from his followers. His books and lectures certainly made him an affluent man. Through the release of various books, lectures and conventions the contactee movement grew through the 1950s, though Adamski would remain the most prominent and influential.

George Adamski was by no means the first 'contactee'. As early as the eighteenth-century people like Emanuel Swedenborg were claiming to be in psychic contact with inhabitants of other planets. A nineteenth century French medium called Catherine-Elise Muller, who went by the stage name Helene Smith, popularized the concept of automatic writing, and was in turn guided by a spirit to document experiences from both fifteenth century India and Mars. However, the pre-1940s contactee accounts do not involve UFOs, and experience of other worlds via psychic connections is more in keeping with the practice of spirit mediums. The eighteenth- and nineteenth-century traditions of séances and other psychic connections were adapted into the emerging flying saucer myth by Adamski and others, including George Van Tassel, Daniel Fry, Truman Bethurum and Buck Nelson, who all emerged to spread the interplanetary gospel.

Daniel Fry claimed he had multiple contacts with aliens beginning in 1949. Fry only went public with these claims in 1954, and shortly after took (and failed) a lie detector test. He then provided photographs and films of UFOs, but analysis soon showed them to be fakes also. Fry later claimed to hold a doctorate, however his 'degree' was from a mail order outfit in London, and was a 'Doctor of Cosmism'.

Buck Nelson was an American farmer living in Missouri who claimed to have encountered a UFO in 1954. He apparently met the inhabitants of this craft, humanlike beings from the planet Venus named Bucky and Bob who had also visited with their dog, Bo. Nelson claims he later went on trips to the Moon, Venus and Mars, and was allowed to keep the alien dog as a gift. After his encounters he claims his chronic back ailment lumbago had disappeared and that his eyesight had improved. Nelson was also given the 'Twelve Laws of God' by the Venusians, essentially a more rambling version of the Ten Commandments from the bible. By 1956, Nelson had become something of a minor celebrity around the Ozark Mountains where he lived, hosting an annual Spacecraft convention on his farm for around a decade. By the late 1960s, he had returned to obscurity.

One of the most successful contactees after George Adamski was Eduard 'Billy' Meier of Switzerland. Since January 1975, 'Billy' has been open about his contact with an alien race he calls the Pleiadian or Plejaren (depending on his mood). He has taken hundreds of photographs of UFO craft, as well as some film footage and sound recordings. He has even provided fragments of evidence to support his claims, such as some metal samples. His accounts have become steadily more far-fetched, moving from sightings and contact, to intergalactic voyages and time-travel.

Meier claims his first experience of extraterrestrial contact occurred back in 1942, when, as a 5-year-old boy he was visited by an elderly humanoid several times. Whether this is true, total fantasy or some odd manifestation of Meier deluding himself about an 'experience' with an old man is unknown. His claims however only get more elaborate. From 1953 until 1964, Meier continued contact with an extraterrestrial he calls 'Asket'. In 1965 he lost his left arm in a bus accident in Turkey, which seemed to put an end to his alien appointments. However, after an eleven-year gap he resumed contact, this time with a female called 'Semjase'. Following this he claims to have visited other worlds and galaxies, been taken back in time, seen dinosaurs and even on one trip met Jesus Christ. He has transcribed his accounts into various (badly written) books.

In 1975, he 'went public' and at the same time established the 'Free Community of Interests for the Fringe and Spiritual Sciences and Ufological studies', or just 'FIGU' for short. Meier also funded a 'documentary' about his claims, with a selection of 'impartial witnesses' (or bad actors in need of a job) woodenly proclaiming to be in awe of his 'evidence'.

In 1997 his marriage to his wife ended acrimoniously, and the aspects of his hoaxing came out in detail. Photographs provided by Meier of 'Asket' were actually photographed stills from the television of Michelle Dellafave and Susan Lund, both members of the dancing troupe 'The Gold-diggers' as often featured on *The Dean Martin Show*. Another photograph from one of his 'time travels' was just a close up from an illustration in the book *Life Before Man!* a children's book about dinosaurs. Most of his UFO photographs were made using miniature models or overlaid photographic cut-outs. His UFOs were, according to his wife, models that he made in the garage out of trashcan lids and other household items. Meier's response to all this was simply that his 'evidence' had been altered by the intelligence agencies.

By the late 1950s, the rather good-natured extraterrestrial encounters as described by the contactees, were being replaced by the slightly more sinister and unwanted abduction cases. The Antonio Vilas-Boas case in 1957 was one of the first. Vilas-Boas was a twenty-three-year-old farmer from Brazil. He claims a 5ft tall alien wearing grey overalls and a helmet, who only communicated in dog barks, seized him and took him aboard a UFO. Vilas-Boas was then stripped naked and covered in gel, and then forced to undergo several medical examinations, before being rewarded with sexual intercourse with an attractive female alien. Twice. Vilas-Boas went on to become a lawyer. His story came to light in 1958, and he was able to recount the event in graphic detail. However, a very similar story was published in the magazine *O Cruzeiro* the year before (*Flying Saucers' Terrible Mission* by João Martins), and several elements also sound a lot like some claims made by George Adamski.

The first widely publicized abduction case was the Betty and Barney Hill incident, reported in 1963, though the alleged incident occurred a couple of years earlier. The Hills were an American couple who were supposedly abducted by an alien UFO in a rural part of New Hampshire, on the evening of 19th September 1961. The case gained wide spread interest, eventually spawning several books concerning the encounter and a 1975 TV movie staring James Earl Jones.

At approximately 10:30 p.m., while driving home from a vacation at Niagra Falls, Betty Hill noticed what she thought was a shooting star while looking out of the window of the car. The 'star' began to move erratically, before getting bigger and brighter. Barney Hill stopped the car to have a better look, and also to let their dog out for a quick walk.

According to what became the Hills' final account of what happened next, Barney observed the strange star through binoculars, only to see a craft of some description, complete with humanoid beings looking out of porthole windows. Running to Betty they both got back into their car and drove off, only to be dazzled by a bright flash. The next thing they knew, two hours had passed and they had no recollection of what had happened during that time. Confused, they drove home. Still feeling strange upon their return, Betty refused to have their luggage brought into the house, insisting it stay in the porch for several days. Over the following weeks they both began to recall strange experiences and feelings: Barney had an overwhelming need to examine his genitals frequently, and Betty had recurring nightmares about being 'examined'. After consultation about these ongoing sensations the pair underwent hypnotic therapy, and the detailed story concerning an alien abduction came out in full.

The details of the Hill case—late night abduction in a rural area, missing time, medical examinations and memory loss—became the archetypal template for many alien abductions to follow. The problem is, the account of this trendsetting original begins to fall apart when it is examined a little closer. The Hills had waited nearly two years before undergoing any form of hypnotic regression, and Dr Benjamin Simon, who conducted the sessions, has gone on to say that statements made under hypnosis are only accounts of what a patient believes themselves, they are not necessarily true accounts of actual events.

The main issue with the story as recalled by the Hills is the fact that Betty Hill was mentally unstable. In the time between the 'abduction' and the hypnosis sessions Betty would frequently record accounts of her dreams, re-write them, add to them and read them out to Barney. She had also become an avid reader of UFO literature, loaning Donald Keyhoe's *The Flying Saucer Conspiracy* book from the local library soon after the 'abduction'. She even went as far as writing to Keyhoe about the incident in 1961, admitting she only began having abduction dreams after reading accounts in his writing. Betty's endless writing formed all the significant details that made up the account as it came out via hypnosis. Betty claimed that following her abduction she would frequently see alien craft in the night sky. She claims she discovered several UFO landing sites, and recalled mysterious piles of leaves being left on the kitchen table, within which were jewelry she had lost the night she was abducted. Betty had spoken about seeing UFOs before any alleged abduction, such as in 1957 when her sister had apparently had a close encounter with one; she also claimed that her family had issues with poltergeists.

Barney's initial recollection was less fantastical, stating that he probably just saw a plane. Their accounts of alien creatures and the spacecraft were also inconsistent, but slowly changed over time, merging into a more unified narrative. The aliens themselves made a radical physical change after one

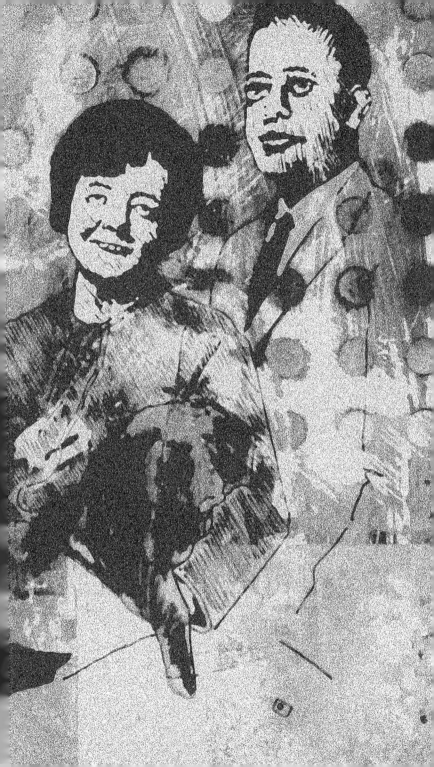

hypnosis session, though such revised descriptions were likely based on a creature depicted in an episode of *The Outer Limits* broadcast just before the session. Barney died in 1969, only a few years after their story broke into the news, and Betty was allowed to develop her own fantastical beliefs as her mental stability undoubtedly worsened. She would later take followers of her story out into fields and point at UFOs that were invisible to everyone but herself. She also came to believe that her cat could fly.

Many still believed the Hills' account and cite it as highly credible evidence of alien abductions. After one hypnosis session Betty produced a star map, a drawing based on a three dimensional model she had apparently seen during her abduction. It illustrated the location of where her captors had travelled. Several years later a schoolteacher by the name of Marjorie Fish assessed the dots and lines and concluded that the alien home world must be the Zeta Reticuli system. The match is dubious at best, and the vague drawing could easily match up with dozens of other constellations just as convincingly.

At a national UFO conference in New York in 1980, Betty presented various photographs of alien craft that she had taken over the years. There were over 200 slides of blurred and out of focus blobs against dark backgrounds. After her talk exceeded over twice its supposed running time, she was jeered off the stage. After seeing something in the sky, she ultimately believed what she wanted to believe, and a mix of various neuroses, paranoia and elements of hypochondria allowed her to create a fantasy world in which to live.

Travis Walton, an American logger, was allegedly abducted by a UFO in 1975, and disappeared for five days. His claim, made November that year, was only a month after the Betty and Barney Hill TV movie *The UFO Incident* was broadcast. His account gained widespread media attention, and he eventually published a book about his experiences, which was then turned into the 1993 film *Fire in the Sky*. Following his initial 'disappearance', Walton would only talk to non-skeptical press, such as *The National Enquirer*, and only those who would pay him. He also took a polygraph test, which he failed. The Walton family had been UFO-obsessed for years, and the witnesses supporting seeing a UFO on the night Travis was 'taken' most likely saw a lit balloon released by Travis's brother. Walton's disappearance was also well timed in getting him out of missing a deadline as part of his logging contract.

The abduction subject gained mainstream attention though the 1980s, mostly by the work of researcher Budd Hopkins and the novel *Communion* by Whitley Strieber. Budd Hopkins was an American painter who became a prominent figure in the alien abduction phenomenon. Hopkins's best paintings are from the 1970s, several of which are included in major collections such as those at the Whitney Museum in New York, MoMA, and the British Museum. Hopkins claims he saw a UFO in 1964, and after trying to report it became convinced of a government cover-up around the issue. Soon after joining a UFO study group he began discussing sightings with UFO researchers.

In 1975 he became acquainted with George O'Barksi, who had claimed to witness aliens disembarking a landed UFO craft. Hopkins wrote an article on the incident for New York's *The Village Voice* magazine soon after. At the end of the article Hopkins invited other witnesses to contact him regarding any sightings or experiences. As the accounts flooded in he became interested specifically in the alien abduction phenomenon, going on to write the book *Missing Time* on the subject. Again this book included a request to contact him regarding any experiences. The resulting 'evidence' sent in by avid readers formed the basis of his second book *Intruders: The Incredible Visitations at Copley Wood*, which topped the *New York Times* bestseller list. This book is often credited with the wider popularizing of the concept of alien abduction and their relation to genetic experiments, which was Hopkins's central hypothesis through the text.

Hopkins soon began to meet self-proclaimed abductees and encouraged them to discuss their experiences by holding free monthly group therapy sessions. Despite having no training in any form of hypnotherapy or psychotherapy, Hopkins began to offer many of the abductees hypnosis sessions, largely based on the rationale that he had seen others do it, and thought he had kind of figured out the process. By 1995 he had delivered his brand of 'therapy' to hundreds of abductees. Psychologist Robert A. Baker is skeptical about this form of hypnosis providing any sort of credible evidence. Suggestive prompts during hypnosis can change a dream or fantasy into a seemingly real event. In many such cases these sessions involved like-minded UFO enthusiasts, and new details concerning the 'discovery' of a past abduction only ever seemed to emerge after consultation with a UFO researcher. According to Baker, people were literally being talked into believing they had been abducted.

One of those people to get the Budd Hopkins treatment was Whitley Strieber. Strieber began his writing career in the late 1970s, after working for an advertising firm. He started off primarily as a horror writer, producing books such as *The Wolfen* and *The Hunger*. In 1987 he wrote *Communion: A True Story*, which is presented as a non-fiction account of periods of lost time and experiences with 'the visitors'. The book is based upon Strieber's 'terrifying flashbacks' experienced after undergoing one of Hopkins's hypnosis sessions. In *Communion*, Strieber claims he was abducted from his cabin in upstate New York on 26th December 1985. He does not clarify if these abductors were alien beings, though he does go into details such as the fact that he received an anal probe. The book went on to sell 2 million copies.

The cover of *Communion* is a painting by Ted Seth Jacobs. The image of a slender humanoid alien, with large black oval eyes is considered one of the most widely recognized depictions of a 'grey alien' within popular culture. Based on a description provided by Strieber, the painting has helped shape the current stereotype and archetypal image of an 'alien'.

The lack of any physical evidence, inconsistencies and implausibilities of many alien abduction stories have led several critics to argue that such memories are based purely on internal imaginations rather than external experiences. Abduction claims are most common in the English-speaking world, and in particular the United States—so much so, that an entire sub-culture has developed around the subject, with support groups and specific myths explaining the reasons for abduction. Due to a lack of real physical evidence most scientists and mental health professionals dismiss the abduction phenomenon as deception, suggestibility, fantasy, sleep paralysis, psychopathology or misinterpretations of environmental factors.

Seventy years of ongoing claims of UFO activity have firmly established the myth of such accounts into the popular consciousness. From misunderstandings of the advances in assisted flight, to religious superstitions, wartime fears, escapist fantasies, sensational media reports, and the wonders of the space age, much has been provided to society to encourage such belief. For many these claims will be nothing more than stories, entertainment to be consumed or disregarded depending on preference. For some these same tales represent a growing mountain of evidence that cannot be ignored. Like Anne Devereux, many claiming experiences of such otherworldly encounters, be they sightings of UFOs or actual alien beings, are likely reflecting on past cultural events, experiences, and folk myths. The more evidence consumed by believers, the more it supports growing belief in the plausibility of such accounts. The fantastical becomes the possible. As more people become open to the idea of extraterrestrial life visiting Earth, more evidence is needed to support the belief structure. More people convinced of the idea propose new sightings and evidence, allowing others to seek out these ongoing claims, and so it becomes a self-perpetuating phenomenon. So develops a conformational bias, as those committed to a belief in UFOs look for more and more support for their cause, going on to see proof wherever they choose. Often ridiculed, but less frequently dissuaded, such devout believers in UFOs have stated their case many times, and a struggle for credibility of their claims remains an ongoing battle against closed-minded scientists and sinister government agents.

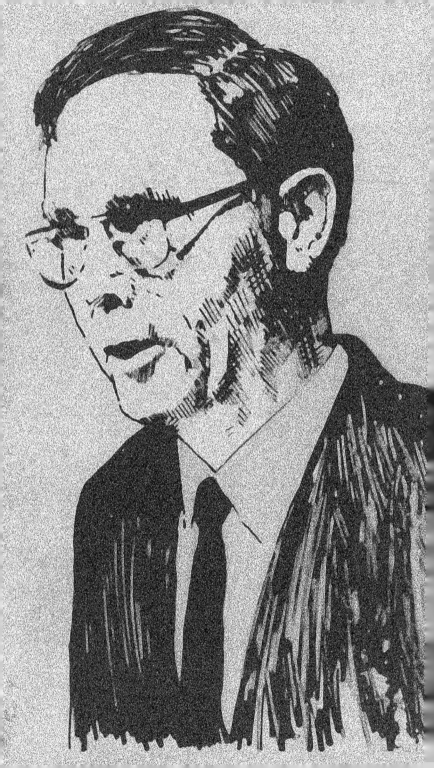

PART TWO
The Truth is Out-There

Many skeptics take great pleasure in picking apart outlandish ideas, such as the one that UFOs are alien craft, and fantastical claims are often debunked by the more rationally minded. Due to the nature of many UFO claims, much of the detail required to conclusively prove anything outright is lacking; things become a battle of the reasonable and the likely against the improbable and the exceptional. Often the rule of Occam's Razor is used as a guide to assess the potential plausibility of UFO accounts. William of Ockham was a fourteenth-century English friar, scholastic philosopher and theologian. His problem-solving principle *lex parsimoniase*, or the law of parsimony, basically translates to the idea that when looking at competing hypotheses, the one with the fewest assumptions should be selected. In basic terms: the simplest explanation is usually correct. Occam's Razor, as it is now commonly known, comes from similar philosophies of Aristotle and Ptolemy. Ockham's principle has been stated in many ways, such as 'entities must not be multiplied beyond necessity'. or 'it is futile to do with more what can be done with fewer', or just 'less is more'. Really the razor is concerned with 'shaving away' unnecessary assumptions around any particular idea or suggestion. The exact implementation of the principle is open to interpretation; what exactly does it mean by 'simple', when does assumption begin and probability end? As a result, skeptics and UFO enthusiasts alike seem to be obsessed with Occam's Razor when discussing the possible existence of UFOs. The simplest explanation regarding a UFO sighting for some may be that it followed a flight path of a plane, so it must have been a plane. For others the fact that the same UFO did not 'act like a plane' means you are making an assumption to suggest it is so, and a simpler solution is that it is an extraterrestrial craft. Without hard facts, assumptions have to be made, and they have to be formed around a person's belief. Some take issue with Occam's Razor, like the Austrian-American mathematician Karl Menger, who argued that entities must not be reduced to the point of inadequacy. Ockham's approach to problem solving is philosophical, not necessarily scientific. Some may argue that anything stepping into unusual assumptions (like the idea of flying saucers) is doomed to be shaved off through Occam's Razor, yet science is plentiful with examples where the simplest and most elegant explanations are not correct. The orbits of the planets, for example, were for some time thought to be perfect circles moving around a fixed Sun, until it was shown the truth was far more complex. Some things are just weird and complicated. Without conclusive evidence, as is the case with many UFO cases, any debate becomes purely conjecture—and again reliant on the belief structure of any party as to what they think most likely.

The best known of the UFO skeptics include Dr Donald Menzel and Philip J. Klass. Menzel was a pioneering theoretical astronomer and astrophysicist who taught at a number of universities throughout America, including Harvard and University of Iowa. During World War II, he worked for the Navy helping to decipher enemy codes and improving the Navy's radio-wave propagation. After the war he became Director of Harvard Observatory and worked as a consultant for the US State Department. Menzel was also one of the first prominent skeptics regarding the ideas that UFOs could be extraterrestrial craft. He began in 1953 with the publication of his book *Flying Saucers – Myth – Truth – History*. Throughout his writings on the subject Menzel maintained that UFOs were nothing more than misidentifications of prosaic phenomena like planes, birds, clouds, or stars. He even appeared before the US House Committee on Science and Astronautics during the 1968 symposium on UFOs where he stated the case for their cause being mundane natural reasons. In 1955 however, Menzel had witnessed a UFO himself whilst returning from a research trip to the North Pole. The experience perplexed him and perhaps only made his resolve to debunk the phenomenon stronger. He was never really convinced he'd seen anything extraterrestrial; rather he just wasn't sure what it was, and later put the sighting down to a mirage of the star Sirius.

Philip Klass was born in Des Moines, Iowa. Working for a number of years in the field of aviation electronics he became a journalist for Aviation Week. Working his way up to senior editor Klass remained a loner and workaholic, not marrying until he reached sixty. He became interested in UFOs in the mid-1960s, and the debunking of fantastical claims became an obsession for him. He began publishing *The Skeptics UFO Newsletter* as well as writing several books on the UFO phenomenon. In 1966, Klass offered anyone $10,000 if they could provide physical evidence of an extraterrestrial craft, or could produce an intelligent physical entity not from this Earth to stand in front of the assembly at the United Nations. By his death in 2005, no one had claimed the prize. Klass also established the Committee for the Scientific Investigation of Claims of the Paranormal, producing numerous articles for their *Skeptical Inquirer* journal.

Disproving the claims of every single UFO report is near impossible, due both to the volume of such reports and also the scant information that is frequently presented, often secondhand or after a considerable period of time since any alleged event. Many UFO claims may fall into common 'debunking categories' as misidentifications are repeated—the sighting of Venus being a frequent one. However, some sightings are genuinely harder to explain. In a rush to disprove evidence of UFO activity, some skeptics have been known to jump to some rather outlandish conclusions themselves. Philip Klass 'debunked' so many UFO cases that just by the law of averages he wasn't going to be right every time. That doesn't mean the cases he got wrong were genuine examples of extraterrestrial visitors; rather he was just too hasty, or missed a key part of the puzzle, and sometimes, it is fair to say, he came out with some total nonsense.

Relatively early into his debunking career, Klass was an advocate of the ball lightning theory as an explanation for a percentage of UFO cases. While he maintained that the majority of cases were misidentifications of things like stars and aircraft there was a more unusual group of sightings that was not easily explained by these causes. In 1968, Klass produced the book *UFOs – Identified*, which argued that some sightings were occurrences of electrified particles that bundled together to form a pulsating ball of plasma. Freak atmospheric phenomena like ball lightning are still very much in the realm of a hypothetical anomaly. The existence of such effects are largely based on the number of reported sightings, as reliable scientific data to support the hypothesis is scarce. It all sounds rather a lot like the belief around UFOs being alien spacecraft due to the number of witnesses supporting the idea. Following further research into the area Klass eventually distanced himself from such a theory, but nonetheless it is a good example of how something more 'scientifically palatable' can be informed mostly by belief rather than actual evidence. Just because a respected skeptic said so doesn't mean it's true. This doesn't mean that because certain cases cannot be easily debunked we must accept the claims of them being proof of anything extraterrestrial. Rather, the burden of proof is still with those making the fantastical claims. Such is the aim of the UFOlogist.

The idea of UFOlogy—the study of reports, physical evidence, documentation and other aspects associated with mysterious aerial sightings—developed during the 1950s as enthusiasts attempted to lend scientific credibility to such claims. The science of such things has not exactly been embraced by academia, and the majority of UFOlogists are enthusiastic amateurs that do not have any focused or consistent approach. As a result, the majority of the scientific community regards such studies as pseudoscience. One of the main problems with UFOlogy is that it often jumps to a conclusion first (such as 'UFOs are alien spacecraft'), and then tries to find supportive evidence for such ideas second. Rumour, exaggerations, opinions and convenient lies add to the body of facts, and things are more likely to be absorbed or disseminated into UFO lore than ever cross-examined or peer-reviewed. Anything that contradicts or creates some serious questions around the main hypothesis is ignored or at least re-appropriated. In fairness UFOlogists rarely lack creativity when coming up with potential ideas, as multiple variations on the phenomenon are explored, each with their own group of devoted followers. The extraterrestrial hypothesis (as in, UFOs are alien spacecraft) may be the best-known alternative explanation for these seemingly unexplained sightings in the sky, but it is in fact just one of several ideas presented by UFOlogy. UFOs may indeed be caused by factors other than alien life, but some have taken this alternative hypothesis into extreme areas.

The American author and blogger Mac Tonnies suggested that UFOs are vehicles belonging to an advanced civilization, but one that resides upon Earth. They are reptilian humanoids from a much older, and therefore more advanced, civilization than our own. These Cryptoterrestrials hide underground or maybe underwater. Tonnies suffered from cardiac arrhythmia, a condition resulting in an irregular heartbeat. He was troubled by ill health and died young at the age of thirty-four. He managed to write a number of fiction works including *After the Martian Apocalypse* and *The Cryptoterrestrials*. The ideas for such stories were developed through his online blog, where he interacted with a small but loyal fan base.

Similar ideas can be found in the earlier writings of Ivan T. Sanderson, a Scottish biologist and writer who was interested in paranormal subjects and sightings to do with things like sea serpents and the Yeti. Once while in Haiti he claims he was briefly teleported to fifteenth century Paris. He also wrote novels as well as articles for magazines like *True*. In 1970, he wrote *Invisible Residents: The Reality of Underwater UFOs,* in which he proposes that UFOs are actually a result of advanced submarine objects belonging to a hidden civilization living at the bottom of the ocean. He claimed UFO sightings were mostly due to these aquatic craft coming up from or returning to their underwater home. Soon after, he wrote about what he called the twelve Devil's graveyards, or the Vile Vortices; geographical areas of paranormal triangles strongly associated with mysterious disappearances. These include areas such as the Bermuda Triangle and the Dragon's Triangle, in the ocean to the south of Japan. In reality any accounts of missing ships or planes are to do with the higher chance of storms in such regions. The majority of reports associated with these areas are really fiction based on old stories of sea monsters and ghost ships or legends concerning amphibious Gods or underwater cities like Atlantis. Such narratives provide a tradition for these underwater UFOs, or USOs (unidentified submerged objects) as they are sometimes called, which in turn are likely due to the seemingly unusual effects caused by underwater volcanoes, which are plentiful in areas like the Pacific Ocean south of Japan.

In October 1967, a UFO spotted of the coast of Nova Scotia disappeared into the waters around Shag Harbour, and was then said to move undersea up-coast in the direction of Halifax. The event was likely a sighting of some fire balloons, small un-manned hot air balloons, which were popular around the time. No one admitted to the release of the balloons, likely due to press interest and the high expense of various search and rescue missions conducted due to concern that the sighting may have been a crashed aircraft. Residents around Wanaque, New Jersey, reported seeing numerous UFOs around the local reservoir between 1966 and '67, though this was later also shown to be due to a series of hoaxes created by the release of fire balloons. Similar accounts, like those in the Sanchez Stevens-produced book *UFO Contact From Undersea* from 1982, detail tales of UFO sightings and abductions relating to craft appearing from underwater around Florida and Puerto

Rico.

The idea that UFOs may originate from some giant underwater or underground base is shared by a number of UFOlogists. The concept of a hollow core within the Earth itself probably goes back to ancient mythologies concerning the underworld, Hell, or legends like the ancient Buddhist city of Shamballa. Various cultures have their own mythologies around such places, often coupled with some sort of surface entrance, such as the caverns leading to the underworld of the ancient Greeks, the Cruachan cave of the Celts, or various tunnels leading to a subterranean land within Native American mythology. By the eighteenth century, the idea had been dismissed as anything other than folklore or pseudoscience, or a source for fiction. Famous examples include stories like Jules Verne's *A Journey to the Centre of the Earth* or Edgar Rice Burroughs's *At the Earth's Core*. Less well known, but equally fictitious, is the 1964 book *The Hollow Earth* by Dr Raymond Bernard. Dr Bernard himself was a fictional invention, being the pseudonym of Walter Siegmeister, an American writer of various esoteric subjects and alternative health remedies. In his hollow Earth book he makes explicit the idea of UFOs rising up from some great underground civilization. The book claims to be an account of the American explorer Richard E. Byrd, a genuine pioneer known for traveling the polar extremities. Apparently Byrd discovered a vast entrance to a hollow Earth somewhere beyond the South Pole, full of wooly mammoths and blue-skinned beings with advanced technologies. Siegmesiter late wrote a secret diary 'by' Richard Byrd adding further evidence in support of his subterranean adventure. The idea has now intermingled with various theories surrounding UFOs.

Another Earthbound solution was proposed during the 1970s when Professor Michael Persinger developed his tectonic strain theory to explain UFOs. This idea suggests the phenomenon is a result of a type of electromagnetic activity caused by tectonic stresses within the Earth's crust, resulting in bursts of energy and types of ball lightning within the atmosphere. Author Paul Devereux took these ideas further going on to describe such things as 'Earthlights', believing these energy bursts explained not just UFOs but dragons, fairies and bodhisattvas. Devereux asserted that the characteristics of UFOs suggest that such Earthlights may be a form of macro-quantum phenomenon that should only exist at the subatomic level, but had somehow 'broken through' into the macroscopic visible world. Trevor James Constable suggested in his 1959 book *They Live in the Sky* that UFOs themselves might be a type of simple cellular organism that is attracted to electromagnetic energy in the atmosphere. Apparently they are invisible biological entities that migrate around the solar system in search of energy storms. Some suggest such beings exist on the edge of three-dimensional space, allowing them to appear and disappear at random.

There are a number of theories suggesting UFOs may be a result of travels from other dimensions. The idea of inter-dimensional UFO journeys are promoted by people such as Jacques Vallée. The idea being that UFOs travel from alternative realities or dimensions that coexist in tandem with our own. This theory removes the complications associated with vast interstellar voyages and replaces them with the perhaps even more complex task of cross-dimensional travel.

A similar idea considers the traditional grey alien to be simply a human being, in some future stage down the road of evolution, and what we perceive as aliens are actually time-travellers from the future. Whether such visits are with the purpose of warning past selves about some potential danger, history fieldtrips, or time-based tourism is open to debate. Dr Bruce Goldberg believes what he calls human chrononauts have travelled back in time several thousand years from the fifth dimension in order to further our own spiritual growth.

Despite these ideas feeding into the apparent complexities of the UFO phenomenon, they are, even by the standards of UFOlogy, considered fairly fringe beliefs. The extraterrestrial hypothesis has always been, and remains, the primary argument of the main UFO groups. Civilian-based UFO groups go back to the mid-1950s, as individuals with common interests attempted to establish credibility for the study of such things. One of the first was The Aerial Phenomena

Research Organization (APRO), a UFO research group set up in Wisconsin in 1952 by husband and wife Jim and Coral Lorenzen. Jim was an electronics technician and musician who shared an interest in extraterrestrial visitors with his wife. APRO spread through the 1960s and at one point had a number of state branches. The group stressed its scientific approach to field investigations and consulted with several PhD scientists such Dr James E. McDonald.

McDonald was an American physicist who worked at the University of Arizona. From the mid-1960s he campaigned in support of UFOs, a vocal critic of the Condon Report (a University of Colorado report rejecting any extraterrestrial explanation for such sightings). He also interviewed over 500 witnesses and was one of six scientists who testified about UFOs before the US House of Representatives Committee on Science and Astronautics in July 1968. McDonald's research methods were often described as confrontational, and he came under fire from both UFO debunkers like Philip Klass as well as believers like Jacques Vallée. Klass raised awareness to a number of inconsistencies in McDonald's statements and further found him to be mis-using funds from government contracts to support his own UFO research. In April 1971 McDonald attempted suicide by shooting himself in the head. Although he survived he ended up blind and wheelchair-bound as a result of his injuries. He later spent some time at the psychiatric ward of a hospital in Tuscon, Arizona. Two months after his first suicide attempt he was found dead along a creek next to a .38 caliber revolver and a suicide note. It is likely that the suicide was at least partly the result of his wife having an affair, as well as her being increasingly involved in far left politics. McDonald is often presented as one of UFOlogy's heroes; clearly intelligent he could talk the academic talk, and use evidence to produce well-structured arguments. His ongoing insistence around the subject of UFOs, as well as presentations to Congress, suggest his views were based on a genuine belief, rather than the intellectual enjoyment of arguing the ridiculous. It may just be that McDonald, as gifted as he was in the study of atmospheric phenomenon and cloud formation, perhaps lacked a sufficient dose of common sense and understanding of the wider cultural landscape.

APRO's credibility suffered a major blow in the 1970s over their support of the Travis Walton abduction case. APRO had arranged the polygraph test for Walton, which he then failed, and the group attempted to suppress the results while still promoting the case. The group continued but with significantly diminished membership until it dissolved in 1988.

The National Investigations Committee on Aerial Phenomena (NICAP), another civilian-led UFO research group, was active from 1956 until 1980. It was one of the most prominent groups of its type, and like APRO stressed its scientific approach. NICAP was co-founded by Major Donald Keyhoe and Thomas Townsend Brown. Brown was an American inventor who believed he had discovered anti-gravity. His 'ionic propulsion lifters' (which never worked) encouraged a popular idea within UFOlogy regarding how extraterrestrial craft might fly. His claims to being a scientist are dubious. He dropped out of his course at the California Institute of Technology and then later Denison University, after professors had told him his ideas concerning electricity and gravity were impossible. He later developed what he called a Gravitor, some sort of anti-gravity device that he attempted to sell as an idea to the military. After all his ideas were rejected and he failed to gain any funding to further his research, he turned his attention to UFOs. Scientists who witnessed Brown's gravity experiments were highly skeptical about any of the claims he made, and attributed any movement in his anti-gravity drives to well-known phenomenon such as ionic drift or electrohydrodynamics. Brown's association with UFOs and amateur experiments has fueled several ideas within conspiracy theory circles, and his ideas are sometimes attributed to the discovery of 'free' energy and advanced stealth technologies. Despite helping to set it up, Brown was asked to leave NICAP after a year at the organization, as he was spending its funds on his continued anti-gravity research. Delmer Fahrney briefly replaced him as NICAPs Director before Keyhoe took the position.

Keyhoe was an American Marine Corps Naval Aviator.

After being injured in an airplane crash in Guam in 1922, he began writing during his period of recovery. This recuperating pastime turned him into a lifelong avid writer. He began producing fiction in the 1920s, when he had a number of stories published in pulp magazines, such as *Weird Tales*. Many of Keyhoe's stories were science fiction based—a fact not lost on several critics of his 'non-fiction' UFO books. His article 'Flying Saucers Are Real' appeared in the January 1950 edition of *True Magazine*. This article was then expanded into a book of the same name, going on to sell half a million copies. Keyhoe went on to write several more UFO books, including *Flying Saucers From Outer Space* in 1953, which was the main inspiration for the 1956 sci-fi movie *Earth vs. the Flying Saucers*.

NICAP was a non-profit making organization and it faced financial collapse many times due to the bad management of its Directors. Keyhoe helped establish the monthly newsletter *The UFO Investigator*, and would often use its distribution to send out requests for funds to members, as he often found himself personally paying for much of NICAP's operational expenses. It did become the highest profile and most reputable UFO group of its time, especially during the 1960s when membership peaked at 14,000 members. It attempted to define itself as the respectable face of UFO research, rejecting the fanciful claims of contactees and remaining skeptical over abduction cases. NICAP published several 'studies' such as *The UFO Evidence* in 1964 and *Strange Effects from UFOs* in 1969. Throughout its existence NICAP did however argue that there was an organised government cover-up of UFO evidence. Despite this, NICAP and its members did from time to time communicate with the FBI and notable members included Roscoe Hillenkoetter, former head of the CIA.

The late 1960s saw membership numbers drop and Keyhoe faced charges of financial incompetence until 1969 when he was finally forced to step down as Director. Keyhoe was replaced by John Acuff and subsequently Alan Hall, a former CIA employee who took the position as a post-retirement hobby. Infighting and dwindling membership ensured a decline of NICAP through the 1970s, until it finally saw publication of its last newsletter in 1980, and officially dissolved soon after. NICAP's archive of UFO cases was later purchased by the Centre for UFO Studies (CUFOS).

CUFOS was founded in 1973 by Dr. Josef Allen Hynek. Hynek was a US Astronomer, Professor, and UFO researcher, and acted as Scientific Advisor for a number of official government studies into UFOs. He continued his own independent UFO research, going on to develop the 'Close Encounters' classification system. Initially skeptical about UFOs, his opinion changed over time. A pivotal moment came in the early 1950s when he interviewed forty-four astronauts and around five of them claimed they had seen aerial objects that they could not account for. Initially he began to speculate UFOs were some sort of unknown natural phenomenon, later suggesting sightings were a result of swamp gas. Frustrated by growing criticisms of his ideas by skeptics and UFOlogists alike, Hynek began to claim more vocally thoughts that aspects of UFO reports demanded scientific attention. After his position as a government advisor on UFOs began to sour, and his career as an astronomer began to stall, Hynek changed ranks to embrace his personal interest in esoteric subjects. In his teens Hynek had been an enthusiastic student of the occult. He studied subjects such as psychic surgery and developed an interest in secret societies and hidden ancient knowledge, particularly through the writings of the mystic Rudolf Steiner. In 1972 he published *The UFO Experience: A Scientific Inquiry*, the book was an attempt to argue the reality of the phenomenon in an academic way.

Hynek's standing as an academic was damaged as a result of the book, and it made him a controversial figure within the scientific community. He soon resigned from his post at Northwestern University, going on to court fame, making money promoting his ideas through lectures and later speculating that UFOs were psychic projections created by some extra-dimensional intelligence.

CUFOS is still based in Illinois and continues to be a small yet active research organization. Since 1976, CUFOS has published *The International UFO Reporter* and has formed formal ties with other UFO organisations through the UFO coalition. Following Hynek's death in 1986 the group was re-named 'The J. Allen Hynek Center for UFO Studies', and operates under its current Director, Mark Rodeghier.

A key member of the UFO coalition is the Mutual UFO Network (MUFON). Previously known as the Midwest UFO Network, it was founded in Illinois in 1969 by Walter Andrus and John Schuessler. Most of its early members had previously been part of APRO or NICAP, but they had changed membership as the former organizations began to disintegrate. MUFON currently has around 3,000 members worldwide, with the majority still within the US. The group holds an annual International symposium and also publishes the monthly *MUFON UFO Journal*. Researchers working for MUFON must follow their strict 265-page research manual, as well as undergo background checks and sit for various tests. Such a strict set of ethics has not however prevented a few questionable bits of 'research' going out in the name of MUFON. In 1987, then-Director Walt Andrus embraced the Gulf-Breeze UFO photographs, which appeared that same year. Bruce Maccabee, who was part of the MUFON collective promoting the photographs, would not accept, even when proven by independent photo-analysis, that the images were faked – likely due to the fact that he had recently written a book on the case. Continued promotion of these hoaxed photographs also helped boost subscription sales for MUFON; as a result Walt Andrus quickly fired several of his researchers who had proved the photographs hoaxes. More recently, MUFON has aligned itself with billionaire real-estate investor Robert Bigelow. An eccentric entrepreneur, he has ambitious plans to one day construct a space hotel; he is also a believer in UFOs and once bought a 'haunted' ranch in Utah because he thought it contained a hyperdimensional portal. Bigelow is currently funding MUFON to investigate cases of personal interest to him, and is essentially turning enthusiastic volunteers into paid staff. Bonuses and further incentives are apparently available to those who produce reports that contribute support for Bigelow's interests in anti-gravity technologies. It seems MUFON will diligently search for the truth in regard to the

UFO phenomenon, unless there is an opportunity for profit somewhere, and then its scrutiny becomes more flexible.

Previously a member of NICAP and then MUFON, Bruce Maccabee helped set up the Fund for UFO Research (FUFOR) in 1979. According to FUFOR it has provided $700,000 in UFO-based research grants. Interestingly many of these grants went straight into the pockets of members or close friends of the group to produce research studies that would promote the claims or support supposed evidence that related to particular projects being developed by such individuals. It is not a great shock to learn that the first approved FUFOR grant was paid to Bruce Maccabee himself. In 1987 FUFOR paid researcher Stanton Friedman $16,000 to investigate a collection of supposed documents supporting government knowledge of UFOs. Friedman was in the process of writing a book largely based on these documents with FUFOR board member Don Berliner, who went on to become the group's director. The documents were declared by FUFOR to be genuine before the book's release. The book, *Crash at Corona*, was also backed financially by Robert Bigelow.

In December 1995, the UFO research coalition (MUFON, CUFOS and FUFOR) produced and presented the document *Unidentified Flying Objects: The Best Available Evidence*. Written by Don Berliner, Marie Galbraith and Antonio Huneeus, the document aimed to collect the most convincing and carefully documented cases supporting the existence of UFOs as extraterrestrial objects. The document was produced with the aim of briefing influential persons, specifically leaders of government, the scientific community, and the press. The document makes a number of assertions, namely that UFOs are extraterrestrial in origin, and secondly that there is secret government knowledge regarding such craft. There is however no real effort made to cross-examine the case studies provided or to give suitable time to any counter arguments. If the 148-page document was produced with the aim of convincing skeptics about UFOs, then it is an outright failure. There is no real evidence here beyond the usual batch of witness testimonies, out-of-context statements, some radar anomalies, and a few questionable photographs.

Despite being presented in a mildly serious fashion (with appendices, a letter of endorsement, and even footnotes) the case studies begin, slightly embarrassingly, with 'depictions of UFOs' within fifteenth-century paintings. The realization that this will be just the same old collection of UFO yarns becomes quickly apparent. A number of other case studies follow, apparently the best that UFOlogy has to offer. Several are well-known examples, such as the Swedish ghost rockets and the Ken Arnold sighting. Five of the others, apparently some of the most convincing of all time, are discussed below.

For some UFOlogists the RB-47 UFO encounter is considered *the* best encounter ever—that is, the one that provides the closest evidence toward proof of extraterrestrial craft visiting Earth. An RB-47 is a reconnaissance version of a Boeing B-47 jet-powered bomber. These variations were largely used in the early 1950s as part of the Cold War effort. They often ventured into Soviet airspace, sometimes needing to evade Russian craft. These craft contained all manner of equipment, not just radar, but also electronic countermeasures and antennae for detecting active radar from other craft.

In July 1957, a RB-47 on a training exercise flying from Mississippi to Oklahoma claimed that a UFO followed it for over an hour. A number of detected signals suggested there was some mysterious ground radar tracking the RB-47. This signal then seemed to quickly move from ground level to the height of the airplane before moving from one side to another, before then disappearing. Soon after, pilot Lewis Chase spotted what he thought were lights from another jet ahead. The 'jet' became an intense bluish-white light and almost instantaneously changed direction at a speed and velocity not possible by any known craft. The object was identified by advanced surveillance monitoring gear, spotted visually, and followed by ground-radar. The UFO seemed to disappear and reappear on numerous tracking systems at once, including within the RB-47 itself and on the ground.

A debriefing session occurred at Forbes Air Force Base, in Kansas, and a report was sent to the Air Technical

Intelligence Center, mostly to investigate the radar and signal detection anomalies. In November that year, four months after the alleged event, intelligence officer E. Piwetz interviewed the crew. The bulk of the report focused on accounts provided by pilot Lewis Chase and ECM Officer Frank McClure. There was originally some confusion between Chase and McClure as to when the incident occurred; they couldn't recall July or September. Apparently being chased for an hour by a UFO was easily forgettable. Piwetz formed his own conclusions about the observed light being the source of any signals.

The report was filed as an unidentified sighting and promptly forgotten. The conclusions of this report claimed the majority of signs related to the flight path of two American Airlines planes, flight 655 and flight 966, which had engaged in a near miss at around the time of the RB-47 flight. Many UFOlogists have argued that such planes were hundreds of miles away from the RB-47 encounter, which may have been the case, but irrespective official agencies were not concerned about the Piwetz report.

It remained this way until a 1967 conference during which Lewis Chase described the account to a committee looking into Air Force UFO claims. The encounter was not written about as being supportive of UFO evidence until 1969 when Dr James E. McDonald picked it up. In the 1970s, Chase clarified his support of the UFO claim to CUFOS, despite other members of the RB-47 crew being highly skeptical, in particular Frank McClure and co-pilot James McCoid.

Philip Klass suggested that the case could be explained by equipment faults, sighting of an airliner, and reception of intermittent ground radar signals. Such signals likely originated from Kessler Air Force base in Biloxi, Mississippi. UFOlogists like Brad Sparks claim that the base, a training facility, wasn't in use over July and could not have been the source of such signals. This is based on the logic that July is summer vacation and as a result the base was not in use; unfortunately some basic research, like checking term dates, reveal that courses ran back to back, all year round.

Tim Printy has spent some time analyzing the case further

and comes to broadly similar conclusions. The navigation radar used on the RB-47 was designed for looking down (it was a spy plane after all), and not so much concerned with tracking airborne objects. Further, the ECM antennae detected signals of S-band radar, the same frequency often used by the military. If it was a UFO, it was equipped with 1950s American radar equipment.

The light was likely caused by aircraft taking off or landing at either Greater South Western airport or Dallas Naval Air Station, both roughly in the area of where Chase claimed to see the light. In the original report by Chase, there were no claims that this light did anything dramatic. It did not display impossible speeds or rapid maneuvers. Such accounts developed after several retellings; originally the light was just spotted and then disappeared (or perhaps just went out of sight). The UFO wasn't disappearing and then reappearing; rather it was a series of unconnected events that were only grouped together on reflection. Misinterpretation of observation and vagueness of memory do not result in the conclusion of extraordinary explanations.

Another famous case occurred on the early evening of 24th April 1964, when police officer Lonnie Zamora began pursuit of a black vehicle that was speeding out of the town of Socorro, New Mexico. He followed the vehicle to the desert area southeast of town when he heard an enormous roar and saw a long, narrow, funnel-shaped blue and orange flame rising from the sky. Concerned it was an explosion caused by dynamite (not uncommon in that area), he broke off the pursuit of the car to investigate. He heard the roar again, noting it lasted about ten seconds and moved from a high frequency sound to a low frequency one. Coming over a small hill to the source of the noise, Zamora observed a strange shiny object with two figures in white standing near it. The figures soon disappeared to the rear of the craft and appeared to get inside. Zamora then saw the flame again, this time on the underside of the craft. The object then slowly began to rise into the sky. Zamora observed it to be oval in shape, with no windows, some red lettering or symbol on the side, and a number of leg structures beneath it.

Zamora quickly reported the sighting to his superiors, who followed up investigations based on the claims. Two tourists from Iowa, Paul Kies and Larry Kratzer, independently claimed to have witnessed a strange egg-shaped craft in the sky at around the same time and in roughly the same area as the Zamora account. Zamora's earnest nature, matter-of-fact reporting, aspects of physical traces, and the additional witnesses brought the Socorro case to national media attention. A biology student at the University of New Mexico, Mary G. Mayes worked on analysis of materials taken from the site. She claims to have found plant matter completely dried of moisture, unidentifiable traces of unknown organic substances, and a patch of fused sand. Her claims were never verified, and she later stated that she 'forgot' the other people with whom she was working on the project.

It took Zamora three attempts to drive his patrol car over the brow of the hill to get a view of the source of his 'explosion'. Eventually getting out of his car, he was no doubt agitated. He was wearing green sunglasses over the top of his normal prescription glasses, and according to his own account in the rush to get out of the car he bumped into the car fender, dropping both his glasses into the sand. He went on to say that the Sun was to the west (toward the object) and did not help vision. His brief sighting of around twenty seconds was made at a distance, staring into the sun, without his glasses on, shortly after involvement of a high-speed pursuit and coming up on what he thought might be a dynamite accident. It is not unreasonable to suggest that as concise as he attempted his statement to be, it was no doubt a flustered interpretation of something he just hadn't expected to see.

According to Bernard Gildenberg, senior member of the Skyhook balloon programme, and Captain James McAndrew, there were several special tests being conducted at the north end of the White Sands Missile Range on 24th April 1964. Zamora's sighting was within the northern most section of this range.

The tests involved a helicopter carrying an early version of the Lunar Surveyor module. Surveyor was a three-legged

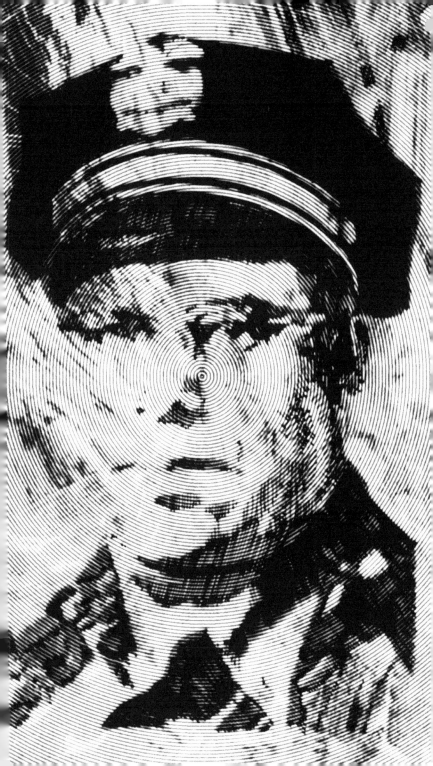

unmanned probe, designed to be used to learn about the Moon prior to the Apollo landing mission. The tests were done using a small Bell helicopter that supported the module on its side, no doubt creating a bizarre-looking profile. The orientation of the landing legs match the imprints found at Zamora's site. The craft used vernier engines to probe and sample soil by blasting them with heat flame. The Surveyor also included a scoop, with a shape that matches the rectangular trough photographed at the 'landing site'. Such test missions would have been manned by a pilot and engineer, two people, both wearing white overalls.

The Surveyor module theory has not been conclusively proved outright, yet it provides a plausible explanation for what Zamora may have seen. This or something similar is most likely at the root of the sighting, but even if it is not, 'flustered police officer see's something unexpected' is still not proof of alien visitors. Zamora became so tired of the subject he eventually avoided both UFOlogy researchers and Air Force personnel, eventually leaving the police to take a job managing a gasoline station.

Another dramatic event occurred over the skies of Tehran, the capital of Iran, in September 1976. Shortly before midnight on the evening of the 19th of that month, a number of Iranian residents telephoned local Mehrabad Airport stating that they had seen an unusual bright light in the sky. Mehrabad's radar was not operational so General Yousefi, Assistant Deputy of Operations at the airport, contacted nearby Shahrokhi Air Force base. Shahrokhi could not detect anything on radar in the rough area described by witnesses. This however did not satisfy Yousefi, especially as looking from the control tower at Mehrabad he was sure he could see a bright light in the sky. Not long after 1am he ordered a F-4 Phantom fighter plane to investigate the sighting. After it could not detect anything, it returned to base and a second F-4 was sent out at around 1:40 a.m.

This second fighter plane, piloted by Lt Parviz Jafari, soon claimed to acquire a radar lock within the vicinity of the bright light. Continuing in pursuit of the object, the pilot soon believed he could make out flashing lights ahead. Upon approach, the F-4 began to register faults with its communication instruments and Jafari then claimed that the UFO moved toward him, dropping a bright object as it did. Thinking it was a missile and that he was under attack, Jafari attempted to engage in combat, only for his electronics to fault further. In panic he quickly returned to base, only for his equipment to rectify itself. Surveillance sweeps by helicopters soon after could not identify any craft or other physical traces. Whatever it was had disappeared.

The documentation regarding the Tehran dogfight comes from a single report, which was written in narrative style and intended as use for an edition of the United States Air Force Security Services quarterly newsletter. The report was based on notes taken by Lt Col Olin Mooy during a debriefing session with the Iranian Air Force. During the mid-1970s, Iran and the USA maintained a strong alliance and many of the Iranian fighter planes were supplied and serviced by American companies. The F-4 Phantoms used at Shahrokhi base were serviced by a mixture of technicians from Westinghouse and McDonnell Douglas, both large American military contractors. As a result there was, at the time, a tight working relationship between the militaries of Iran and the US.

The particular F-4 Phantom piloted by Lt Jafari had a long history of intermittent electrical outages and equipment failures that technicians had not been able to fix. Its radar system was also later repaired for being faulty. American contractors at the base had frequently complained about low quality record-keeping and poor workmanship that meant defective aircraft were being kept in use.

Philip Klass has suggested that the original bright light as seen by General Yousefi and others was actually the planet Jupiter. Also, during September the trail of Halley's comet had left a shower of meteors to fall over the Middle East and parts of the Mediterranean. Any bright lights or 'missiles' seen by pilots are likely explained by these sources, especially as Lt Jafari had no prior experience flying at night. The radar sighting was limited to the faulty F-4, and neither the Air Force base, nor a passing commercial aircraft located any objects visually or on radar in the area of the alleged UFO. Jafari did however keep up the UFO story, later participating in a National Press Club conference, demanding a worldwide investigation into UFOs in 2007.

Another case involves a conventional aircraft and a close encounter with a UFO. On 17th November 1986, a Japan Airlines Boeing 747 cargo plane, JAL 1628, was en route from Paris to Tokyo. Just after 5 p.m., whilst flying over an eastern section of Alaska, the flight crew claimed to witness two UFOs to their left. Contact with nearby Anchorage Air Traffic Control established that no other craft should have been in the area. After a time the two UFOs disappeared, only to be replaced by a third, much-larger craft that seemed to be in pursuit of the Japanese Airliner. Further communication with Anchorage resulted in changes of direction and even a dramatic 360-degree maneuver in an attempt to shake off the UFO. A passing United Airlines flight was close enough to see JAL 1628, but was unable to identify any additional craft. Finally, due to ongoing concerns, a scrambled military jet was sent to investigate. Again it could not identify any other craft in the area other than JAL 1628. Shortly after, at around 5.50pm just over Mt. McKinley the mysterious UFO disappeared.

When the Japanese Airline eventually made it to Tokyo there was a detailed debriefing of the crew. Captain Kenju Terauchi described in detail what he had witnessed, describing a giant walnut-shaped craft. However, when co-pilot Takanori Tamefuji was interviewed, his statement was quite different. He did not witness any walnut-shaped object, rather just some lights that Captain Terauchi was very agitated about. When asked if the lights he saw were particularly distinguishable from stars, Tamefuji said that they were not. Undeterred, Terauchi later went to the press with his story, something that was not looked on with great approval by his employers; Japanese Airlines soon grounded him as a result of his outburst and transferred the pilot to a desk job. Terauchi had a history of reporting UFOs, and didn't stop after his famous walnut sighting, going on to report another UFO as soon as January 1987.

The Belgian UFO wave concerned a series of sightings between November 1989 and March 1990. Despite claims by a number of UFO groups that this constituted a unified invasion, the key sightings during this period have very little, if anything, in common, and were really nothing more than a brief media flap. During the night of 29th November 1989, two policemen reported seeing an unusually bright light in the sky. Such lights were apparently seen by a number of other witnesses and it was suggested a UFO was heading over the town of Liege and toward the border with Germany. The initial police report however described a light that was in the same position in the sky as Venus, and further lights were shown to be emitting from a local disco.

This didn't stop the sightings being reported in the media, and soon various other reports began to come in from the public. Many subsequent accounts described the UFOs as triangular, generally black and silent and identifiable only by three points of light at each tip of the triangle. In the night sky it is pretty easy for the eye to create a triangle by three points of reference, from light produced by conventional aircraft, stars and satellites; in most cases this seems a highly likely explanation as to what people were seeing. Although the Belgian wave is generally associated with these black triangles, a number of reports were also received describing cigar-shaped craft, rectangular platforms, and classic flying saucers. Many of these sightings were later shown to just be observations of helicopters in the night sky.

A second key event occurred on 30th March 1990 when unusual lights moving toward Thorembais-Gembloux, to the southeast of Brussels, were reported, and an air traffic control centre at Semmerzake also picked up a number of radar confirmations in roughly the same area. This ultimately caused the Belgian Air Force to dispatch two F-16 fighter planes to investigate. Neither F-16s spotted any UFOs. Evidence later emerged that the lights were a result of helicopters, and the initial radar sightings were caused by faulty equipment.

The Belgian UFO group Société Belge D'Etude des Phénomènes Spatiaux (SOBEPS) was largely responsible for the promotion of such collective reports as some sort of cohesive UFO invasion. The creation of the Belgian black triangle myth was mostly down to the ongoing campaign by SOBEPS to promote four-months-worth of sporadic reports as one focused mass. It has been argued by UFO skeptics such as Marc Hallet that SOBEPS were spreading misinformation through various media sources. One of the key pieces of evidence in their promotion campaign was a photograph allegedly taken in the Petit-Rechain area depicting a triangular UFO with glowing lights at its tips and within its centre. The creator of the image, Patrick Marechal, has since admitted it to be a hoax. The UFO is actually a model made from polystyrene, back lit by an orange spotlight. Patrick made the image initially as a prank to fool some work colleagues, but the image soon leaked out of the workplace and into the hands of SOBEPS.

The lack of any other black triangle photographs was explained by UFO enthusiasts as being caused by infrared light emitting from such crafts, which then made them disappear when exposed to film. A number of people did manage however to capture the triangular UFOs on video. One video was later shown to be a close up of a street lamp. The best-known, produced by shopkeeper Marcel Alfarano, is just a film of what are clearly ordinary aircraft lights in a roughly triangular formation. Even SOBEPS admits this video is nothing special, though the same may not be true for Mr. Alfarano - as he has since claimed to be in telepathic contact with the visiting aliens.

There is a pattern that quickly emerges when looking at such cases, and it seems that the majority can be explained by sightings of fairly standard celestial objects like planets, stars, and falling meteors. Faulty radar equipment, too, plays a large part, and there is a reliance on such equipment to provide unfaltering hard evidence, when in reality it cannot. With the exception of Lonnie Zamora, no one ever got close enough to really see anything (if you discount fantasist Captain Kenju Terauchi), so the assumption from witnesses that such things are alien spacecraft suggests a pre-disposition to explain anomalies as such.

Sightings that cannot be explained are just unknown things, and unknown things are not by definition alien spacecraft. If rational prosaic explanations are not always totally persuasive, the only conclusive thing such accounts prove is that something was spotted and its exact cause is still unknown. The assumption that these UFOs are anything exotic falls back again to notions of belief. Such sightings provide just as much evidence for demons, angels, super-secret military craft, and flying unicorns, as they do aircraft, stars, or a flock of birds. Unidentified flying objects can support all these claims in equal measure, depending on what you believe most likely, yet on their own ultimately prove none of them.

The acceptance from a lot of UFOlogists that a number of unexplained aerial sightings are extraterrestrial craft, and further that the government of America (and maybe a few other countries) is aware of this, is firmly established. Perhaps if you say something often enough, and enough people listen, and eventually enough people start to believe it themselves, then maybe you can start to claim it is true.

In many ways the Disclosure Project typifies what UFOlogy has become. Established by Dr Steven M. Greer in 1993, the intention of the project was supposedly to de-classify and disclose all information regarding UFOs. The end result is presumably some all-embracing love-in between government agencies, UFO groups and aliens, and the dawn of a new age of interplanetary possibilities, free energy, advanced technologies, and peace, love, and harmony for everyone else. Although it sounds like the wishful ideals of someone who has watched one too many episodes of *Star Trek*, it is really just another version of a scheme to manipulate people's beliefs for the personal gains, both financial and egotistical, of one or a few individuals.

The National Disclosure Project was presented to the media on 9th May 2001. The launch conference hosted around twenty witnesses, mostly ex-military, who provided statements regarding UFO sightings and other evidence. These individual testimonies were presented as a collective mass of evidence, though on comparison few have any actual connection to one another and none are in any way verifiable. Most claims have since been rejected following independent scrutiny, and the majority of 'witnesses', such as Walter Haut, astronaut Gordon Cooper and UFOlogist Nick Pope, had already 'come forward' many times. Such information is clearly hot property, as Greer is now claiming to have a 'dead man's trigger' installed somewhere on his person—so if he were to be killed various sensitive documents would be instantly sent out to influential people. He has never gone into detail as to how this might work, or the content of such documents, nor felt the need to release any of this supposed information via his Disclosure Project. When the Disclosure Project didn't set the international media world alight, he later blamed the 2001 terrorist attacks of September 11th; apparently they were, according to Greer, engineered by the government to distract attention from coverage of his project.

Steven Greer is a retired medical doctor, and trained Transcendental Meditation teacher, who claims to have seen a UFO when he was about eight years old. He founded the Center for the Study of Extraterrestrial Intelligence (CSETI) in 1990. Soon after he set up what he called Project Starlight and began sending freedom of information requests and UFO related junk mail to the US government. He has later claimed this amounted to him being a personal advisor to President Bill Clinton on the subject of extraterrestrials. In April 1997, CSETI made statements to US Congressmen on their collective evidence surrounding UFOs. Around this time he also ran into copyright infringement issues by claims from the UFO research coalition, for alleged duplication of their *Best Available Evidence* document.

Since the early 1990s, Greer has also been taking people into the desert to shine flashlights at random things in the sky, with the hope that any perceived flicker from a star or aircraft is taken as a sign of interstellar communication. Greer claims many alien craft are 'trans-dimensional', and so not visible to the human eye, perhaps explaining why his UFO stakeouts never have a particularly great hit rate. In 2004, Greer began providing a chance to spend five nights with him at his farm in Virginia (for a fee of $600 per person). Here, as part of his Truth for Sale initiative, he extols the nature of reality and the experience of higher states of consciousness. Such opportunities are targeted at focused groups of fifteen people, who must agree to stay for the full duration. In what sounds increasingly like the formation of a UFO cult, Greer also explains why mainstream religious views on spirituality are wrong (and presumably that his own are not), and that he is specially placed to hold the blueprint for the Golden age of Humanity. His claims of alien contact are edging close to 'contactee' territory, more recently going into detail about his telepathic contact with extraterrestrials, or 'coherent thought sequencing' as he calls it.

To boost his ego a bit more he has co-produced and written a 2013 'documentary' about the life and claims of Dr Steven M. Greer. This documentary, *Sirius*, promotes various ideas concerning UFO disclosure, Greer's tireless work, and the revelation that he has discovered physical evidence of an alien body. The claims of evidence of a physical alien, a central plug in his movie, turned out to be nothing more than a human child skeleton from South America.

Steven Greer uses other people's unfounded accounts to promote his own personal gains. This currently involves the promotion of his own UFO-based phone app, organised UFO trips, and promotion of his own movie. CSETI has claimed to have raised close to $5 million to pursue its goals, however Greer has since been accused of using funds raised through Disclosure for personal real estate and sexual recreation services.

His ongoing claim that 'full disclosure of UFO information is imminent' is starting to wear a bit thin; a fair few years have now passed since 1993. Such rhetoric seems more in tune with the accounts of contactees like George Adamski and Billy Meier than any attempt at real scientific investigation into the UFO phenomenon. It seems evident that 'disclosure' is probably the last thing that Greer wants. Without the ongoing quest for this almost-but-never-quite-reachable revelation, he is not able to exploit the particular niche in society he has discovered that allows him to satisfy both his ego and his bank account.

Another UFOlogist to gain an almost cultish following in recent years is Richard Dolan. Born in Brooklyn, New York, Dolan claims to be an academic historian who has gone in search of the 'truth' regarding the UFO cover up. Dolan makes a big deal about his academic background; listening to him you would be sure he was a PhD with many years of a scholarly career behind him. After 'tiring of the academic life', he became a self-employed 'business writer'. His only employment in an educational capacity is teaching the Introduction to UFOlogy module at the International Metaphysical University. He gained an undergraduate degree in History and English Literature from Alfred University, a tiny private university primarily known as a School of Art and Design. He makes big claims about further studies at the University of Oxford in the UK. Technically he did do a course there, but it was not a degree. He earned a 'certificate' in Political Theory, through what sounds very much like a two-week summer school, where the only entry requirement is a cash transfer. He did gain a Master's degree (not a doctorate as he sometimes suggests) in History from the University of Rochester, where he spent some time studying the Cold War. Obviously he could knock out a PhD, he just can't be bothered right now. It was during this time that he began researching and writing about UFOs. He has since written several books including *UFOs and the National Security State*, and *AD After Disclosure: When the Government Finally Reveals the Truth about Alien Contact*. Dolan argues the grand conspiracy claim: that the government is 'in on it' and is hiding the evidence of UFO contact. This is nothing new; it's really just a rehash of UFO stories that have been around for decades. But he presents it all repackaged with an academic twang, talks quite well, and makes a big deal about his detailed research, even though the bulk of his data comes straight from back copies of the MUFON journal. He has some idea of how to write text flavoured with a dash of critical reasoning, which puts him above the research standards of most UFOlogists. His books *appear* well-researched, they *look* like an academic approach, but the fact that he understands what a footnote is does not make him a scholar. His arguments are superficial, nothing is cross-examined in any depth, social and psychological issues around sources are ignored, and his standards of proof are very low. Still, all of this has made him a fast-rising UFOlogy star. He is becoming a kind of rock 'n' roll UFO researcher, even ditching his early academic-geek look for a shaggy haircut, fashionable beard, and open collars.

Dolan has been involved with Disclosure, appearing at the Citizen's Hearing on Disclosure in 2013. Organised by Stephen Basset, the initial attempt for this event was to arrange a hearing in front of Congress on Capitol Hill. When this clearly wasn't going to happen, Basset hired a room and held his own 'hearing', inviting members of Congress to attend. When none showed an interest he reached out to former members of Congress, still with no interest. He then offered to pay any current or previous member $10,000 to attend. He had to double this figure to $20,000 per person, to eventually persuade six former members of Congress to listen to various statements regarding UFOs and an alien cover-up. As well as Dolan, those providing evidence included the likes of Steven Greer, Stanton Friedman, and Nick Pope.

Basset is the Executive Director of the Paradigm Research Group, which is obsessed with lifting the lid on government knowledge about extraterrestrials. He assisted Steven Greer with his 2001 Disclosure Project briefing and wrote a book *UFOs and US Presidents: The Secret History*, which provides all the proof you need about any cover-up. Basset got into UFOs after spending time with Dr John E. Mack, and worked as a volunteer for his Program for Extraordinary Experience Research. Mack was a Harvard University psychiatrist who studied people said to have had encounters with alien beings, many of whom had been referred to him through Budd Hopkins. In 1994, Mack wrote the book *Abduction: Human Encounters with Aliens*, where he argued that such experiences represented spiritual implications for society, going on to suggest that his ex-wife's gynecological problems may have been due to aliens. He also received a $200,000 advance for the book, which may have been a key motivational factor to Basset's following work.

Another person to get swept up with the Disclosure Project is Gary McKinnon, a systems administrator and hacker from Glasgow, who was accused in 2002 of perpetrating the biggest military computer hack of all time. McKinnon claims he was only looking for evidence of free energy suppression and the government cover-up around UFO activity. He states that his motivation was the 2001 Disclosure Project presentation, saying that he found it all 'very credible'. As a teenager he was a member of the British UFO Research Association (BUFORA), a move encouraged by his stepfather who was both an avid sci-fi fan and believer in UFOs.

McKinnon subsequently hacked into ninety-seven US military and NASA computer systems from his girlfriend's aunt's house. It is claimed he paralyzed several munitions deliveries for the US Navy's Atlantic fleet and caused around $700,000 worth of damage to IT security systems. In November 2002, he was indicted by a Federal Grand Jury in Virginia and sentenced to seventy years in prison. McKinnon, who was later diagnosed with Asperger's Syndrome and clinical depression, began an appeal that led to a judicial review to consider blocking his extradition on grounds of his mental health. A bizarre mix of supporters came forward on the side of McKinnon, including David Cameron, Terry Waite, Sting, Stephen Fry, Bob Geldof, and pop groups Marillion and the Proclaimers. Pink Floyd's David Gilmour also released a song to promote the case. McKinnon claims to have made several otherworldly discoveries during his hacking, including high-resolution photographs of UFOs and lists of 'non-terrestrial operatives'. He has since admitted to smoking a lot of pot during the process and neither saved any of this data nor remembers enough detail to expand on any of his claims. On 16th October 2012, then-British Home Secretary Theresa May withdrew her extradition order to the United States. He has now re-invented himself as an online search expert.

Most of the fun is really in the chase, the search for the truth—or at the very least a compelling story. UFOlogists and skeptics alike are guilty of offering their own opinions to explain the cause of any unknown phenomenon. By the simple lack of real evidence such opinions must be based on assumptions and rational, or irrational, beliefs. William of Ockham would have a field day. Many UFO groups have attempted to start a serious discussion about extraterrestrial craft visiting Earth. They have attempted to amass compelling evidence to support such an idea, but so far have not done enough to impress much of academia. There is however one group that has put more time, effort, and resources into the study of UFOs than NICAP, MUFON or CUFOS combined. If academia has never really taken research into UFOs all that seriously, then the major governments of the West have more than made up for it.

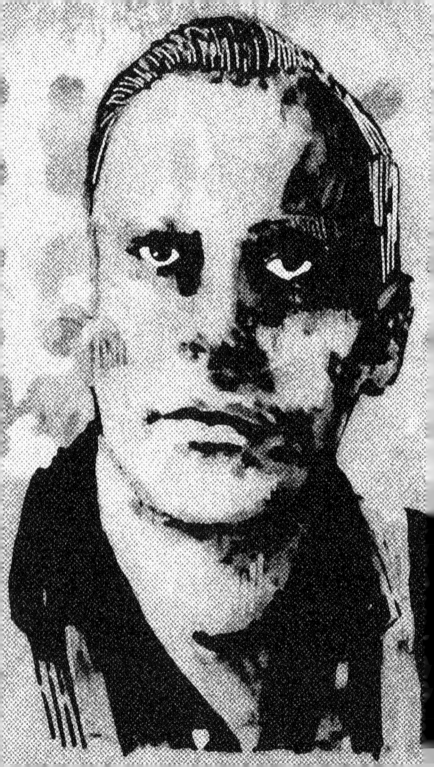

PART THREE
Invaders From a Foreign Land

By the late 1940s and early 1950s fears of an internal Communist subversion in America had reached unprecedented levels of paranoia. Despite there only being 50,000 Americans (out of a population of 150 million) being registered as members of the Communist Party, suspicions ran high and many people found themselves investigated for un-patriotic acts. In 1954 The US Communist Control Act was passed with overwhelming support, and after very little debate, in both houses of Congress.

Joseph McCarthy was an American politician who served as a Republican US Senator, becoming the most visible face of American anti-Communism during the early 1950s. In February 1950, McCarthy gave a Lincoln Day speech to the Republican Women's Club, at Wheeling, West Virginia. During this speech he made claims about the State Department being infiltrated with Communists and produced a list of what he claimed was 200 names of individuals who were known Communists working for the State. Such claims may well have been wide speculation by McCarthy, but it was a pivotal moment to the development of attitudes that followed. Many factors contributed to what became known as McCarthyism, which probably has its roots in the first 'Red scare' of 1917, when following the Bolshevik Russian Revolution many Americans feared a similar radical change was imminent within the US. During the first half of the twentieth century, Communism had risen to become a viable political force and a genuine alternative to the Capitalist democracy of the West.

As well as McCarthy, J. Edgar Hoover, Director of the FBI, was one of the most fevered anti-Communists active during the 1950s. During this time the FBI operated a secret Responsibilities programme, which distributed anonymous documents of evidence on behalf of teachers, lawyers and other professionals. Many individuals were accused of Communist affiliations due to these accusations and lost their jobs as a consequence. The FBI also engaged in a number of illegal practices in search of Communist sympathizers, which included illegal phone taps, checking of mail, and burglaries. They also passed information to prosecuting attorneys in anti-Communist cases that detailed the planned legal strategies of defence lawyers.

It was within this post-war climate of paranoia that the UFO phenomenon developed within America, feeding on people's genuine fears and beliefs about a corrosion of their way of life from some invading other. The war had given many much to fear in the sky, from bombers to spy planes and from long-range missiles to Kamikaze pilots. In July 1947, Pentagon officials were expressing concern about recent UFO reports, primarily those of Ken Arnold, as well as a number of close encounters near Muroc Army Air Base in Southern California. There were some concerns these reports could be sightings of genuine Soviet surveillance craft, or that the reports themselves were a Communist plot to spread further fear and paranoia.

By late 1947, the US Air Force had amassed 109 UFO reports. General George Schulgen ordered a review of this UFO data and had General Nathan F. Twining tasked with leading the investigation. The result was Project Sign, the first official US Government study into UFOs, which was active for most of 1948. The final Project Sign report published in 1949 stated that while some UFOs appeared to be actual aircraft, there was not enough data to determine their origin. A number of personnel involved with Sign speculated about the potential extraterrestrial origin of some craft, including project Director Robert Sneider. This opinion was however officially rejected as Sign was dissolved and quickly replaced by a second study.

The second attempt was Project Grudge, a short-lived project that ran for less than a year during 1949, issuing four summaries and a formal report in August of that year. Its final 600-page report concluded that 'there is no evidence that objects reported upon are the result of an advanced scientific foreign development, and, therefore they constitute no threat to the National security'. Two years after Ken Arnold's sighting, such government studies had officially put an end to the idea of UFOs as anything of any significance. Though apparently not everyone was convinced.

On 19th July 1952, Washington air traffic controller Edward Nugent spotted a number of objects on his radar. No known aircraft were supposed to be in the area and Harry Barnes, senior air-traffic controller, contacted Andrews Air Force Base. Some confusion at the base (caused by someone seeing a shooting star out of the window) resulted in several military craft being prepped for take-off. The sightings made headline news in a number of papers, such as the *Cedar Rapids Gazette*, which claimed Saucers swarmed over the Capital. This was followed by stories in *The New York Times* and the *Washington Post*.

The following week on 26th July, a National Airlines flight into Washington observed strange lights above their aircraft. Radar trackers at National Airport and Andrews Air Force Base soon began tracking the unknown objects. By the evening radar centres were picking up signals in all sectors over Washington. Two military jets were then scrambled and reports leaked revealing that the jets had been ordered to shoot down any UFOs they encountered. No action had been taken in the sky, but public interest in potential alien craft flying over the Capital was heightened.

In response to these recent reports, the Pentagon held

the largest press conference since World War II on 29th July. Presented by Major Generals John Samford and Roger Ramey, the various sightings over the Capital were explained as stars and meteors, and the radar signals explained as being caused by temperature inversions, where warm air causes radar beams to bounce off the air itself. UFOlogists screamed about a 'cover-up', convinced that these radar signals could not be false.

Much is made of radar signals as hard evidence of UFO activity. The attitude toward radar, certainly during the mid-twentieth century, was very much like the attitude toward photography in the early twentieth century. The 'photograph doesn't lie' was a common perception until of course people realized it could. The same is relatively true for radar; if it has detected a signal then this is often taken as proof that something noteworthy must be there. Radar technology developed steadily through the twentieth century and radar systems used today are far more sophisticated beasts than those of the pre-digital age. Radar is susceptible to noise and clutter generated by frequency echoes returned from targets that are not generally of interest. The source of such clutter can frequently be things such as flocks of birds, snowstorms, hail, sandstorms, atmospheric turbulence, movements in the sea, high areas of ground, buildings, or meteor trails. Radar can also suffer from intentional or accidental interference as certain radio frequencies can jam such object-detection systems. On top of all this is the issue that radar is essentially electronic equipment that can fault or break as much as anything else, and regular calibration is required by technicians to ensure things are working properly.

Clutter can also be caused by reflections caused in certain atmospheric conditions, as temperature inversions can cause radar to bounce off heat patterns within the air itself; this is rare, but by no means unheard of. These signals are often referred to as 'ghosts' or 'angels', a term coined by radar operators during World War II in reference to fallen comrades. Such anomalies are well-known to skilled radar operators, who understand the differences in general between 'interesting' objects and 'angels'. Equipment is calibrated to filter out noise, and things such as pulse-doppler processing and signal-to-noise ratio settings work toward reducing such clutter as much as possible. Radar operators know what they are looking for and also learn to filter out any remaining clutter in order to differentiate a flock of birds from an aircraft, at least most of the time. Radar is not a foolproof certainty. In other words, just because there has been a radar blip, it does not mean unquestionably that there is an object of interest in the sky. Like photography, radar is easily capable of not quite telling the truth.

A reduction in 'angel' sightings has also paralleled the development in digital radar technologies, as systems have just become better at filtering out anomalies. However mistakes will still be made from time to time. The general ignorance of radar anomalies from the wider public provides convenient 'hard evidence' for UFOlogists to exploit when looking to support fantastical claims. Most people are just not that interested in the particulars of radar detection systems; stories about aliens flying through the skies are typically far more interesting.

By August 1952, *Life* magazine was reporting stories of UFOs flying over the White House. Such descriptions have grown over time and become fueled by supposed documentation of such events. A now infamous photograph apparently depicting a string of illuminated craft flying over the White House has entered UFO folklore as evidence of such an event. There have been many versions of the photograph circulated through books, magazines, documentaries, and now via online forums. The actual photograph is real, in so much as the original image is not faked or manipulated, but it is frequently cropped and presented out of context. The image was not taken in 1952 but rather 1965, and was first associated with UFOs when it was used as the cover to an edition of *Flying Saucers* magazine in summer 1973. The image actually depicts reflections of street lamps and lawn illuminations from the front of the White House. The reflections in the sky are actually lens flare, existing only through photographic reproduction. Such streetlights are often cropped out of the image, as the matching pattern of lights tends to make the true source of the UFOs fairly apparent. Versions of this photograph have even been animated to create film footage of the event. Created through computer image manipulation software, the earliest appearance of such footage was not until October 2005.

Around fifty-five separate UFO reports were received during July 1952, an extremely high number that disturbed both the Air Force and the CIA. Both groups suspected an enemy nation was attempting to flood the US with false reports of UFOs in a bid to cause mass panic. A memo on the subject of UFOs as a possible cause for concern sent by CIA director Walter B. Smith resulted in the creation of the Robertson Panel. This group met formally for the first time in January 1953. Headed by consultant physicist Howard P. Robertson, the panel was assembled by the CIA and the Intelligence Advisory Committee to assess and review all of the official UFO files. The panel met for twelve hours over the course of four days and reviewed the best evidence from official UFO reports, concluding that most UFO reports had prosaic explanations, and that all could no doubt be explained with further investigation. The main concern proposed by the panel was the fact that increased public interest in UFOs could lead to government departments receiving overwhelming quantities of reports from the wider public, which in turn could result in a security threat as agencies may miss genuine threats within such noise. There was also a concern that civilian UFO groups could become a hotbed of subversive ideas and be open to manipulation by nefarious individuals. As a result, the panel recommended a public relations campaign aimed at 'debunking' the UFO phenomenon.

Due to the advice of the Robinson Panel, increasing Cold War tensions, and the Korean War, USAF Director of Intelligence Major General Charles P. Cabell ordered the formation of a new investigation to monitor UFO reports. Project Blue Book was the third official US Government study on the subject, as well as its longest-running and most in-depth one. It was active up until January 1970 and over this period the project collected 12,618 UFO reports, going on to conclude that most of them were misidentifications of natural phenomena or sightings of conventional aircraft or weather balloons.

Twenty-eight-year-old Edward J. Ruppelt was originally asked to oversee Project Blue Book by Lt. Col. N. R. Rosegarten, partly because he had a reputation as a good organizer and was critical of some of the lack of scrutiny in the early Project Sign. However, Ruppelt was ultimately frustrated by his assignment to Blue Book, seeing it as a rather pointless paper exercise. This was compounded when later in 1953 his Blue Book staff was reduced from ten to three, and he subsequently asked for re-assignment. Despite being credited with coining the term Unidentified Flying Object, Ruppelt's 1956 book *The Report on Unidentified Flying Objects* assessed UFOs as a 'space age myth'. He died young, of a heart attack in 1960 at the age of thirty-seven, and as a result became part of the great UFO cover-up conspiracy.

Project Blue Book collated sightings, analysed the probable cause and classified such reports into groups like 'Balloon', 'Aircraft' or 'Birds'. A small percentage of Blue Book reports were classified as having 'insufficient evidence' to satisfactorily determine their cause, while another group was classified simply as 'unknowns'. This last grouping has often been pounced upon as evidence of alien craft by UFO researchers. However the cases are simply what they are classed as: they are just unknown. An 'unknown' report might be a sighting of a balloon, or aircraft, some natural phenomenon, something of pure invention—but this would be just speculation. The difference between 'insufficient evidence' and 'unknown' is largely due to the clunky definitions established by the group at the time. Cases with 'insufficient evidence' would be reports with a level of description to suggest possibilities for an explanation, but not enough data to draw any real conclusions. For example, 'I saw a strange craft with flashing lights' might suggest conventional aircraft, but on its own isn't conclusive. An 'unknown' would be a report so vague or outlandish that there would be simply nowhere for any investigation to go; the detail of such reports would basically amount to 'I saw something in the sky'. The idea that these 'unknowns' are alien craft doesn't even make sense within the logic of the study, as in order to have made such conclusions, these reports would have needed substantial amounts of data and so would have been removed from such a classification in the first place.

Project Grudge had produced four reports on UFO sightings between November 1951 and February 1952, after which Project Blue Book began issuing monthly reports, the first of which became report 5. Reports 1 – 12 were essentially status reports on the projects, but a special in-depth report 14 (there seems to be no report 13) attempted to analyse the data collected by the studies so far. Produced in 1954, Project Blue Book Special Report 14 suggests that out of 434 reports classified as unknown, there were in fact only 12 sightings (2.7%) that were genuinely unusual and unexplainable, having been documented and reported in a way as to provide a good deal of information about the sighting. However even in these cases it was ultimately concluded that the lack of any real evidence beyond a witness statement suggested that the chance of such a sighting being a 'flying saucer' was remote. Further, it was stated that a good deal of reports that were ultimately classified as 'knowns' appeared in their first instance to be equally bizarre until a rational explanation was deduced.

Despite this, reports of UFO sightings and even landings, with occasional glimpses of actual aliens, became frequent and public interest continued to grow both in America and overseas. Magazines began to print more stories on flying saucers and TV networks like CBS produced programmes devoted to the topic. Popular celebrities, such as Sammy Davis and Johnny Carson, came forward to speak of their own UFO experiences. As public fascination increased, House Republican Leader Gerald Ford of Michigan (later the 38th President of the United States) formally demanded a Congressional hearing and investigation into these flying saucers. Donald Keyhoe, Director of NICAP, backed such requests. Ford's demands were met when limited open Congressional hearings were held by the House Armed Services Committee and Air Force officials for one day in April 1966. Witnesses testifying about such sightings included Dr J. Allen Hynek and Harold Brown, Secretary of the Air Force. Nothing of great significance regarding alien craft was revealed at this committee, however, what was noted was the massive financial burden such investigations had been having on the Air Force. Money was being wasted and attempts to rationalize mysterious sightings were only feeding public paranoia.

Due to ongoing public pressure regarding UFO activity, the Air Force explored the potential of a contract with a leading university to undertake an intensive independent investigation into UFO sightings. The aim was to ease public concerns that the US government was concealing what it knew about UFOs and also unload the ongoing pressures of dealing with reports of such sightings. As a result, the University of Colorado accepted a $325,000 contract with the Air Force to undertake an eighteen-month study.

The Condon Committee was the informal name for the University of Colorado UFO Project. It was funded by the US Air Force between 1966-'68 under the direction of Edward Condon. Condon was a distinguished American nuclear physicist, a pioneer in quantum mechanics, and was also involved in the development of nuclear weapons during World War II. Neither Condon himself nor other members of the university were that keen on conducting such a study but were persuaded to do so for financial reasons by Robert Low, Assistant Dean of the graduate school.

In July 1968, the Committee on Science and Astronautics held the US House of Representatives Symposium on Unidentified Flying Objects, the second of only two formal hearings on the subject. Statements were given by six scientists in regard to the subject of UFOs, including those from Dr J. Allen Hynek, Dr James E. McDonald, and Dr Carl Sagan. Further supporting papers were provided by Donald Menzel, Leonard Sprinkle, and Stanton Friedman. The committee met for one day on July 29th in Room 2318 of the Rayburn House Office Building. Several of the scientists, in particular Hynek and McDonald, recommended conducting further official study into the area of UFOs, yet such action was what the Condon Committee report (which at this point had not been released) was expected to counter.

By this point in his relationship with UFOs, Hynek had started moving toward the idea that there was more to them than misidentifications of weather balloons and swamp gas. His 1968 statement is suitably non-committal on his belief in an extraterrestrial source, but by the late-1960s his tenure as official scientific advisor to Project Blue Book was coming to an end, and business rather than scientific priorities were soon to take precedent.

McDonald provides a large number of detailed cases, answering questions such as 'Why don't pilots see UFOs' and 'Why don't astronomers see UFOs?' His point being that they do see them, or at least report that they believed they saw them. Interestingly, most of the cases McDonald cites come from a limited number of sources, namely Donald Keyhoe (fiction writer and Director of NICAP), NICAP records, and APRO records. His statement that UFOs are likely extraterrestrial craft is formed, by his own admission, not from the strength of the actual supporting evidence, but rather on the fact that he didn't find any of the alternatives adequate. McDonald attempted to form alliances with a number of members of the Condon Committee in an effort to influence their findings and also undermine Condon's leadership.

After examining hundreds of UFO files from Project Blue Book, as well as those from several civilian UFO groups, the Condon Committee produced a final report in April 1969 that stated 'the study of UFOs was unlikely to yield major scientific discoveries'. In response to this report the US Air Force closed Project Blue Book in an attempt to put a stop to the ongoing UFO fascination. The official line was that there was nothing of concern regarding any sightings of flying saucers, and there was no cover-up regarding government knowledge of extraterrestrials. However, the fact remained that some UFO reports were potentially also sightings of test reconnaissance planes, such as the U-2 or A-12, and for a period the intelligence agencies encouraged the perception of UFOs over identification of secret military projects.

It should also be considered that the idea of a flying disc-shaped craft is a fairly established man-made concept. Although such shapes have never become part of mainstream aviation design, they have been frequently experimented with, especially during the first half of the twentieth century when there was less of a preconceived idea about what aircraft should look like. The McCormick-Romme Umbrella Plane was developed in 1911, a nonagon-shaped doughnut with a pilot precariously balanced on an exposed central seat. Following several design modifications it made a successful flight, reaching thirty-feet into the air, but after two years of development the design was scrapped. Other similar designs followed, including the Lee-Richards Annular Monoplane developed in 1913.

The 1930s saw a renewed interested in circular aviation concepts. The Arup S-1 was the first of a range of aircraft developed by Cloyd Snyder. A propeller-driven glider, the craft was tested a number of times, starting in 1932, but had very poor controllability. The glider had to be towed into the air and, once airborne, was powered by a Henderson motorcycle engine. The design was refined, culminating with the Arup S-4 in 1935, though it did not perform much better than its predecessors. Most of the Arup craft were ultimately turned into scrap during World War II. The Nemeth Roundwing, which first appeared in 1934, faired marginally better. Designed by Paul Nemeth and built by students at Miami University, it eventually managed airborne cruising speeds of 100mph.

The period toward the end of World War II was marked with a number of experimental innovations in aircraft. These were the last throes of the propeller age and the dawn of the jet engine, and some weird and wonderful designs were around for a short period. Alexander Weygers's flying saucer-looking Discopter was designed on paper in 1944. The Vought-XF5U 'Flying Flapjack' was an experimental US Navy Fighter developed during World War II. The unusual design consisted of a flat, somewhat disc-shaped body. It was small and maneuverable with a top speed of 475mph. Not many were made and production of the model was cancelled in 1947. It did however feature on the cover of *Mechanix Illustrated* in spring 1947, just before an outbreak of flying saucer sightings. The Northrop YB-35 'Flying Wing' was an experimental heavy bomber aircraft used by the US Army Air Force toward the end of World War II. Its successor, the YB-49, essentially the jet-powered replacement, made its first flights in 1947.

Whether sightings of military craft explain various UFO

accounts or just that the rumours of such a craft's existence is in the back of the minds of witnesses is unclear. However, the changing shapes of experimental craft do often parallel the changing shapes of reported UFOs. The high altitude testing of secret reconnaissance craft between 1954 and 1974 no doubt led to a huge increase in such reports. It is estimated that half of the reports received by Project Blue Book from the late 1950s through to the late '60s were a result of the testing of craft like the U-2. This led the Air Force to make several misleading and deceptive statements to the public in attempts to protect national security. Such deception only added fuel to conspiracy theories and cover-up controversies that later developed.

No matter how much data was released to debunk claims, or how many studies on the topic were conducted, people continued to believe in UFOs and that there was a cover-up going to the very top of government. After the closure of Blue Book, Walter B. Smith encouraged the CIA to continue to monitor UFO reports but urged them to conceal such interests from the media and public, so as to reduce potential alarmist tendencies. Smith also wanted to know what use could be made of the UFO phenomenon in connection with psychological warfare techniques. UFOlogist Leon Davidson has since claimed that the CIA was solely responsible for creating the flying saucer myth as a tool for Cold War psychological warfare. Sinister motivations and cover-ups concerning the CIA and other secret government agencies has become a staple of UFO folklore, represented in part at least by the Men in Black.

During the early 1950s, Gray Barker was working as a theatrical film booker in West Virginia. About this time he developed an interest in the 'Flatwoods Monster' – an alleged extraterrestrial sighting reported near the town of Flatwoods by a pair of young brothers, Edward and Fred May. The story was soon reported to local officials by the boys' mother, Kathleen May, in September 1952. The descriptions provided by the boys have been suggested to be rather similar to that of a barn owl, and it may have been a simple case of them unexpectedly coming face to face with one and being startled by it. Barker had begun collecting stories on the incident and soon had enough to produce an article on the case, which was then published in *Fate* magazine. After this initial success, Barker began writing more pieces on UFOs and related issues on a regular basis, often for publications such as *Space Review*. Although his accounts were always written as if fact, they were intended by Barker to be works of fiction. Many years later a reworking of his 'Flatwoods Monster' article was produced, where he wrote about an alleged creature known as the 'Mothman'. This preceded John Keel's better-known *The Mothman Prophecies* book by several years and may have been a key influence on Keel's supposed accounts of such creatures spotted in West Virginia in the late 1960s.

Barker was largely skeptical about UFOs and other paranormal phenomenon, writing books and articles principally for money, but also to satisfy his own unique sense of humour. He has confided to fellow UFO enthusiasts James Moseley and John Sherwood that he enjoyed seeing when one of his hoaxes had deceived a UFO devotee. He sometimes employed a more direct approach, such as when he wrote a fake letter to George Adamski, claiming to be from the US Department of State, saying how pleased they were with Adamski's UFO work.

In 1956, he wrote the book *They Knew Too Much About Flying Saucers*, which introduced the concept of the Men in Black to UFO mythology. In this book Barker describes the account of Albert K. Bender (who also happened to be the Director of the International Flying Saucer Bureau), who after seeing a UFO and trying to tell others about it, was confronted by three men in black suits driving a black car. After this encounter Bender was too frightened to ever discuss the details of his UFO sighting, though presumably not the encounter with the mysterious suited men. In the late 1960s Barker collaborated with John Sherwood on a fictional story featuring the Men in Black, later published as 'fact' by Raymond Palmer in his *Flying Saucers* magazine. In 1962, Barker wrote a second book on the Men in Black, *Flying Saucers and Three Men*, and shortly before his death in 1983 he produced a final book, *M.I.B: The Secret Terror Among Us*.

In popular culture the Men in Black are often implied to

be government agents, either working for the CIA, FBI, or some other top secret 'official' organization. In some accounts they are even implied to be aliens themselves. Barker's writings inspired the *Men in Black* comic book series by Lowell Cunningham, which in turn inspired the 1997 movie of the same name starring Will Smith and Tommy Lee Jones.

The idea that UFO secrecy goes to the very top of government is common amongst certain UFO believers. As a result, much has been made of such grand conspiracies and supposed encounters between aliens and US Presidents. President Dwight D. Eisenhower was rumoured to have had many encounters with UFOs and aliens, though it seems clear that this is mostly, if not completely, the invention of a small group of individuals. The idea was further encouraged by the writings of British UFO researcher Timothy Good. Eisenhower reportedly witnessed a UFO while onboard the USS Roosevelt in 1952. The story wasn't reported until 1997, when it featured in an edition of the *New York Post*. In 2010, former Federal Relations and Veteran's Affairs committee member Henry W. McElroy, Jr., 'went public' regarding an encounter between Eisenhower and an alien.

In 2012, Senior Editor of the *Veteran's Today* website, Gordon Duff, recounted a claim that he once saw a document in the early 1980s that was dated August 1977, and which itself referred to an incident in 1953 – where Eisenhower had a meeting with an 'alien power'. Allegedly, during this meeting a deal was made to allow aliens to harvest citizens from the United States. It's nice to know the aliens ask permission first. Duff is also a firm believer in Zionist conspiracy theories, certain that 9/11 was an inside job. Eisenhower is also supposed to have met aliens at Edwards Air Force Base (at the time known as Muroc Air Field). The story has its basis in a supposedly unexplained disappearance of the President whilst on vacation at Palm Springs. Press Secretary James Haggerty has later revealed that the President had damaged a tooth while eating fried chicken, and had gone to a dentist to get the problem fixed.

President John F. Kennedy had some alleged involvement with UFOs, too. He supposedly wrote a top secret memo to the

Director of the CIA requesting a detailed review of all UFO intelligence files, with any 'unknowns' affecting National Security to be shared with NASA. Eleven days after writing this memo JFK was assassinated. An alleged CIA document from 1962 also revealed that Marilyn Monroe was planning to give a press conference about what President Kennedy had told her concerning a visit to an Air Force facility where he observed the remains of a crashed UFO. The document was dated 4th August 1962, the day before Monroe died. The supposed document emerged in 1994 from Milo Speriglio, a writer whose previous works had included *The Marilyn Conspiracy* and *Marilyn Monroe: Murder Cover-Up*. The CIA document was actually a hoax, produced by Tim Cooper, a Security Officer from California who was personally acquainted with Speriglio. After receiving the memo from Cooper, and believing his story about it coming from a CIA agent, Speriglio attempted to use it to reignite the success of his 1980s Monroe conspiracy books. The memo has now featured in a range of UFO books, and even a few mainstream Marilyn Monroe biographies, but by 2009 Cooper had admitted that such documents were nothing but fabrications.

Richard Nixon was the President who finally managed to cash in on the ambitious space programme announced by Kennedy in the early 1960s. He also managed to stick around for long enough to announce the development of the space shuttle. Despite this, his was a presidency defined by scandal and cover-up, one that cemented a distinct distrust of the American government in a significant number of its citizens. The Watergate scandal and President Nixon's subsequent resignation seriously damaged America's faith in its own government, adding evidenced events to back up stories concerning the shady conspiracies often popular within the UFO community. The war in Vietnam had a major impact, too, on Nixon's reputation, being a long and ugly campaign that ended in 1975 when US troops withdrew from South Vietnam, only for the Communists to take over the area soon after. In 1973, Nixon took a trip to Florida where he met comedian Jackie Gleason to open a charity golf tournament. According to

Gleason, the pair became good friends, bonding over a love of golf and apparently a shared fascination regarding UFOs.

Gleason has gone on to claim that Nixon once took him to a secure area at Homestead Air Force Base and showed him the remains of alien bodies. Gleason was a long-time UFO fan. He was also an insomniac who read UFO books frequently until the early hours. After his death a collection of 1,700 books of his on the subject were donated to a local university. Gleason had personally financed psychic research into extraterrestrial and supernatural areas, as well as having bought several artifacts, such as jars of 'ectoplasm'. He even had a house built in New York, which the architects based on the shape of a classic flying saucer, later named 'The Mothership' after its completion.

Jimmy Carter is sometimes referred to as the UFO President. Carter reported seeing a UFO in 1969, before he was President. He claims to have seen a bright object, 'luminous, as bright and as big as the Moon', in the night sky above Georgia. Carter has described the event many times, saying that he was impressed with what he had seen. Upon revision of his sighting it seems most likely that he actually just saw Venus, bright in the night sky.

The Freedom of Information Act (FOIA) was passed in America in 1966. When Carter took office in 1976, he removed further barriers around the confidentiality of Government documents, opening up the viability of further FOIA requests. He also introduced the 'Public Interest Balancing Test' in 1978, forcing courts to examine levels of public interest when considering declassification requests made under the FOIA. Carter had set the stage for the release of many official UFO documents. While campaigning for President he had promised, if elected, 'to make every piece of information this country has about UFO sightings available to the public'. He didn't quite manage that, however, during Carter's administration the FBI released 1,600 pages and the CIA 892 pages of UFO documents.

Ronald Reagan is another US President who allegedly witnessed a UFO. Reagan reportedly saw two UFOs while he was Governor of California. The first sighting occurred while he was on his way to a Hollywood party. He arrived in a very excitable state telling actress Lucille Ball of a UFO he had just spotted along the LA coastal highway. Ball later commented that she often wondered if Reagan would have been elected President if he had told everyone he'd seen a flying saucer. Reagan's second encounter occurred in 1974, when he spotted a strange light behind the Cessna jet plane he was travelling in. Reagan has also confided to Norman Miller, the Washington Bureau Chief for the *Wall Street Journal*, that both he and his wife Nancy had done personal research into UFOs and were particularly interested in 'references' to UFOs in Egyptian hieroglyphics. Ultimately Reagan refused to state outright that he believed in UFOs, but also would not deny their possible existence.

President Bill Clinton mentioned the idea of UFOs and aliens around twenty-five times on the record during his time at the White House. He has since admitted that he began looking into UFOs during his second term in office, close to the fiftieth anniversary of the Roswell crash, and has since stated he believes it increasingly less likely that we are alone. Clinton's Chief of Staff, John Podesta, has gone on record demanding that the government declassify further knowledge about UFOs; as he said in a 2002 press conference 'it's time to find out what the truth really is'. Podesta continued to work as an advisor to President Barack Obama and most recently acted as campaign chairman for Hillary Clinton's 2016 presidential campaign. Podesta has stated that his biggest regret working with Obama was not securing release of classified UFO files. He may have had more luck with Hillary Clinton, who is apparently open to the idea that Earth has been visited by aliens, and has said that she wants to disclose all the government knows about UFOs. Despite his greater acceptance of several conspiracy theories, such as ideas that climate change is a hoax, President Donald Trump has so far remained silent regarding anything to do with UFOs.

The American government is not alone in exploring the UFO phenomenon. When a reconnaissance plane was returning from a mission over Europe during World War II, it claimed it was approached by a metallic UFO which then continued to follow it. Upon hearing of the incident, British Prime Minister Winston Churchill became so concerned that he made records of the incident classified for fifty years over fear their release would cause mass panic, he was also concerned it would 'destroy one's belief in the Church'. The decision was made after a meeting with US President Dwight Eisenhower over the best ways to approach the UFO problem.

As a result, the Flying Saucer Working Party (FSWP) was set up in October 1950. It was chaired by G. L. Turney, and became the UK Ministry of Defence's first official study into UFOs, which had its roots in a study commissioned by the then-Chief Scientific adviser Sir Henry Tizard, who had worked on the development of Britain's radar defences prior to World War II. FSWP operated under such secrecy that its existence was known to very few; the group comprised of only five technical intelligence specialists, who produced reports for Winston Churchill's government. After ongoing pressure from people such as Air Chief Marshall Hugh Dowding and Lord Louis Mountbatten, Tizard, too, became convinced such sightings demanded further investigation.

Lord Hugh Dowding, an Air Chief Marshall of the Royal Air Force and former head of the RAF Fighter Command during the Battle of Britain, made several statements about UFOs in 1954, claiming that many sightings were of objects 'not manufactured by any nation on Earth'. He was also a spiritualist and ghost hunter who had produced a number of books on psychic phenomena, such as *Lychgate: the Entrance to the Path* in 1945. He was also an active member of the Fairy Investigation Society.

Lord Louis Mountbatten, 1st Earl Mountbatten of Burma, believed UFOs were extraterrestrial; he claimed a UFO once landed in the grounds of his estate at Broadlands in Romsey, Hampshire, in 1955. Mountbatten was also uncle to Prince Philip, the Duke of Edinburgh, and husband to Queen Elizabeth II. The Prince has been strongly rumoured to have a keen interest in UFOs, demonstrated in a statement from 1954 when he said, 'there are many reasons to believe that UFOs do exist, there is so much evidence from reliable witnesses'. Desmond

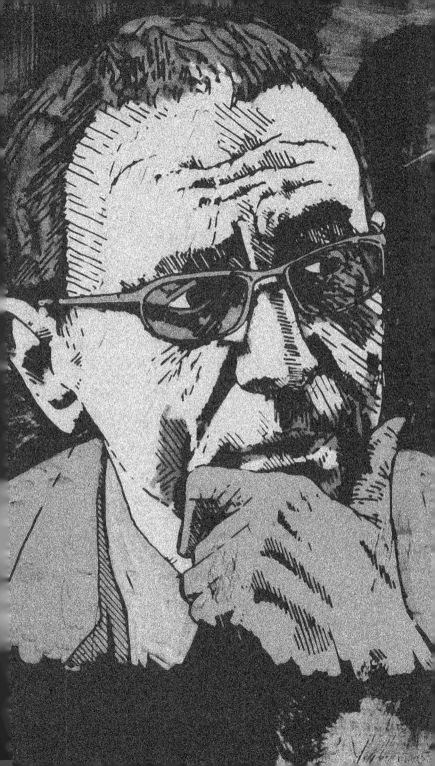

Leslie was an eccentric aristocrat and author of *Flying Saucers Have Landed* with George Adamski. His father was first cousin to Winston Churchill, and also had links to Prince Philip. On instruction from the Prince, Air Marshal Peter Horsley, formerly a Deputy Commander-in-Chief at HQ Strike Command, undertook a study into UFOs while working as a Royal equerry.

Despite such external pressures, the FSWP's Directorate of Scientific Intelligence Report Number 7 concluded that all UFO sightings could be explained as misidentifications of ordinary objects or phenomena, optical illusions, psychological delusions, or hoaxes. As a result, the FSWP was officially dissolved in 1951, but government interest in the subject did not end with it. After the 1952 Washington sightings, Churchill sent a memo to Lord Cherwell, Secretary of State for Air. Confused about the recent UFO outbreak in America, Churchill asked, 'what does all this stuff about flying saucers amount to? What can it mean? What is the truth?' Cherwell referred Churchill to the official studies of both the US and UK, holding to the conclusions that such things had prosaic explanations. However, further confusing events were soon to cause the British government to re-question such findings.

In September 1952, a NATO exercise called Operation Mainbrace aimed to simulate a Soviet invasion of Western Europe. The exercise involved personnel from the UK, USA, France, Norway, Canada, and others. It was part of a series of NATO programmes involving around 300,000 military personnel who engaged in various maneuvers from the Arctic Circle to the Mediterranean Sea. On September 13th, the Danish destroyer *Willemoes* was performing exercises north of Bornholm Island as part of the Mainbrace exercise. During the night, Lieutenant Commander Schmidt Jensen observed a UFO moving at an estimated 900mph over the ship.

Less than a week later, Lieutenant John Kilburn observed a silvery object following an RAF jet at Topcliffe, North Yorkshire. Around a month after that, over rural Gloucestershire, Flight Lieutenant Michael Swiney spotted three circular craft while in the cockpit of a Meteor trainer jet. He described them as white and possibly supernatural. Interestingly, Swiney's flight instructor was Air Marshall Peter Horsley, who at the time was being encouraged by Prince Phillip to interview aircrew involved in the earlier Topcliffe incident.

In December that year, the CIA's Assistant Director of Scientific Intelligence, Dr H. Marshall Chadwell, reported on the incidents which occurred in September at RAF Topcliffe as well as that during October at the RAF flying school in Little Rissington, Gloucestershire. As a result the Ministry of Defence covertly reformed the Flying Saucer Working Party under the Direction of Dr Reginald Jones, who was also Director of Scientific Intelligence at the MoD. The Mainbrace sightings led the RAF to officially recognizing the UFO phenomenon as a potential issue, and shortly after two RAF officers travelled to Wright-Patterson airfield in Ohio to visit America's Project Blue Book staff. By 1953, the decision was made that the British Air Ministry should investigate UFO reports on a permanent basis.

A memorandum on aerial phenomena was later prepared for a meeting of the Cabinet Office's Intelligence group in April 1957, as the Air Ministry were concerned that a number of UFO reports were still shrouded in mystery. The same year a secret investigation was launched by a research branch of the RAF into ongoing unexplained radar anomalies; the study concluded the radar systems had simply been tracking migrating flocks of birds. During the Cold War, RAF planes were scrambled around 200 times to investigate UFOs over the UK air defence region. These invariably proved to be anti-submarine or long-range reconnaissance aircraft from the Soviet Union.

Interest in UFOs continued over the following decades at an influential level. William Francis Brinsley le Poer Trench, the 8th Earl of Clancarty, who was a friend of Desmond Leslie, helped to found *Flying Saucer Review* magazine, of which Prince Philip was alleged to be a regular subscriber. Le Poer Trench went on to write a number of books on UFOs himself, including *The Sky People* and *Reptiles from the Internal World*. A firm believer in UFOs, le Poer Trench soon set up his own UFO group, Contact International. In 1975, he gained a seat in the House of Lords following the death of his half-brother and used his time to establish a UFO study group, push for declassification of UFO data, and chair a number of UFO-based debates. He promoted some strange ideas: that UFOs originated from the hollow earth, that the North Pole did not exist, that various characters from the bible, such as Noah, were from Mars, and that he himself was a descendent of a 65,000-year-old alien species.

The House of Lords All-Party UFO Study Group was set up by le Poer Trench in 1979 and included members such as Lord Hill-Norton, once Admiral of the Fleet and Chief of the Defence Staff, the Earl of Kimberley; Lady Falkender, former aide to Harold Wilson; and Ralph Noyes, private secretary to Vice-Chief of the Air Staff. Noyes believed he witnessed a UFO in 1956, and went on to write UFO spy-themed fiction as well as non-fiction accounts of crop circles, such as *The Crop Circle Enigma*. By the early 1990s, he was entertaining UFOlogists such as Timothy Good and Nikolai Lebedev at his flat in London and soon after his retirement he began writing letters to the Ministry of Defence concerning all manner of UFO issues.

Of particular interest to Ralph Noyes was an incident that occurred over winter 1980 at an air base near Rendlesham forest, in part of Suffolk. The story was reported in various media during the early 1980s, such as when the tabloid newspaper *The News of the World* broke the story in October 1983, running the incident as a front-page headline: 'UFO Lands in Suffolk – and that's Official'. It was followed by an article in *Omni* magazine soon after. In 1985, David Alton, a former Liberal MP for Liverpool and now member of the House of Lords, also wrote letters to then-Minister of Defence, Michael Heseltine, about the Rendlesham UFO incident.

The Rendlesham Forest case is sometimes referred to as the 'British Roswell'; in truth the reality of each case is equally mundane. The two Royal Air Force airfields, RAF Brentwaters and RAF Woodbridge, are around two miles apart near the east coast of England, just past Ipswich. During the Cold War the US Air Force operated both areas. Across several nights over Christmas 1980, strange lights were spotted in the night sky, which were then tracked, and witnesses observed an 'alien craft' in nearby Rendlesham forest. The witnesses included multiple military personnel and a senior official at the base, Lt. Col. Charles Halt, filed an official report concerning the incident.

The reality is perhaps not as dramatic as any of that sounds, and the incident has been thoroughly debunked by a number of people, in particular Ian Ridpath and Brian Dunning. 25th and 26th December 1980 was a particularly good period for observing meteors and shooting stars, especially in south and east England, making it a fertile site for would-be UFO spotters. In fact, many UFO reports were received in the area over this period.

On 26th December, after a security patrolman reported seeing some 'strange lights in the sky', several airmen from Woodbridge Base went to investigate. The reports of both the patrolman and the airmen suggest that they had in fact just seen shooting stars. However the airmen also noticed a pulsing light coming from the forest, which they thought might be a downed aircraft. It wasn't. Behind the one mile stretch of forest is Orford Ness lighthouse. The UFO research group Citizens Against UFO Secrecy (CAUS) later conducted and then, ironically, suppressed witness testimonies of those involved in this first night of sightings. The statements, in particular those of John Burroughs and Ed Cabansag, largely supported the lighthouse sighting rather than any alien spacecraft hypothesis, but by the time these documents were released to a wider readership, UFO themes had already taken root.

On a different night another group of airmen, this time led by Sgt. James Penniston, spotted 'a mechanical object with red and blue lights' moving through the edge of the forest. This would eventually become known as the 'alien craft'. USAF Military Patrolman Kevin Conde has later admitted to being part of a practical joke, staging his police car to frighten the guard at the east gate of the base. As Conde has said, 'It was fertile ground for practical jokes, and practical jokes are a tradition in the security police'. The 'craft' wasn't a UFO; it was a 1979 Plymouth Volare.

The strange sightings obviously caused a bit of commotion at the base, and Col. Halt eventually decided to take the investigation into his own hands. He decided this during the base Christmas party, going off into the woods at around 10pm on 28th December. Halt and some men later found 'evidence' of where a craft had touched down – three impressions in the ground. Local forestry commission worker Vince Thurkettle later examined the 'landing site', and recognized the impressions as rabbit diggings. Other pieces of evidence, such as 'burn marks' on trees were simply shown to be axe marks left by foresters to indicate which trees were ready to be chopped down. Recordings of average levels of background radiation have also been cited as evidence by people such as Ministry of Defence official Nick Pope, who doesn't seem to really understand much about background radiation. The evidence provided by Pope in his later book, *Open Skies, Closed Minds*, to support the idea that radiation levels at Rendlesham were high actually comes from comments in the ITV programme *Strange but True? With Michael Aspel*. Halt also noticed the pulsing light of the lighthouse, looking at it through a starscope magnifier.

Halt later sent an official memo regarding the event to his superiors. The fact that he didn't send this until sixteen days after his findings suggested that he wasn't in total fear of an immediate alien invasion. He also got several facts wrong, including the date of the first sighting. He did however also expand on the sightings, discussing his own dramatic account of what was likely misidentification of some stars viewed through a telescopic lens re-interpreted as flashing alien craft. The British MoD made a cursory investigation and didn't feel it even necessary to interview any witnesses. The incident was regarded with little importance, no further official report was made, and no further action taken.

As is often the way, however, the truth shouldn't get in the way of a good story. And as with all good UFO folk myths, the 'facts', 'evidence' and 'witness statements' have evolved and grown substantially over time, in particular in this instance those of James Penniston and Charles Halt. In more recent TV interviews, Penniston claims to have witnessed the craft flying up out of the trees. He has expanded this even more, saying he was able to examine the craft in detail before it left, took photographs of it, and even claimed to have touched the craft.

Pictures taken were of course seized and destroyed by the Air Force. He also displayed his notebook with drawings of the craft supposedly made during the incident, however this notebook had never been seen by anyone else until twenty-three years after the 'sighting' and is also annotated with an incorrect date. Penniston underwent hypnotic regression in 1994, encouraging his ideas about a landed craft. He has since claimed to be in telepathic contact with the pilots of the alien craft, and that the aliens were time-travelling visitors from the future.

Charles Halt has gone as far as to produce an affidavit stating that the UFO sightings were fact (despite the affidavit conflicting with details within his own previous report of the incident), and that the security services of Britain and America conspired to subvert the truth around what occurred. Halt has radically expanded on the stars he saw through his telescopic lens, claiming craft shot over the top of him, and shone lazer beams onto storage hangars, further going on to say that craft split into groups and exploded in flashes of light. None of these events were documented on the evening they are alleged to have occurred by any personnel, including Col. Halt. Although Halt recorded his own audio commentary while investigating the UFO sightings, apparently seeing craft explode and fire laser beams onto nuclear storage bunkers must not have been significant enough an event for him to mention in it. Other officials at the base, particularly Col. Theodore Conrad, who now considers the former senior officer an embarrassment, have disputed the statements by Halt.

In 1994, Nick Pope instigated a cold-case review of the Rendlesham forest incident. Pope was an employee at the British Government's Ministry of Defence from 1985 until 2006. Since then he has promoted himself as an independent journalist and 'expert' on UFOs. In 1991, he was assigned to a new section of Secretariat (Sec(AS)2a to be specific) where one of his part-time duties included investigating reports of UFO sightings and assessing any defence significance. Pope became obsessed with the UFO sightings; though the majority, he admitted, were mundane, he claimed several stood out as unusual. After the 1994 review of Rendlesham forest and associated press interest (largely encouraged by Pope himself), he was subsequently 're-assigned'.

Pope has gone on to make a living off the back of his brief role at the MoD, writing several books on UFOs (most notably the 1997 best-seller *Open Skies, Closed Minds: Official Reactions to the UFO Phenomenon*) and regularly appearing on UFO documentaries, at conferences, and as a frequent guest on America's Coast to Coast AM. Pope has claimed he was a senior MoD official who 'headed up' the British UFO desk at the MoD. He has styled himself as the British go-to authority on all things UFO and a 'real life version of Fox Mulder' – the fictional FBI agent from the TV show *The X-files*. Such a comparison is very much his own invention; the reality of his role was essentially sorting out paperwork reports that no one else wanted to organize. It was a general, non-technical, junior administration post with an emphasis on correspondence with the public and documenting voicemail messages left by people regarding UFO sightings.

Speaking in 1997, Pope's former Head of Department at the MoD described him as a junior desk officer who was not in charge of, or Head of, any part of Secretariat. There was no UFO project and handling of UFO sightings was a very small element of the job. Pope's courting of media attention around the Rendlesham forest case was likely an aspect of his re-assignment in 1994, and his ongoing attention-seeking would be no doubt partly the reason why the MoD was flooded with freedom of information requests concerning their UFO records. In 1999, *The Sunday Times* reported that Nick Pope had made claims suggesting aliens abducted him and his girlfriend in Florida in 1991, though Pope now denies he ever made such a statement, despite supporting information appearing in Pope's interview with Jane Goldman in the book *The X-Files Book of the Unexplained (vol 1)*.

He has frequently been involved with marketing and PR agencies, working on promotional campaigns for films and video games, often in an underhand way. In June 2012, Pope warned to expect mass UFO sightings during the 2012 London Olympic games. His 'warnings', which made the national news, were later revealed to be nothing more than a publicity stunt for a Sony Playstation game *Resistance: Burning Skies*. This is not an isolated incident, and a number of his appearances to discuss UFO-related issues are essentially a thinly veiled promotion for whatever campaign he is currently being paid to promote. From the DVD release of *Species III*, to promotions associated with movies like *Battle: Los Angeles*, *The Day the Earth Stood Still* re-make, and a 7-Eleven campaign based around the JJ Abrams movie *Super-8*. By his own admission his interviews and appearances aimed to blur the lines between reality and fiction, and to encourage mention of whatever product he was plugging. He has also written several science fiction novels, such as *Operation Thunder Child*, about government agencies establishing dialogue with a captured alien.

Pope's promotion of official investigations into the UFO phenomenon, as well as increased public interest due to the release of movies such as *Independence Day* and *Men in Black*, also likely encouraged ongoing debate regarding the topic during the 1990s. In 1996, Labour MP Martin Redmond addressed GCHQ's monitoring of UFOs during a debate at the House of Commons. He also pushed for an investigation into a UFO sighting spotted near Skegness by police officers and demanded to know why such sightings were not considered to be of any defence significance. The RAF eventually looked into it, concluding that the lights spotted by police were just bright stars.

Prime Minister Tony Blair received a briefing from the MoD about UFOs in 1998, while making preparations for the introduction of the Freedom of Information Act. Blair was concerned about possible disclosure of classified information after being pressed in regard to making government UFO reports publicly available. The concerns were raised after UFO writer Nick Redfern wrote to him questioning the alleged government UFO cover-up. The then Prime Minister responded saying that there was no government-sponsored research into the UFO phenomenon and there were no plans to initiate such work. The statement wasn't however strictly accurate, as there was at the time an ongoing government study into the topic. Project

Condign was the name given to a secret UFO study undertaken by the British Government's Defence Intelligence Staff, which ran between 1997 and 2000.

The results of Project Condign were compiled into a 400-page document titled *Unidentified Aerial Phenomena in the UK Air Defence Region*. It drew on approximately 10,000 sightings and reports that had been gathered by the DI55, a section of the Directorate of Scientific and Technical Intelligence within the Defence Intelligence Staff. It was released into the public domain on 15th May 2006 after a Freedom of Information Act request by UFO researchers Dr David Clarke and Gary Anthony. According to the report, the majority of UFO sightings can be explained by the misidentification of common objects, such as aircraft and balloons, while the remaining unexplainable reports were most likely, it claims, the result of supernormal meteorological phenomena not fully understood by modern science.

Dr David Clarke is a research fellow in journalism at Sheffield Hallam University. His background is in the study of folklore, and he has, since 2008, been working with The National Archives as a consultant regarding the release of their UFO files. Clarke has written several books on the subject, including *The UFO Files: The Inside Story of Real-Life Sightings*, *How UFOs Conquered the World: The History of a Modern Myth* and *Britain's X-traordinary Files*. Clarke adopts an open-minded yet ultimately skeptical view of the phenomenon and approaches the topic as a form of modern day folk narrative.

Several FOIA requests by David Clarke have also been made in an attempt to gain understanding of how the MoD viewed Nick Pope's exposure of UFO cases while he was still an employee, however the release of such insight was blocked by Pope himself. To save on administrative costs, the MoD decided in 2008 to release various UFO documents into the public domain. Despite Pope's previous claims to the contrary, these reports where in the most part just many pages of mundane misidentifications of helicopters, weather balloons, and satellites. With Pope's information cache now within easy public access, he has kept his profile relatively subdued, with only the occasional appearance at UFO conferences or whenever he has been paid to plug a UFO-themed product.

All the Ministry of Defence UFO files have now been released in batches, starting in 2008 and completed by March 2017, (with the exception of anything prior to 1967, which was routinely shredded). This has now amounted to around 52,000 pages of data on UFOs from the MoD. These files include official policies, reports, correspondence with Ministers and freedom of information requests. The release of the files was widely reported and even contributed to a small UFO flap as UFO sightings over the UK increased in the wake of the exposure. In particular, *The Sun* newspaper ran frequent UFO-themed stories during 2009, such as 'Army Spot UFOs over Shropshire' and 'UFO hits wind turbine'. Gordon Brown's government eventually closed the Ministry of Defence UFO desk in 2009, putting a final full stop to official UK government interest on the matter.

The subject refuses to die. Many conspiracy theorists, such as Robert Hastings and Richard D. Hall, believe the release of the MoD files is just a smokescreen to placate the general masses and provide cover for the real truth regarding UFOs. Liberal Democrat MP Norman Baker, who acted as Home Office Minister under the Conservative-Liberal coalition government until his resignation in 2014, had strong views on freedom of information and also some very liberal ideas concerning decriminalization of drugs. More interesting, however, is his ongoing fascination with all things conspiracy theory and UFO. In 2007, he wrote a book, *The Strange Death of David Kelly*, concerning the suspicious death of the weapons expert blamed for 'sexing up' the Iraq War weapons of mass destruction dossier. He has also argued that the September 2001 attacks on the World Trade Center were an inside job, and that there is currently a global micro-chipping agenda run by a group of secret Nazis. He is a firm believer in UFOs, suggesting that they need proper investigation. Even after the release of volumes of official UFO data, he has repeatedly asked questions in parliament to support further study.

Official investigations into the UFO phenomenon ultimately only seem to feed the notions of a wider conspiracy, as such studies fuel notions of cover-ups and secret knowledge. It is not just America and the UK who have had an ongoing interest in UFOs. Many governments around the world have studied and reported on such phenomenon, from Denmark to Chile and Australia to China.

France has the biggest space agency in Europe; it is also the only country to maintain a full-time and state-run UFO department. The group, Groupe d'Études et d'Informations sur les Phénomènes Aérospatiaux Non-identifiés, better known as GEIPAN, is a unit of the French Space Agency, whose brief is to investigate unidentified aerospace phenomenon. The first organization for the study of UFOs in France was set up in 1977, created by the Director of CNES (the National Centre for Space Studies), Yves Sillard, and Claude Poher after meeting with J. Allen Hynek. By the turn of the twenty-first century, the department was almost non-existent, closing and reopening a number of times under slightly different guises and remits. In July 2005, the new Director of CNES, Yannick d'Escatha, pushed to create a department for the study of UFOs once again. By January 2006, GEIPAN had announced that it was to put all of its UFO files into the public domain and published 480 files online the following year. This has amounted to nearly 100,000 pages of witness testimonies, photographs, and archived reports.

Agencies such as GEIPAN assume, by the nature of their being, that there is an inseparable link between UFOs and outer space. The possibilities implicit within space exploration have helped maintain interest around UFOs as extraterrestrial craft. Simply put, we do not know enough about what is out there to conclusively state if other intelligent life does, or does not, exist. It remains theoretically plausible that alien life occurs in other parts of the universe; our own planet is proof that it is possible for various forms of life to exist. It is yet to be decided if life such as that found on Earth is a bizarre anomaly or a far more common occurrence. The Cold War, and the space race that was a product of the technological competition between two superpowers, resulted in the most accelerated period of discovery in regard to space flight. The age of paranoia became the age of wonder as manned exploration of space became a reality. As humans took their first steps into the great cosmos, perhaps the aliens were watching.

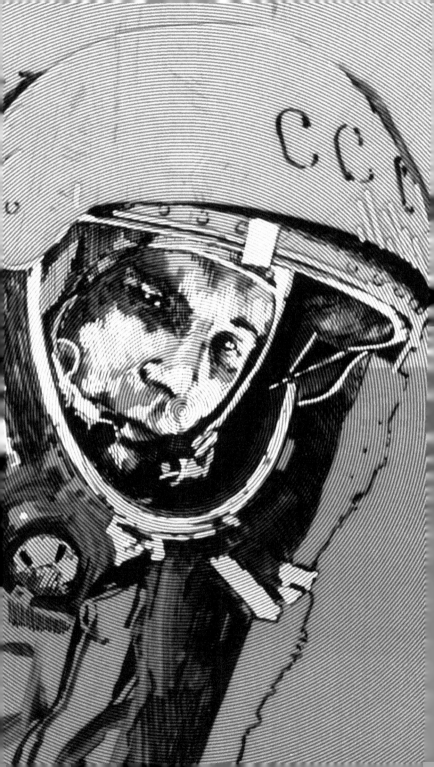

PART FOUR
To Bodly Go

The perceived government knowledge of UFOs no doubt has some of its roots within the secrecy surrounding the American use of German scientists following the end of World War II – particularly as such 'foreign knowledge' contributed greatly to the development of the American space programme. The exploration of space in the second half of the twentieth century provided much inspiration for those hopeful of evidence of extraterrestrial life. Ironically the same agencies who paved the way for such wonder are the same ones that have ultimately become accused of corruption and hidden agendas in regard to the UFO phenomenon. If the US government were indeed happy to allow former members of the Nazi party to work on top-secret projects, then surely they would not be averse to forming alliances with other 'foreign' bodies.

Operation Paperclip ran from 1945 all the way up until 1990. The programme was organised by the US Office of Strategic Services, with the aim of bringing various German scientists, engineers, and technicians to the United States following the end of World War II. America wanted to take advantage of the knowledge-base of what was left of Nazi Germany, principally around military technology. An important secondary purpose of Operation Paperclip was also to ensure that the same technology did not fall into the hands of the Soviet Union. Following the end of the war, as various individuals evacuated the ruins of Nazi Germany, those with special skills or knowledge, or even those suspected of having useful skills, were taken to detention and interrogation centres. Here around 1,800 scientists were held during the years after the war, some for several months at a time. Paperclip eventually imported 1,600 men to the United States, as part of intellectual reparations claimed owed to America; such scientists were essentially the spoils of war. Key individuals involved in Paperclip included the physicist Hubertus Strughold and rocket scientists Kurt H. Debus, Arthur Rudolph, and Werner Von Braun.

Von Braun was an aerospace engineer who pioneered rocket propulsion and went on to become an influential architect of the American space programme. He invented the German V-2 rocket and was a key figure in the development of much of the Nazi rocket technologies. Toward the end of the war Von Braun was based at Peenemunde where the V-2 was developed; it was also the centre of the 1946 Swedish Ghost Rocket sightings. As a result of his inventions, Von Braun was at the top of the United States' Black List of German scientists targeted for interrogation at the end of the War. It wasn't long before his skills were re-focused to advance the West.

By 1950, Von Braun was claiming it was possible to send a rocket to the Moon. Such speculation fed into the growing public appetite for space exploration and the rapid growth of sci-fi based popular culture throughout the rest of the decade. Von Braun also developed designs for various space structures, including a rotating space station. The idea was never realized, but it did provide a key influence upon the designs used for Stanley Kubrick's film *2001: A Space Odyssey*. He continued to ambitiously speculate about advances in rocket technology to reach the stars. As well as working out concepts for a manned mission to Mars, he also produced a number of TV films about space exploration for Walt Disney. Von Braun eventually became

Director of the Marshall Space Flight Centre; developing the Saturn V rocket, he became a central member of the Apollo Moon programme. During this time he also worked closely with fellow Paperclip convert Kurt H. Debus, who became the first Director of the Kennedy Space Centre.

That an ex-Nazi helped develop NASA's space programme was no doubt a bitter pill for some Americans to swallow, and the logic in some circles that Nazi technology was the result of extraterrestrial influence (rather than just a talented German) may have been more palatable, however far-fetched the idea. As well as his connection to the Swedish ghost rockets, some UFOlogists have also made claims that Von Braun saw the alien bodies from the Roswell crash, and was able to examine the remains of their craft.

The German military machine was developing all manner of strange and advanced weaponry towards the end of World War II. German Landkreuzer tanks, staffed by 100 men, only existed in plan form, but were mind-bogglingly big. Even more ambitious was the heliobeam, a theoretical orbital weapon that would use an orbiting concave mirror to reflect sunlight onto a specific concentrated area. A frequently cited weapon, 'Die Glocke' or 'The Bell' was an alleged saucer shaped aircraft being developed by the Nazis. In all of the data and materials captured by occupying forces nothing remotely like 'The Bell' was ever discovered. The closest thing to a German flying saucer was probably the Sack AS-6, a round-winged experimental plane that never made it past the prototype stage. Designed by Arthur Sack, a farmer with a passion for aero-model building, he entered his design into the 1939 National Contest of Aeromodels held at Leipzig-Mockau. The plane was a poor flyer, often needing a literal 'push' to get going, but Sack continued to work on models through the war. By 1944 he had constructed bigger and better models out of wrecked Messerschmitts and homemade plywood wings. The craft never really managed more than a brief hop into the air before landing and inevitably damaging part of its landing gear or rudder. It is doubtful Sack was aided by advanced alien technology.

Regardless of this, the idea of 'Nazi flying saucers' is

common within fiction, and taken seriously in some corners of UFOlogy and other conspiracy theories. The origins of The Bell are probably connected to the reports of foo fighters and the Swedish ghost rockets. A circular jet aircraft, the VZ-9 Avrocar, developed in Canada in the late 1950s, has also been attributed to Nazi technologies, but only on the say-so of German Georg Klein. The prototype vehicle was actually designed by Englishman John Meadows Frost. A blue-sky research project, the aircraft was unstable, slow, and canceled after two years and a cost of $10million.

In the 1970s, German Holocaust denier Ernst Zündel wrote books about secret Nazi weapons launched from underground bases in Antarctica, such as *UFOs – Nazi Secret Weapon?* in 1974. Zündel was followed by Miguel Serrano, a Nazi sympathizer from Chile who claimed Hitler was communing with Hyperborean gods in an underground Antarctic base. In the late 1980s, Austrian authors Norbert Jürgen-Ratthofer and Ralf Ettl produced the document *UFO – Secrets of the Third Reich*. This created a new wave of Nazi UFO myths involving ancient Babylon and an extraterrestrial civilization in the solar system of Aldebaran. Both Jürgen-Ratthofer and Ettl were members of the German far-right group Tempelhofgesellschaft, founded by former policeman Hans-Günter Fröhlich. After their writings gained support, they formed their own splinter group called Order of the Black Sun. This group aimed to make preparations for the Aryan race to meet up with advanced beings living within the hollow Earth.

German conspiracy writer Jan Van Helsing (real name Jan Udo Holey) has produced a number of books since the mid-1990s about various theories concerning Nazi-mythology. These are often to do with Zionist global domination, Hitler's Antarctic base, the hollow Earth, and Nazi UFOs. Helsing writes about the Vril Society of Berlin, a fictitious group of rocket engineers interested in the occult. Writers Jacques Bergier and Louis Pauwels invented the Vril Society in the early 1960s, based on ideas from Willy Ley's 1947 article 'Pseudoscience in Naziland' and the 1871 novel *The Coming Race*, by Edward Bulwer-Lytton. Van Helsing claims the society, which he insists was genuine, made contact with extraterrestrials and soon became dedicated to making spacecraft so they could again meet up with the aliens. When the war ended with the defeat of Nazi Germany, the Vril society, and their flying saucers, retreated to Antarctica and entered the hollow Earth to meet up with Hitler and a race of advanced beings living deep underground.

The inspiration for many things discussed today concerning Nazi flying saucers comes from the 2000 book *The Truth About the Wunderwaffen* by Igor Witkowski, a Polish magazine editor. The specific idea of 'Die Glocke' in fact only made its debut in these twenty-first century writings, though apparently Witkowski claims it was discovered in the secret transcripts of an interrogation of Nazi SS Officer Jakob Sporrenberg at the end of the war. No other writing supports this alleged account from Sporrenberg, who never held any technical or scientific position in the SS and was a Gruppenführer in charge of a team of police in Minsk and later Norway. Witkowski claims that these top-secret craft were able to decompose plant matter and turn blood into gel. American writers like Jim Marrs and Henry Stevens have further promoted the idea of Nazi UFOs, going on to speculate that such craft provided the ability to see images from the past during operation. Since 2004, author Joseph Farrell has written numerous books concerning all sorts of links between Nazis, UFOs, conspiracy theories, and the global finance system, such as *Reich of the Black Sun: Nazi Secret Weapons & the Cold War Allied Legend*. Farrell has also presented an alternative theory concerning the Roswell crash, speculating it was a downed secret Nazi aircraft, in *Roswell and the Reich: The Nazi Connection*.

In 2008 the Discovery channel series *Nazi UFO Conspiracy* suggested links between Die Glocke and a crashed UFO in Kecksburg, Pennsylvania, in the mid-1960s. This was followed by similar claims a year later on an episode of *UFO Hunters*, and again in 2011's *Ancient Aliens*, which suggested Nazi SS Officer Hans Kammler escaped the end of the war via a time-travelling UFO. He evaded capture by use of top-secret alien technology, only to crash land in 1960s America, and then integrate himself into post-war society. Most of these ideas come from the 2001 book *The Hunt for Point Zero: Inside the Classified World of Antigravity Technology* by Nicholas Cook. Over the fifty years since its occurrence, the Kecksburg sighting has developed its own UFO mythology, but one that has gone through various phases. This has included alien UFO craft, Soviet satellites, Nazi time machines and a NASA cover-up.

In the late afternoon on 9th December 1965, a young boy playing outside believed he saw an object crash land into some nearby woods of the town of Kecksburg. Several other witnesses had seen a similar bright object in the sky, but such observers were spread over a much larger area than the small town fifty miles southeast of Pittsburg. Reports were received throughout Pennsylvania, and also Ohio, Michigan and parts of Canada. The *Greenburg Tribune-Review* reported on the story the next day, claiming 'Unidentified Flying Object falls near Kecksburg'. Due to insistence of some reports a number of state police, military engineers, and civilian scientists did conduct a survey of the woods near Kecksburg soon after the alleged crash, but found nothing.

Later analysis of a series of photographs taken by Richard Champine resulted in the object being identified as a meteor. Astronomers Von Del Chamberlain and David Krause, of Michigan State University, traced the path of a meteor, which came down at around the time of the sightings – but in south Ontario, not Kecksburg. It is often impossible to accurately estimate the distance of such things from the ground, and witnesses frequently believe objects to be much closer than they actually are.

The story faded into obscurity until the NBC TV show *Unsolved Mysteries* re-invented the story as a crashed UFO in September 1990. The account of a small number of locals redeveloped the events much in the model of the more famous Roswell crash of 1947. Resident Bill Bulebush makes claims of seeing an acorn-shaped UFO crashing in the woods, and insists many others support his claims – unfortunately they just don't want to come forward. Such people include his wife, who has since stated that she ignores his UFO stories. In fact more than fifty residents of Kecksburg wrote in to NBC to complain about the *Unsolved Mysteries* episode, citing various inaccuracies in the programme. There however remain a handful of local supporters of the UFO narrative, including Mabal Mazza and Bonnie Milslagle, who have constructed a tale around the crash involving their former respective employee and husband, John Murphy. The account only appeared twenty years after Murphy had died and is not verified by anyone else.

There was later speculation that the crashed object was actually part of a Soviet satellite, Kosmos 96. An investigation in 1991 concluded that a fragment of the Kosmos satellite had crashed in North America, but it came down over Canada, and around thirteen hours before any of the reported Kecksburg sightings. There has been a push by UFO-obsessed journalists like Leslie Kean for NASA to release documents it must have on the subject of the crash. Despite obliging several freedom of information requests, NASA divulged very little on the incident, principally as they had very little information on it. Kean was not convinced and filed a lawsuit against NASA to get them to search more diligently for records concerning the incident. Likely Kean's lawsuit was just a publicity stunt for her own investigation into the UFO aspect of the incident. Since the early 2000s, she has been associated with a range of sensationalist stories, often with very scant supportive evidence. More recently she promoted a UFO video taken from El Bosque Airfield in Chile, though it was later shown by UFO debunker Robert Sheaffer to just be that of a fly. Kean spent four years bombarding NASA with freedom of information requests, eventually publishing her book *UFOs: Generals, Pilots and Government Officials Go on the Record*.

Dr Carol Rosin, who claimed to be close friends with Werner Von Braun, described his knowledge of extraterrestrials and made a link to the Kecksburg incident. No such relationship was mentioned until twenty years after Von Braun's death, when Rosin had chosen Steven Greer's Disclosure Project as a platform to reveal this. It is alleged that Hans Kammler was the senior officer who supervised Werner Von Braun, giving Von Braun exposure to the anti-gravity propulsion systems of the time travelling UFO that crashed in Kecksburg. This combined with access to the secrets of NASA allowed for the development of space travel technologies. NASA covered up all such evidence, permitting the Nazi scientists to develop a secret space programme based around alien technologies.

While it may be the Nazi party who maintain the most legitimate claim to have contributed to the technological development of the American space programme, it was certainly the Russian Communist party who maintained the strong impetus for its continued progression. The Space Race between America and Russia was a symptom of the ongoing Cold War and was just as much, if not more so, about demonstrating technological superiority than actual exploration.

By the mid-1950s, President Eisenhower had become acutely aware of the progress the Soviets were making on their Sputnik project due to imagery captured by secret spy planes. In an attempt to display technological and scientific superiority, America confidently moved forward with Project Vanguard, with a goal of launching the first artificial satellite into orbit. In 1955, the US Naval research laboratory began preparations for launch of the first Vanguard mission, with a schedule date for a historic launch of September 1957. Unplanned delays and rocket failures pushed the deadline further toward the end of the year. Despite a focused effort, the first successful orbital launch from Earth was the unmanned Soviet Sputnik 1, which penetrated the atmosphere on 4th October 1957. Fear that the same Soviet rockets could be capable of sending nuclear warheads anywhere in the world soon became a genuine concern.

Paranoia was ripe when no image of Sputnik was released by the Soviets until five days after the launch. Many had started wondering just what it was that was up there. It is no great shock that there was a spate of UFO sightings through America over the time Russia was launching its Sputnik satellites, as many people stared into the sky in an attempt to see the orbiting objects.

In December 1957, the United States failed to replicate the success of Sputnik with the unsuccessful launch of the first Vanguard satellite. The Vanguard TV3 was the first attempt by

America to launch a satellite into space; it rose 1.2 meters into the air before falling back onto the launch pad and exploding. The technological failure was a loss of prestige for America and an international embarrassment. Russia had put a satellite into orbit; America could not even get their rocket off the ground. The American space programme struggled to keep pace with the Russians, coming second in groundbreaking achievements on a number of occasions. For America, the dent to national pride only encouraged the US Government to invest more and more focus and resources on the space race with Russia. To improve focused effort and resources, in July 1958, Eisenhower signed the National Aeronautics and Space Act, which established NASA. The administration became operational later that year with a staff of 8,000 and an annual budget of $100 million.

By the time America eventually replicated Russia's initial orbital success with Explorer 1, the USSR had since put an animal (the dog Laika) into orbit and, in 1959, succeeded with the unmanned probe *Luna 2* becoming the first man-made object to land on the Moon. In April 1961, the Soviet Union reached another milestone when *Vostok 1* took the twenty-seven-year-old cosmonaut Yuri Gagarin into orbit for just under two hours. The achievement resonated around the world and the dreams of a human exploration of space had become a reality, though for many Americans it was not looking like a reality their nation would share.

As a feat of human exploration, Gagarin's accomplishment is without question a significant achievement. His was the first tangible opportunity for a human to escape the confines of Earth and step into the great vast expanse of outer space. It is no surprise either that such an event has provided inspiration for the UFO community. In alleged documents supplied by Dr Rimili Avramenko, Yuri Gagarin is recorded as stating that after his experience in orbit he believed UFOs to be real, and shortly before his death in 1968 was prepared to go on the record about such claims.

Gagarin died during a training exercise using a MiG jet, and although the mysterious death was finally revealed as an accident with a second plane, there have been speculations that he was assassinated due to his knowledge of UFOs, or even that a UFO itself caused Gagarin's plane to crash. Avramenko's account of Gagarin's UFO belief only surfaced through Philip Corso's 1997 book *The Day After Roswell: A Former Pentagon Official Reveals the US Government's Shocking UFO Cover-Up* and he may indeed be a fictional fabrication by the author; other than Corso's work, no other reference can be found to Avramenko, the alleged senior engineer who apparently worked for America's Strategic Defense Initiative. Corso's work is largely regarded as a fraud, even within the UFOlogy community, although his son continues to add to the mythology, more recently claiming that the Roswell UFO was, like the Kecksburg UFO, in actual fact a time machine.

In response to Gagarin's milestone, President John F. Kennedy made official the ambitions to put an American on the Moon. In May 1961, Kennedy made a speech before Congress announcing an ambitious goal to send an American to the lunar surface and back before the end of the decade. The race to reach the Moon dominated the American space programme during the 1960s, as this one great remaining milestone was seen by many in America a way of winning the race they were currently losing. It was a high profile and very public effort to reassert the technological superiority of the US. Though Kennedy had privately admitted that the space race was a waste of money, he continued to push the initiative to exploit rewards he believed could be reaped from a frightened electorate. Despite these views, his assassination in 1963 only strengthened the resolve to make it happen, and by the end of the project, the Apollo programme had cost around $25.4 billion to achieve its goal.

Launching on 16th July by a force of 7.5 million pounds of thrust, the Apollo 11 mission became the first manned landing on the Moon. Apollo 11 took a further four days before eventually landing on the Moon's surface, some 239,000 miles away. Neil Armstrong had to manually pilot the Eagle Lander to a suitable spot on the Sea of Tranquility, before eventually taking his first steps onto the lunar surface. His famous 'one small step for man' line is still engrained in the popular consciousness.

An estimated 600 million people witnessed the first

Moonwalk live through television and radio. It was a major cultural event, seen by many as a defining moment of the second half of the twentieth century. The achievements of NASA, and in particular the Apollo space programme, can be seen as a milestone both in technological accomplishment and human exploration. The Apollo 11 mission was by no means the only trip to the lunar surface; NASA managed repeated visits to the Moon, and a total of five further moonwalks before ending the programme in December 1972. Despite the huge cultural influence of the 1969 landing, public obsession with the Moon missions began to subside into the 1970s. After NASA had proved such things were possible, recurring missions seemed by some to be an expensive indulgence.

Initial skepticism of NASA during the late 1960s was concerned with the continued high level of funding and political prominence given to the space programme, seemingly at the expense of combating issues closer to home, such as inner city violence and racial tensions. Some developed the perception that cash was being spent on getting to the Moon, but not on caring for the poor and vulnerable. Poet and musician Gil Scott-Heron makes the tension apparent in his 1970 track *Whitey on the Moon*; 'I can't pay no Doctor bill – but Whitey's on the Moon', he riffs. Over the following years the Watergate scandal and Richard Nixon's subsequent impeachment did much to damage faith in official bodies, and the use of technology for the space programme began to be seen skeptically as a thinly veiled excuse for the development of equipment to be used primarily for war, especially in Vietnam. Accusations surrounding a NASA conspiracy began to surface after the mid-1970s, when several questions emerged regarding wider trust in the American government and other official agencies.

Within certain UFOlogy circles, NASA now has an ongoing association with UFO cover-ups and conspiracy theories, and seems universally mistrusted by those who often support more outlandish claims. The threat of *the other* has progressed through World War II-era Nazis and Cold War Communists into sinister government agencies like NASA, who seem, in the eyes of some, to be all deeply interconnected. As well as the historic mistrust of German scientists working for American agencies, such paranoia may well also be fueled by as simple a thing as the fact that NASA and Nazi sound quite similar. As ridiculous as that seems, other conspiracy theories have developed around the fact that Osama Bin Laden and Barack Obama are vaguely similar names (Obama Sin Laden) and therefore are both in allegiance, or that the spread of the Ebola virus is related to a secret plot on the basis that British Army Soldier Fusilier Lee Rigby was murdered by Michael Ad-*ebola*-jo.

The International Flat Earth Society was one of the first groups to actively start promoting the idea that NASA was corrupt and deceptive as per their belief that Earth could not be a spinning globe. By the 1970s, UFOlogy had begun revisiting the space programme with claims of UFOs following certain Apollo missions, sightings of strange objects by Astronauts, speculation about extraterrestrials witnessed on the Moon's surface. NASA's main objective was supposedly to hide UFO evidence, with corruption going so far as to fake the Moon landings altogether.

Not long after the 1969 Moon landing, rumours of a bootleg tape concerning communications between astronauts and NASA began circulating around certain UFO groups, supposed proof of the Apollo astronauts witnessing UFOs. The claims first appeared in a September 1969 edition of *National Bulletin* magazine, in an article written by Sam Pepper. The secret communications were reproduced as a transcript evidencing sightings of UFOs made by Apollo astronauts, though no individuals are identified, and certain phrases such as 'mission control' are not consistent with vocabulary used during such NASA communications. Further stories then began emerging of UFO sightings linked to the Apollo 11 mission, such as that produced by Curtis Fuller, editor of *Fate* magazine, who wrote in 1970 about mysterious spaceships spotted by Neil Armstrong, Michael Collins, and Buzz Aldrin.

Others soon began to add to the growing mythology of NASA's knowledge of UFO activity. Otto Binder was an American author of science fiction and comic books, best known for his *Superman* stories from the 1950s, as well as work on comics such as *Captain Marvel* and *Captain America*. Binder was also a believer in several fringe ideas concerning UFOs and alien life. He wrote extensively about UFOs in magazines, such as articles like 'Mankind Child of the Stars', which argued that modern humans are actually half-human/half-alien crossbreeds. He wrote a number of articles for *SAGA* magazine, which during the 1970s was regularly producing UFO supplements. One such article, 'Secret Messages from UFOs' written in 1972, included a transcript supposedly between an Apollo 11 astronaut and NASA's mission control. Binder wrote it under the guise of an 'insider' who claimed the exchange was acquired by radio Hams listening in on NASA broadcasts. The truth is a Ham radio operator by the name of Larry Baysinger did actually manage to intercept around thirty minutes of conversation between NASA and the Apollo 11 astronauts back in 1969. Using modified radio equipment from an army tank radio receiver, Baysinger hoped to hear unedited dialogue of the space mission. To Larry's disappointment the conversation he intercepted was exactly the same as the one being broadcast to the public on television. There was no editing of communication.

In 1974, Bill Kaysing wrote *We Never Went to the Moon: America's Thirty Billion Dollar Swindle*, eventually self-publishing it two years later. Here Kaysing introduced many of the standard conspiracy theory arguments against the Moon landing, such as the absence of stars in photographs and absence of blast craters beneath the lunar modules. Kaysing worked as a furniture maker before becoming librarian for Rocketdyne, the major engine supplier for NASAs Saturn rockets. The same year a Japanese UFO group, the Cosmic Brotherhood Association, published a number of photographs allegedly from the Apollo 11 mission showing a pair of UFOs. Accusations began to take pace, as the following year Bob Barry produced the one edition magazine *The UFO Report*, claiming NASA was hiding evidence of UFOs.

Maurice Chatelain claimed to be the former Chief of NASA Communication Systems and encouraged a number of UFO-related ideas associated with the Apollo space programme.

These were mainly to do with a UFO spotted by astronaut Jim McDivitt, as well as claims that Neil Armstrong and Buzz Aldrin saw UFOs on the Moon. He has also claimed that the problems experienced by the Apollo 13 mission were as a result of alien interference. Chatelain was actually a low-level engineer who worked briefly for North American Aviation, a sub-contractor used occasionally by NASA whilst they were developing their communication systems in the mid-1960s. Chatelian never worked on projects for NASA and was no longer employed by North American Aviation when Apollo 11 landed on the Moon.

Vladimir Azhazha often crops up as an independent scientific supporter of Chatelain's claims. Azhazha describes himself as a Professor of Mathematics at Moscow University. Unfortunately Moscow University doesn't exist, and Moscow State University has never employed anyone of that name. He did however act as editor for a number of MUFON UFO journals during the 1970s, including the November 1977 edition where he concludes that information provided by Chatelain proves that the Moon is a 'transhipment base for UFOs'. Chatelain went on to write the 1978 book *Our Ancestors Came From Outer Space*, which describes Neil Armstrong witnessing two UFOs whilst doing his famous lunar walk.

The mainstream media continued to promote the UFO narrative throughout the 1960s and '70s. CBS had previously made a 1966 UFO special, *UFO… Friend, Foe or Fantasy? with Walter Cronkite*. Cronkite was a respected American journalist, and best known as the anchorman for the CBS Evening News from the early 1960s through to the early 1980s. As well as covering major stories of the time such as the Kennedy assassination, Watergate, and the long running conflict in Vietnam, he was well known for extensive coverage of the American space programme. He received the Rotary National Award for Space Achievement's Corona Award for a lifetime of achievement in space reporting, and later became the first non-astronaut to receive NASA's Ambassador of Exploration Award. Considered by many at the peak of his career to be one of the most trusted figures in American news, he was a dominant voice for several decades.

By 1973, CBS was looking to make a further documentary based on the UFO phenomenon and Cronkite was the obvious choice to front the programme. In October that year, *The UFO News Report* was broadcast. UFO researcher Bill Knell claimed that Cronkite had lunch with him in advance of interviewing guests for this new UFO documentary. According to Knell, Cronkite was interested in his work around Air Force UFO stories. This conversation then led to Cronkite confiding in Knell with regard to a UFO sighting the news anchorman had experienced in the 1950s. It involved witnessing a large UFO whilst in the South Pacific to report on testing of Air Force missile systems: a large grey disc-shaped UFO hovered close to the ground, and used a blue beam to freeze missiles (and security dogs) in midair. Cronkite was instructed by an Air Force Colonel never to report the incident, but had over time confided to 'the right sort of people'.

Knell has appeared on various UFO-related talk shows, such as *Coast to Coast AM*, promoting his extraterrestrial research. As well as the Walter Cronkite story, he makes claims about a UFO spotted by President Kennedy and crashed alien wreckage seen by Howard Hughes and Jackie Gleason. He has been in legal troubles many times, for fraud, copyright infringement, and child neglect. Knell later went on to form the company arizonapuppies.com with his wife, a profiteering scam aimed at selling non-existent guide dog puppies to blind people. Knell tricked many people out of money before eventually being caught. Cronkite did produce a news report in 1973 that included an interview about a UFO with Ohio Governor John Gilligan, but not with Bill Knell. It is unlikely the pair ever lunched, especially as Cronkite has later stated he has never even heard of Bill Knell, and it took until 1998 for Knell to produce his version of the account.

In 1976 an alleged interview with Walter Cronkite appeared in the *National Enquirer* tabloid. Freelance writer Robin Leach produced the article claiming to be based on an interview with Walter Cronkite regarding his belief in UFOs. During the article Cronkite describes evidence supporting a huge cylindrical object spotted by Neil Armstrong and the subsequent cover-up by NASA. After Cronkite complained to the *National Enquirer* editor about the fraudulent article (there was never any interview), Leach was fired as a writer, but the magazine refused to retract the story. Robin Leach later found fame in the mid-1980s hosting the TV show *Lifestyles of the Rich and Famous*.

The persistence of NASA conspiracies, UFO cover-ups, and the Moon landing hoax theory is also possibly symptomatic of a level of disappointment amongst parts of society; man travelled to the Moon in the late 1960s, yet we are not in the age of deep space exploration as quite many had predicted during the same decade. The energy crisis of 1973 saw basic fuel for heating and travel become expensive and restricted. Rather than a new dawn of space adventure, many Americans were faced with a future struggling just to get to work. The perceived damage to NASA's integrity that developed during this era is something that still lingers today amongst conspiracy theorists.

James Oberg is an American space journalist, best known for his work around the Russian space programme and his work for *Skeptical Inquirer*, mostly in regard to presenting counterarguments to conspiracy theories surrounding the Moon landings and various UFO sightings by astronauts. In 2002, he was commissioned by NASA to produce an official response to the Apollo hoax accusations, though the contract was later canceled after negative media attention. Oberg has however remained a voice of authority on space race folklore, debunking many claims concerning NASA hoaxes and astronaut-related UFO sightings.

Skylab 3 was the second manned mission to the American space station Skylab, beginning July 1978 and ending around two months later. In September that year, astronauts Alan Bean, Owen Garriott, and Jack Lousma witnessed a glowing red UFO through a window for a period of around twenty minutes. The sighting was recorded in Bean's personal diary and then mentioned in Robert Emenegger's 1974 book *UFOs, Past, Present and Future*. The case has since been more widely promoted by UFOlogists Bruce Maccabee and Brad Sparks. James Oberg has spent time looking into the account, including a number of discussions with the astronauts themselves. The conclusion reached was that the UFO was actually a small piece of debris from Skylab itself, reflecting the Sun as it drifted pretty close to the window from which it was viewed, indeed similar debris was observed on other Skylab missions.

J. Allen Hynek's 1976 book *The Edge of Reality: A Progress Report on Unidentified Flying Objects* presents within its pages a list of unusual sightings by astronauts as comprised by George Fawcett. This list includes a number of astronauts and cosmonauts claiming to have witnessed UFOs, although these include a number of outright forgeries, such as the account of Joe Walton, and even the book's authors were not convinced by the legitimacy of several claims. Most are accounts that were never claimed to be UFOs in the first place. For example, in June 1965, astronaut Edward H. White (the first American to walk in space) photographed a weird-looking metallic object from a Gemini spacecraft, the pictures of which were never released. They were however likely to be just flakes of ice off the super-cold fuel tanks.

Some of the accounts were claimed to be genuine, such as those made by Major Gordon Cooper. Cooper was for some time considered an American hero, being one of the original seven astronauts from Project Mercury. He piloted the longest Mercury spaceflight in 1963, which included conducting a risky (and unplanned) manual re-entry using only the visible stars as a guide. Despite this he left NASA in 1970 under something of a cloud, resigning in protest after having been relegated to third back-up for the ongoing Apollo programme. The fact was he had become complacent, missing training sessions and not reading up on all the technical data before missions. It was soon after leaving NASA that his claims regarding UFOs began to emerge. By this point, Cooper was out of pocket and short on attention after his 1960s-era celebrity had faded. His early comments were cautious and well-worded, but as time progressed his accounts became more embellished and far-fetched.

An account of a UFO sighting at Edwards Air Force base in 1957 changed from Cooper recounting something that somebody else had seen, to Cooper having seen a film of a

UFO, to finally his being present to see the UFO firsthand and even the one who made the supposed film. He claims there was a NASA cover-up, no doubt the reason why no film ever materialized and no one else came forward to support his claims. In 1963 (in orbit this time), he claims to have seen a glowing, greenish object, which was then picked up by tracking radar. The sighting was reported but the press was told that they would not be allowed to question Cooper about the incident.

Cooper has gone on to claim that incriminating orbital images he took of Edwards Air Force Base were confiscated, apparently to 'hide' all the UFOs that they must have had in full view at the base. It has however since been proven that such photographs as described by Cooper couldn't exist anyway, as they were beyond the range and ability of any camera taken on any manned space mission. As time progressed Cooper claimed to have received telepathic messages from aliens, instructing him how to rectify a design flaw in the space shuttles. There is no record of either the 'flaw' or subsequent 'design modifications' as described by Cooper relating to any aspect of the space shuttle development.

The fact is Cooper enjoyed visiting UFO conventions and relished the attention that his stories received. His career post-NASA had not been a great success. During the 1980s and '90s he was involved in several companies, for which he collectively managed to create a loss of $2million. He also briefly worked for Walt Disney Productions to help develop ideas for theme-park rides and solve some technical issues. Disney decided that not a single one of his ideas was worth implementing and they soon parted company. He had burnt bridges with NASA and failed a number of times in business. People however did want to hear his UFO stories, and as time went by he became happy to tell them.

Another astronaut with a keen interest in UFOs was Dr. Edgar Mitchell. Mitchell was the sixth man to walk on the Moon and, along with fellow astronaut Alan Shepard, holds the record for the longest ever moonwalk. Upon returning to Earth as part of the *Apollo 14* mission, Mitchell claims he had a powerful *savikalpa samādhi* experience – an awareness of a great spirit beyond creation. Essentially a form of religious ecstasy or what has been described as the overview effect, it is a sensation reported by a number of astronauts whilst viewing Earth from orbit, as the overwhelming fragility and inter-dependence of all life is plain to see when the world is viewed in whole. Mitchell also had a lifetime fascination with psychic powers, such as remote viewing and telepathy, which all pre-date his spiritual awakening whilst in orbit. He even conducted an extra sensory perception experiment during his Apollo mission.

He became founder of the Institute of Noetic Sciences in 1973, a nonprofit research and education organization aimed at exploring 'collective transformation through consciousness research'. It conducts research into psychokinesis, alternative healing practices, and paranormal phenomena. The Institute managed to employ a number of staff, including Dean Radin, a leader in the study of global consciousness, and Rupert Sheldrake, the world's leading advocate for the psychic ability of dogs. Mitchell also believes a remote healer by the name of Adam Dreamhealer cured him of kidney cancer. He is '90% sure' that the many accounts of UFOs reported are genuine sightings of visitors from other planets. Talking in December 1991, Mitchell called for a serious investigation into the UFO phenomenon and a release of government knowledge on the subject. His hometown of Artesia, New Mexico, is forty miles south of Roswell; he was sixteen when the Roswell story appeared in the summer of 1947 and, till his death in February 2016, he believed that what crashed there was a genuine alien spacecraft.

Mitchell is not unique in experiencing a profound psychological impact as a consequence of being in space. Astronaut Jim Irwin revealed he had felt the presence of God whilst on the Moon, eventually leaving NASA to become a Baptist minister. Buzz Aldrin suffered too with depression and alcoholism after the intense public attention as a result of his involvement in the *Apollo 11* mission.

Astronauts are just people, and are as susceptible to fear, delusion, paranoia, or misidentification of objects as anyone else. Their chosen profession does not exclude them from these human traits. They may well have specialist skills, training, and knowledge relating to space flight, but space is still a largely unfamiliar and unnatural environment for our species. It is not beyond reason to suggest that when in such extreme surroundings, someone, who is essentially exploring the 'unknown', sees something, or thinks they see something that is unfamiliar or strange-looking.

The basic truths and statements regarding unusual sightings by astronauts have also undergone exaggeration, confusion, and embellishment as they have been reported, retold, and re-packaged into news stories, UFO books, and documentaries. For example, stories of UFOs following the Apollo 12 Moon mission actually derive from a transmission by Charles 'Pete' Conrad and Richard Gordon joking about being followed; in reality they were referring to rocket debris. The press however got hold of the transmission transcript and published snippets out of context in order to create a story. Jim McDivitt's photograph of a UFO taken from a Gemini-4 capsule was later shown to be lens flare from the Sun, reflecting off metal bolts outside of the capsule. Footage of the 'snowman' UFO taken by Buzz Aldrin was again just a magnified window reflection in the lunar module. It is worth considering that at various points any spacecraft will be surrounded by debris; fuel leaks, dumped water, frayed insulation and ejected equipment. Windows on these craft are tiny, and often smudged by sealant or rocket fuel.

Despite efforts by some to discredit NASA, the American space programme has had an impact culturally, not just in the US but also globally. The continued progression of space technologies, such as the payloads of NASA space shuttles, have allowed for the growth of communication satellites and continuous research and development into new technologies. The Apollo programme and the Space Shuttle in particular have captured public interest and imagination, impacting consumerism, film, television, art, music, photography, and the career ambitions of young aspiring Americans from all corners of society. During the shuttle era, millions of people purchased space-themed products: spaceships, both realistic and fantastical, and pretty much anything imprinted with the

NASA logo, from t-shirts and mugs to stuffed toys and replica spacesuits. IMAX films recorded several of NASA's in-orbit operations, such as the spacewalk of Kathryn Sullivan. Various IMAX films, such as *The Dream is Alive* and *Destiny in Space*, allowed viewers to experience in crisp detail the wonders of space. The shuttle programme had an impact on Hollywood, too, as various fictional accounts of shuttle missions became the subject of movies such as *Space Camp*, *Space Cowboys*, *The Core*, and *Moonraker*. West coast American architects like John Lautner used as inspiration shuttles and satellites to transform the look of cities and highways. Upswept, wing-like roofs, satellite shapes, and dome tops became a dominant language in the construction of motels, diners, and gasoline stations. More recently international architects like Richard Rogers and Zaha Hadid have explored similar aesthetics evoking a high-tech look that can trace a lineage back to shuttle-esque surfaces.

The space programme still represents technological advancement, the extremes of human exploration, international collaboration, and the possibilities of a very different and exciting future. The explorations of space made the wider cosmos seem less unreachable, and future journeys to other planets surely became plausible in the minds of many individuals. Deep space exploration, into areas of space beyond the solar system, is still largely theoretical. Equipment like the Hubble space telescope captures tantalizing glimpses of the vast complexities of the wider cosmos, teasing the possibilities of further exploration. Practical issues, such as how to travel such enormous distances, what would power such flight, unfeasible costs, and the huge amount of time required for such journeys have provided obvious barriers to greater manned-explorations of deep space.

The nearest star to Earth beyond our Sun, Proxima Centuri, is 4.3 light years away (over 25,000-trillion miles away), and even travelling at the speed of light (around about 670 million miles per hour) the journey from here to there would take over four years just one way. The same practical issues would obviously impact on any alien life interested in exploring Earth. This is assuming our nearest star system is home to advanced alien life. If planets orbiting Proxima Centuri do not house intelligent beings with the required technologies, then the logistical difficulties of such a trip becomes even greater. Perhaps Luhman 16 at 6.59 light years away or Sirius at 8.58 light years are home to such life, or maybe even Zeta Reticuli at 39 light years away. Betty Hill came to believe she was abducted by aliens from Zeta Reticuli, and perhaps aliens from there did take a near-eighty-year roundtrip to spend two hours with a husband and wife from New Hampshire, but any imagined reasoning as to why such a trip would happen seems absurd. If alien races had the technologies to travel at close to forty times the speed of light, in a way that was cost effective, then the journey seems more reasonable. However the ability to do so, even in the wildest of theoretical senses, seems so beyond the laws of physics, as we know them, that either such feats are impossible or our understanding of the universe is so naive that advanced races would look on us with as much interest as we might garden snails.

So far as we know the speed of light is also the speed of causality; it is the maximum speed at which two particles can transfer information between each other. Breaking this barrier would at the very least result in some strange physics, as matter would essentially struggle to keep up with itself. To maintain these speeds, the effects of such travel would need to begin happening before whatever caused the travel in the first place. Cause must be followed by effect, not the other way around. Essentially a UFO moving at speeds way beyond that travelled by light would have to arrive somewhere before it had left where it originally came from, and according to physics, as we understand it, this isn't possible. In terms of special relativity, it is theoretically possible for an object to accelerate up to the speed of light, but not beyond it. Only tachyonic particles can, hypothetically, move faster than light. In fact, these particles always only move faster than the speed of light. The characteristics of a taychyon is however purely an idea; no compelling evidence for their existence has yet been found, and many physicists think they cannot exist.

Such principles of physics owe much to the work of Albert Einstein. His 1905 paper 'On the Electrodynamics of

Moving Bodies' introduced his special theory of relativity. Much of what Einstein argues has only been reaffirmed over time, rather than discredited. Due to the practical limitations of intergalactic travel as suggested through relativity, many UFOlogists see such laws of physics as simply ideas to be broken. Einstein's German heritage may, too, play a part in the continued skepticism. Harassed and denounced by the Nazis before he left Germany in 1933, Einstein campaigned for a number of improvements in civil rights when he became an American citizen.

Alternative modes of propulsion have been suggested and experimented with over the years. Things such as nuclear propulsion, matter-antimatter annihilation rockets, gravity propulsion, solar electric propulsion, and Ion propulsion have been theorized and even tested, though none claim energy efficiencies powerful enough to break the light barrier. The Alcubierre drive is a speculative idea proposed by theoretical physicist Miguel Alcubierre. The idea involves achieving faster-than-light travel but without contradicting the rules of general relativity with a craft capable of contracting space in front of it while at the same time repelling space behind it. It is a manipulation of spacetime itself, where the destination and start point are pulled closer together. Although the idea is not impossible from a theoretical and mathematical point of view, in reality it may well be extraordinarily unlikely. The amount of energy required to produce such an effect, if it is even possible, would be of a magnitude greater than the estimated mass of the observable universe, an outburst of energy that would in all probability destroy not only any craft itself, but also the entire area into which it was travelling.

Despite these practical issues, several members of the scientific community have not been put off in their ambitions to communicate with distant intelligent life. The desire to contact other civilizations through any serious attempt goes back to the early nineteenth century, when astronomers were still speculating about life on Mars, Venus, or even the Moon. German mathematician Carl Friedrich Gauss suggested drawing a giant Pythagoras triangle across the Siberian tundra, with ten-mile-wide strips of pine forest and fields of rye, in an attempt to communicate with nearby interplanetary neighbours. Another idea from Austrian astronomer Joseph Johann von Littrow involved using large parts of the Sahara desert to draw shapes in, with twenty-mile-wide trenches filled with water and ignited at night with kerosene. During the 1890s physicist Nikola Tesla suggested his electrical transmission system could send signals to Mars. He even thought at one point that he had detected a signal from the planet; though it turned out to be nothing, it fueled speculation that contact via radio-waves could be possible.

In June 1952, J. Allen Hynek conducted a survey of astronomers, with several, including Clyde Tombaugh and Lincoln La Paz, reporting that they had observed sightings that they could not fully explain. Clyde Tombaugh was self-taught in the study of astronomy, but so dedicated was he that by his early twenties he was offered a job at the Lowell Observatory in Flagstaff, Arizona. His job involved use of the 13" telescope to image the sky. In February 1930, he discovered Pluto, going on to discover new comets, stars, and galaxy clusters.

Lincoln La Paz, an astronomer at the University of New Mexico, became interested in the idea that several green fireballs observed over southwest America might be alien probes rather than meteors. Media reports on the claims mixed up Tombaugh's work with La Paz's more far-out theories, as well as several articles written by Donald Keyhoe concerning military witnesses of UFOs. The result was the claim that Tombaugh and the US Military were actively searching for extraterrestrial satellites. To add further confusion, Tombaugh reported seeing a UFO in 1949 in New Mexico, and again observed another two years later while at the White Sands observatory.

In 1959, physicists Philip Morrison and Giuseppe Cocconi suggested the possibility of searching the microwave spectrum for signs of intelligent communication. Harvard astronomy professor Harlow Shapley also began speculating on the probable number of inhabited planets in the universe. Soon after, American astronomer Frank Drake began work on what would become Project Ozma, using a bank of eighty-five-foot-wide radio telescopes from the National Radio Astronomy Observatory at Green Bank, West Virginia, to search for signs of life in distant space.

In 1961, astronomer Carl Sagan joined a semi-secret society, later dubbed The Order of the Dolphin. The group gathered at Green Bank Observatory with the aim of establishing ways in which to detect evidence of intelligence life outside our own solar system. Members included J. Peter Pearman, Melvin Calvin, and Frank Drake, as well as the neuroscientist John Lily. Lily was a researcher interested in languages of communication used by dolphins; he was also interested in sensory deprivation and psychedelic drugs, often in combination. He developed a series of experiments in which he would ingest ketamine either in an isolation tank or in the company of dolphins, sometimes feeding the dolphins LSD so as the two species could better communicate. By 1974, Lily had come to believe in the existence of a hierarchical group of cosmic entities controlled by a Cosmic Coincidence Control Centre.

Lily helped popularize the idea that dolphins have their own language and possess a kind of intelligence equal to our own. The Order of the Dolphin group used the principles of how you might decipher dolphin language as a template for understanding potential alien languages. More recent research into dolphin language has suggested it is far less sophisticated than once thought.

As part of the meeting held in 1961, Drake developed an equation to help predict the difficulty of detecting signs of extraterrestrial life. There are so many variables and unknowns that the Drake equation can't be used in any real practical sense, beyond it being a theoretical guide as to the plausibility of extraterrestrial life. Using the Drake equation has resulted in figures of intelligent lifeforms beyond ourselves within the Milky Way Galaxy being anywhere between zero and 15,785. Carl Sagan once suggested the number may be as high as one million, though soon relented that it was probably much smaller. The mathematical physicist and cosmologist Frank Tipler suggested that on average each galaxy would only have one, or less, advanced civilization comparable to our own.

The Fermi Paradox takes its name from a question posed by Italian physicist Enrico Fermi in the early 1950s. Similar to observations made by people such as Konstantin Tsiolkovsky in the 1930s, Fermi asked in response to claims of apparent UFO activity, simply, 'Where is everybody?' His paradox is essentially concerned with some of the high estimates of probability for extraterrestrial life and the complete lack of tangible evidence to support such claims. There are many reasons to explain this, ranging from life simply being very rare to the impracticalities of huge distances between any potential civilizations, other species simply being too alien for us or them to comprehend each other, or the chances of intelligent life developing in line with ourselves – and close enough to communicate – being prevented by common extinction events.

By the early 1970s, NASA had begun funding several Search for Extraterrestrial Intelligence (SETI) projects, such as research into Project Cyclops, a 1,500-dish radio telescope array. The construction estimate of $10 billion meant such an installation was never realized. Many of the principles suggested in the Cyclops report did however provide a template for much of the SETI projects to follow. Due to the high costs of any attempt to search for alien life via the use of deep space probes, the decision was made for the far more economical approach of searching for signs of signals.

The Ohio State University radio observatory, also known as 'Big Ear', was part of the university's SETI project. The observatory was designed by Dr John Kraus and constructed mostly with the assistance of eager students. Big Ear was built between 1956-61 and finally became operational in 1963. Ten years later and up until 1995 the observatory was used to search for extraterrestrial radio signals, as part of the Ohio sky survey project. On 15th August 1977, a strong narrowband signal was detected by volunteer astronomer Jerry R. Ehman, working at Big Ear. Lasting seventy-two seconds the signal was perceived to come from the direction of the constellation Sagittarius, though the specific area was one containing no planets or stars. The alphanumerical code that caused excitement, 6EQUJ5, described observation of a sustained kHz frequency transmitted close to the hydrogen line. '*WOW!*' wrote Ehman next to the print out. Big Ear has since detected thousands of narrowband pulses, from all over the sky, though all last less than ten seconds, never appear in the same place twice, and have never had the strength of the Wow! signal.

Despite repeated attempts, the Wow! signal has never been found again. Through 1987 and then 1989, astronomer Robert Gray searched for the source of Wow! but found nothing. Another search was attempted in 1999 by Dr Simon Ellingsen, which again found nothing. Ehman himself searched for it around fifty times, becoming sure that the signal was not of extraterrestrial origin. Later analysis suggested that the signal was an earthbound artificial radio signal that has been accidentally picked up by Big Ear.

By the late 1980s, Big Ear's future seemed uncertain. An old IBM 1130 computer borrowed from Green Bank Observatory, which was used to continuously process fifty channels of Big Ear's searches, was eventually destroyed by a mouse who had built a nest in the computer's air intake. This cut off the air supply to the disc drive, which then overheated beyond repair. The University had been attempting to sell off the land since 1982 and Big Ear was eventually bought in 1998, with the land being turned into a golf course. In 2012, thirty-five years after Wow!, the National Geographic channel began collecting messages from the public through social media, eventually compressing the messages into a digital package to be beamed into space. More than 20,000 people provided messages for the project, which was sent in the direction of the original Wow! signal, two and a half quadrillion miles away.

The Allen array is the result of collaboration between the SETI institute and University of California, Berkeley. It currently has forty-two radio telescope dishes at the Hat Creek Radio Observatory in California. After a cash injection of over $11 million, the project finally became operational in 2004, and has spent the majority of years since searching the stars for alien life (with some pauses due to lack of funding and forest fires).

The Allen Array has identified several signs of potential

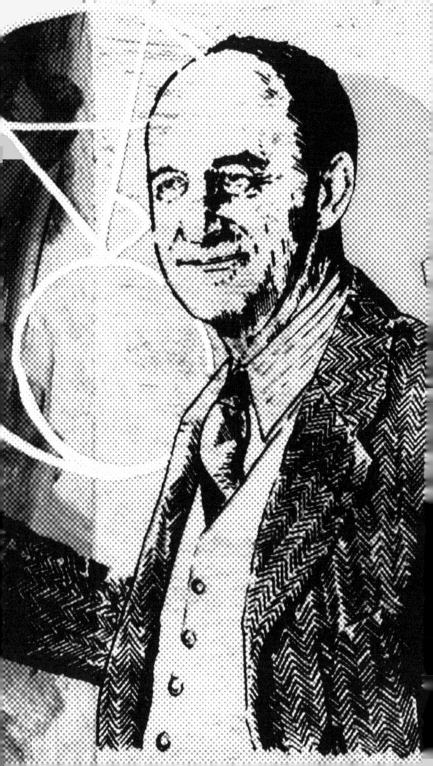

interest in deep space. One example is KIC 8462852, also known as 'Tabby's Star', a star in the constellation Cygnus approximately 1,480 light years from Earth. Since 2011 unusual observations have been made concerning light fluctuations around the star. While some scientists suggest a likely cause to be a passing swarm of dusty comet fragments, others have speculated about the remote possibility that it could be a sign of alien technology.

The Ratan-600 telescope located in Zelenchukskaya in the Caucasus Mountains, part of southwestern Russia and just north of Georgia, is used to scan the skies for signs of extraterrestrial intelligence. In May 2015, a strong signal in the direction of HD164595, a star in the constellation of Hercules around 94 light years away, was detected, though the discovery was kept secret for over a year. Nikolai Bursov of the Special Astrophysical Observatory in Zelenchukskaya encouraged sustained monitoring of the area for further signs of what potentially could be evidence of intelligent life. SETI later joined in the search positioning their large Allen array to scan the same area. Like the Wow! signal of 1977, HD164595 has not it seems replicated the impressive signal. SETI remain skeptical and after further investigation, Yulia Sotnikova of the Russian Academy of Sciences has suggested analysis of the signal revealed its most likely cause was terrestrial interference.

In July 2015, a $100 million initiative was launched by the Breakthrough Initiatives Group at the Royal Society in London. Launched by Professor Stephen Hawking, the ten year project will use power telescopes and listening equipment to scan the million closest stars to Earth in a bid to find evidence of intelligent life. Perhaps such initiatives will eventually identify intelligent civilizations in the far reaches of space, though some believe evidence of extraterrestrial life may still be found much closer to home.

The Moon still remains the only celestial body to have been visited by human beings. Its size in the night sky makes it far more tangible a destination than the distant dots that make up the other visible planets of the solar system. In the fifteenth century, Leonardo da Vinci believed the dark areas of the visible Moon were landmasses and the lighter areas oceans. In the early nineteenth century, Bavarian astronomer Franz Von Paula-Gruithuisen claimed to have glimpsed cities on the Moon with his telescope. Around the same time British astronomer Frederick William Herschel believed that the Moon, other planets, and even the Sun contained life, comparing the probable landscape of such bodies to that of the English countryside.

Vladimir Terziski, self-proclaimed President of the American Academy of Dissident Sciences, who is actually an engineer from Bulgaria, claims that the Nazis landed on the Moon as early as 1942 and soon established a base there. Terziski appeared in UFO circles during the early 1990s after he produced the book *Close Encounters of the Kugelblitz Kind*. According to Terziski the first man on the Moon was German theoretical physicist Werner Heisenberg, who in reality was Professor of Physics at the University of Berlin. Terziski also believes the Moon has an atmosphere along with water and vegetation and that the Moon base currently has a population somewhere in the region of 40,000 people.

By the 1950s, John J. O'Neill, science editor for *The New York Herald Tribune*, discovered what he thought was a bridge on the surface of the Moon. In 1958, the comic book artist Jack Kirby produced a story called *The Face on Mars*, in which a large face served as a monument to an ancient humanoid race from Mars. In more recent times the person most influential in promoting the idea of evidence of ancient civilizations on the surface of other celestial bodies is Richard Hoagland. Hoagland has made claims that advanced civilizations exist or once existed on the Moon, as well as some of the moons of Saturn and Jupiter; he his best known however for his insistence on such civilizations existing on Mars.

Hoagland claims that NASA routinely censors or edits photographic material before anything is published in any public forum or catalogue. He suggests that an extraterrestrial race used the Moon as a terminal station and ruins of cities, transparent dome structures, basements, and tunnels stretching many kilometers are apparent on the lunar surface. Hoagland is not against the idea that the Nazis landed on the Moon.

Hoagland was largely self-taught in regard to his science education, having no academic qualifications beyond his high school diploma. This hasn't stopped him positioning himself as an equivalent to the likes of Carl Sagan, with whom he has a particular obsession. Hoagland claims he was a curator of astronomy and space science at the Springfield Science Museum during the mid-1960s. The Museum is a Natural History centre, which is also home to the Seymour Planetarium. On the subject of Hoagland, the Museum has stated that no person of such name has ever been an employee there. Previous employee Rich Sanderson and the previous Director Frank Korkosz have confirmed Hoagland was involved in some of the Planetarium presentations during the 1960s, but not that he was a paid employee and certainly not a curator. It seems likely that Hoagland was actually a volunteer who worked as an occasional presenter for the Planetarium shows, though by all accounts he was good at it, displaying a natural charisma and ability for storytelling. Through his time at Springfield, Hoagland came into contact with J. Allen Hynek when the Museum hosted a WTIC-AM radio show in 1965, which covered the Mariner IV fly-by of Mars. Hoagland had been assisting WTIC announcer Dick Bertel, and was presumptuously described by the coverage as a 'Museum Curator'.

In July 1976, NASA's *Viking 1* spacecraft orbited Mars, capturing a number of photographs of its surface. One of the images, over the region known as Cydonia, captured a rock formation with the appearance of a humanoid face. The 'face' was first described as such by NASA themselves, when the image was released as a curiosity with the caption 'huge rock formation which resembles a human head'. Chief NASA scientist at the time Gerry Soffen dismissed it as nothing more than a trick of light and shadow. This dismissal didn't stop Hoagland producing the 1987 book *The Monuments of Mars: A City on the Edge of Forever*.

Other 'structures' discovered on Mars as a result of Hoagland's research include a bust of Queen Nefertiti, an adjustable wrench, and a replica of the restaurant at the Los

Angeles airport. More recently, in 2014, UFO enthusiast Scott Waring (creator of UFOsightingsdaily.com) claims to have identified various relics of ancient Martian civilizations after studying images from the 1997 Sojourner mission.

The human mind is prone to what is known as apophenia, the experience of seeing meaningful patterns or connections in random or meaningless data or imagery. Any meaning gained through an episode of apophenia is entirely a self-referential one, the 'results' of a Rorschach test being a common example. A specific type of apophenia is called pareidolia, which specifically deals with how the mind processes seemingly random imagery to create recognizable forms. Common examples are perceived images of faces in patterns, cloud formations, industrial objects or rocks. The subconscious brain processes random shapes in an attempt to make sense of it by association with commonly recognized objects.

The sixteenth-century artist Giuseppe Arcimboldo exploited pareidolia by creating 'faces' using arrangements of vegetables, meats, books, and flowers. There are many examples of natural formations in rocks producing faces, animals, and religious deities. For example, the profile of Stac Levenish Island in Scotland or the human face on Pedra da Gavea in Rio de Janeiro. The Face of Mars is certainly another example, as more recent, higher resolution imagery has shown the exact same outcrop to be a rather un-face-like rock formation.

Mike Bara, author and Richard Hoagland's protégée, claims that pareidolia is not a real phenomenon. He has also claimed, in his book *Ancient Aliens and Secret Societies*, that NASA is run by mystics who worship Egyptian Gods. He co-authored the 2007 book *Dark Mission: The Secret History of NASA* with Richard Hoagland, and like his co-author has only a high school diploma to his name. That hasn't stopped him confidently making claims along the lines that global warming is a scam and evolution is wrong.

Ironically, the scientific community is edging toward a point where they are increasingly optimistic that they may indeed find evidence of alien life, as more probes, satellites, and high power telescopes search the cosmos. Chief NASA scientist Ellen Stofan thinks that this discovery may be in the next ten to twenty years, though added it would most likely be a microbial lifeform. Such 'life' may be simple bacteria, but such a discovery would be profound evidence that life on Earth is not utterly unique. Such a discovery is yet to be made, and perhaps it will be an awfully long time until it is. Professor Stephen Hawking shares the view that life most likely exists in addition to that found on Earth. He adds that if we are to come across any other life form, certainly an intelligent one, we better hope we are the more advanced and not the other way around, as the history of advanced races meeting more primitive ones never turns out well for the primitive ones. Contact with the advanced technologies of the Europeans was not, for example, an advantageous experience for the Inca and Mayan societies.

The idea that alien life may most likely be very alien-looking microbial growths sits in contrast to the many examples of sightings describing humanoid beings. Exactly how alien bacteria manufacture and pilot craft with beyond light-speed capabilities remains to be seen. Consideration of rational practicalities suggests that aliens and UFOs are indeed far more likely a manmade phenomenon, evidenced perhaps most strongly in the physical similarities between humans and the humanoid appearance of most *aliens*. The effects of evolution seen on our planet alone suggest life is capable of producing a wild variety of forms and sizes, and the chance therefore of an intelligent alien species resembling a human seems remote.

Like the fear and paranoia felt in the West as a result of first Nazism and then Communism, the concept of the alien becomes a useful tool from which to express concerns through the development of myth and stories. Concerns around German scientists and Russian space activity may be a much greater influence on the development of such stories than any actual visitors from space. If Frank Tipler is right in his estimation that each galaxy would only ever be home to one or fewer advanced civilizations, then the reality is that any great neighbouring alien race would likely have existed a long time ago in a galaxy far, far away…

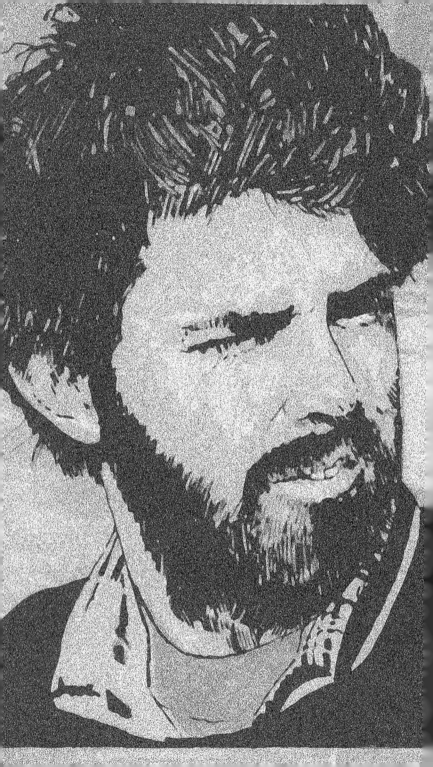

PART FIVE

Fairy Tales From Mars

George Lucas's 1977 feature *Star Wars* had a massive cultural influence. Released at the end of a turbulent decade for the West, it was a space age fairy tale filled with visual spectacle and feel-good escapism. *Star Wars* exploded into the perfect pop-cultural storm; it was a refreshing distraction from a decade tired of serious issues and scandals: a messy war in Vietnam, the Watergate scandal, a recession, and the energy crisis. The 1970s was a decade greatly defined by somber and serious cinema – *The Deer Hunter*, *Taxi Driver*, *The Exorcist*, *The French Connection*, *The Godfather*, *A Clockwork Orange*, *One Flew Over the Cuckoo's Nest*, and *Chinatown* – although all great movies, they don't exactly fit the 'Fun for all the Family' market. The 1970s film previously closest to capturing the buzz of *Star Wars* was probably Steven Spielberg's 1975 feature *Jaws*, a tension-filled monster-movie featuring an exaggeration of a real world shark terrorizing a small community and eating several inhabitants (including children) in the process. It's no wonder audiences devoured the bubble gum escapism of *Star Wars*.

Lucas's film takes as inspiration the 1930s and '40s sci-fi serials such as *Commando Cody* and *Flash Gordon* (he initially wanted to produce a re-make of *Flash Gordon*, but couldn't acquire the rights). It also borrows liberally from several comic book sources, most notably Jack Kirby's *New Gods*, with its all-encompassing power 'the source', which Lucas copied and re-named 'the force'. Frank Herbert's novel *Dune*, first published in 1963, also provided a strong source of inspiration for Lucas's *Star Wars* saga. Herbert himself took as inspiration Shakespeare, Greek tragedy like *Oedipus Rex*, and the writings of Fyodor Dostoevsky. *Star Wars* displays its fairy tale template gleefully; the opening caption 'A Long Time Ago in a Galaxy Far, Far Away…' is an obvious play on the 'Once Upon a Time…' phrase often found at the start of children's stories. Its use of a Princess held captive by a Black Knight (Darth Vader) in a castle (in this case the Death Star) plays with classic fairy tale motifs. Dashing young peasants (like the farm boy Luke Skywalker) must rise to become noble Knights (or Jedi in this instance). Magical old wise men have supernatural powers, as do the evil fairies of the Dark Side. Although such conventions are often subverted, adapted into a science fiction language, or used playfully, the fairy tale influence upon *Star Wars* is strongly evident, and indeed intentional.

The period around 1977 ushered in a new phase in the exploration of space: by 1975, the United States and the Soviet Union had achieved the first international human spaceflight with the Apollo-Soyuz Project, 1977 saw the launch of *Voyager 2*, and 1981 saw the launch of the space shuttle, the first re-useable spacecraft. *Star Wars* clearly fit the mood of the time and soon became the most financially successful film of the decade, spawning an almost unprecedented wave of imitators, with an influence that spread beyond cinema into everything from toys, games, books, clothing, music, political speeches and breakfast cereals. Pop culture went space crazy. The aesthetic of Hollywood was fundamentally changed as a new emphasis was placed on spectacle and increasingly impressive special effects. Movies with a space theme remained dominant for a number of years after the release of *Star Wars*, including films such as *Close*

Encounters of the Third Kind, Alien, ET: The Extra-Terrestrial, The Black Hole, Moonraker, Star Trek: The Motion Picture, Flash Gordon, Battle Beyond the Stars, The Last Starfighter, Flight of the Navigator and the first of the *Star Wars* sequels, *The Empire Strikes Back*.

It is not a surprise such a phenomenon had an impact on UFO sightings. One example, the Spanish Turis landing case of July 1979, described a sighting of alien beings dressed in shiny white suits with helmets featuring protruding black spectacles. These sound very much like the *Star Wars* Stormtroopers. Though drawings provided by Spanish farmer Frederico Ibáñez make the creatures look more like the movie's Jawa traders, the source is clear: these are *Star Wars*-inspired creatures. The rise in popularity of triangular-shaped UFOs following the release of the film and into the 1980s probably has more to do with the general shape of spacecraft depicted in Lucas's movie as it does sightings of any advanced military aircraft. One case from November 1977 involved a couple from Plymouth, New York, who spotted a huge triangular shaped craft. Moving slowly overhead it made a loud noise like a rocket and had four glowing engines at its rear. The description matches exactly the iconic opening scene of *Star Wars*, as a giant triangular-shaped Imperial Star Destroyer passes menacingly overhead, eventually filling the screen with a number of bright, roaring engines. In 1978, brothers Gary and David Oickle observed a huge triangular UFO with large windows moving very slowly above Patapsco State Park, Maryland, and in January 1979, Albert Chop witnessed a triangular UFO moving slowly over the mountains southeast of Palm Desert, California. The object was described as extremely large and much brighter that the stars in the background, much like the large, light grey Star Destroyer designed to stand out vividly on screen against its dark space backdrop.

Society feeds pop cultural trends, but equally fashionable pop cultural trends influence inclinations within society. This concept relates to what is known by some as cultural tracking. This broadly means that the beliefs that people hold tend to follow the culture in which they are immersed. As cultures change, so do beliefs, and vice versa. As a result, philosophical, ethical, and social customs and beliefs inform the culture produced and consumed during any particular era and, in turn, that same cultural product can impact on beliefs and customs. Cultural phenomena like *Star Wars* superficially influence other things for purely commercial reasons, but also indicate a wider appetite from a society hungry to engage with the themes of that same cultural trend.

In 2010, all six *Star Wars* movies were re-released in theatres in a 3D format, and rumours began to circulate about the possibility of further installments to the series. Later that same year, UFO enthusiast Scott Waring claims to have found what looks like a *Millennium Falcon*-shaped craft (another iconic *Star Wars* spaceship) partly obscured by a hangar in part of Area 51. The image was obtained by a study of Google Maps, and can only be viewed by following specific instructions allowing the viewer to travel 'back in time' through the viewer to 1989. In June 2011, an account was made of a UFO shaped like the *Millennium Falcon* discovered at the bottom of the Baltic Sea. Claims made by the Swedish Ocean X Team who discovered it, Peter Lindberg and Dennis Åsberg, include its ability to disable any electronic equipment when divers approach within 200 feet. Geologists have suggested it most likely is a natural formation or sediment dropped by a fishing trawler.

In regard to cultural narratives informing sightings of UFOs, the idea relates to what is called the psycho-cultural or psychosocial hypothesis, a concept developed during the 1980s by writers such as Jacques Scornaux and Michel Monnerie. Basically the hypothesis argues that sightings of UFOs and related events are best explained psychologically or through social means. Such ideas have their roots in the writings of Carl Jung, especially his 1958 work *Flying Saucers: A Modern Myth of Things Seen in the Skies*. His suggestion is that as belief in the reality of UFOs remains resilient despite the lack of any tangible evidence, there is therefore a strongly implied psychological explanation at the heart of the matter. In Jung's words, UFOs essentially act as a type of 'technological angel'. In simple terms, an individual will unconsciously use a cultural reference to engage with or explain a particular event, feeling, or issue experienced within society. In the unconscious, wonder about the possibilities of space exploration could mix with imagery from science fiction, and in turn transform a genuine sighting of a bird into something otherworldly.

The idea around the psycho-cultural hypothesis is that belief in UFOs and visiting aliens is a result of a narrative formed from a collective enchantment with the concept of spaceflight and intelligent alien life. Such a phenomenon has evolved on the back of developments in actual space exploration, science fiction stories, and adaptions of age-old myths concerning spirits, gods, the unknown, and the unexplained. Sightings of UFOs are able to encapsulate wonder, spiritual awakening, terror, salvation, discovery, and a world of secrets and new possibilities.

The idea that the traditions, cultural practices, ingrained beliefs, stories, concerns, and desires of a society inform their folklore is not a new one. Researchers such as Linda Dégh and also Howard Peckham have approached the UFO subject as a folk tradition. Linda Dégh would argue that UFO sightings provide examples of a continuation of traditional folk narratives presented through a filter of contemporary concerns and fascinations. Their principle idea is that modern aliens are really just an updated form of fairies or spirits. To somewhat counter these ideas, some UFO researchers have essentially argued the opposite. For example, Jacques Vallée wrote *Passport to Magonia: from folklore to flying saucers* in 1969 and John Keel produced *UFOs: Operation Trojan Horse* a year later, exploring the connection between Celtic mythologies, folklore, and fairy tales with modern day accounts of UFOs and aliens. The intended thesis in both books was to illustrate that UFO encounters had been an ongoing occurrence dating back centuries, and that similarities between folk myths and alien encounters was proof of extraterrestrial visitations way before the mid-twentieth century.

David Sivier, a writer often interested in fairy mythology, UFOs, and the supernatural, has examined the inter-relation between all three genres and would argue that comparisons in regard to the central motifs of fairy lore and alien encounters are many: from otherworldly lights in the night sky to strange visitations, abductions, little green men, circles left in fields, hidden underground lairs, secret knowledge through magic or advance technology, and the ability to appear at will from a mysterious *other* realm. These are all enough of a similarity to suggest that there must be some connection between the various tropes. Many UFO and alien encounters also compare strongly to the structure of supernatural myths of the incubi, succubi, witches, and ghouls with tales of forced sexual encounters, bizarre experiments, or spells requiring animal parts, shape-shifting, and the harvesting of vulnerable humans. It is worth looking at the trends of such folktales through the ages and into the birth of the UFO phenomenon in the mid-twentieth century to see exactly what the most likely root of such accounts is.

Celtic traditions can be dated back to cultures from around 1000 BCE due to identifiable artifacts found on the bank of Lake Hallstatt in Upper Austria. The Celts were one of the first cultures to develop the concept of immortality, specifically the idea that the soul transferred to an Otherworld. They believed that after death, a Celt was given a new life, though different from the idea of reincarnation, it is perhaps the origin of the spirit form as different from the physical form. Celtic tradition includes references to hundreds of Gods and Goddesses, though not all have any clear function. They would make offerings and sacrifices to such Gods, including animal and occasionally human sacrifice in order to pacify Gods and ward off bad spirits. There was also a strong belief in many spirits and supernatural beings occupying parts of the natural world. Things such as rocks, rivers, and trees were believed to contain a spirit, and such things would react in certain ways depending on how they were treated. The Celts were not a single uniformed tribe or culture. Societies that can be described as Celtic shared some similarities in language and traditions but were only grouped into a collective whole by the Greeks and Romans. The term Celts in fact only came into common use during the seventeenth century through the writings of Welsh naturalist Edward Lhuyd.

These cultures first appeared in recorded writing around

600 BCE through writings made by Greek travellers. Due to certain mystical significances given to the written word, the Celts themselves did not document much of their own culture, and it was not until the Christian period that any Celtic literature developed. Such writings, mostly produced by devout Christian monks, re-evaluated such narratives via Christian beliefs and the ancient myths concerning Pagan gods were reinvented as tales of wizards and sorcerers. Even the term Pagan is a Christian invention, essentially describing a follower of some other lesser religion, as opposed to a greater Abrahamic one.

The stories from Celtic literature, such as the *Leabhar Laignech* (The Book of Leinster) tell of mythical invasions from 'the ever-living ones', such as the Children of Danu, and were produced by a number of people including Áed Ua Crimthainn, abbot of the monastery of Tír-Dá-Glas through the second half of the twelfth century. Other texts, such as *Lebor Gabála Érenn* (The Book of Invasions), purports to be an ancient Celtic history of Ireland going right back to the creation of the world. For a long time the text was considered to be an accurate account of history, but more recently it is viewed as mostly myth; some historians believe parts to be loosely based on real events, others believe it essentially to be a work of fiction.

The Welsh *Mabinogi*, another key piece of Celtic literature, contains a number of mythological tales and romances. An early example of prose literature from Britain, the collection of tales within the *Mabinogi* was also complied during the twelfth century and was based on a number of earlier oral traditions. Tales such as *Pwll Pendefig Dyfed* involve various legendary figures, princes, Lords of the Otherworld, and fairy folk. Common themes in such mythology involve trips to mysterious lands, sexual relations between humans and fairy folk, shape-shifters, and frequent use of magic. The concept of magic, as distinct from any religious belief or practice, was first widely separated through the teachings of Judaism, which defined the practices of pagan worship involving any God other than Yahweh as 'magic'. During the Middle Ages, the Christian Church rejected magic as a whole because it was viewed as an unnatural way of interfering with the natural world. Magic, and by default many pagan traditions, became associated with sorcery, witchcraft, and the occult; as a result, Celtic customs and beliefs became transformed through Christian intervention into underworld spirits, fairies, and magic folk.

These ancient myths have become fragmented through such revision and adaptation. Several may have developed from Indo-European myths, such as the sky-god Dyaus, which through Greek recording became Zeus, and again through Christian Latin morphed into Jove. In Irish Celtic tradition, Dyaus slowly became Lugh Lámhfada (the bright one), who was slowly demoted into Stooping Lugh before being Anglicized into the Leprechaun.

Although similar folk tales are found all over the world, particular versions will often reflect the values, traditions, and customs of the society and culture from which they come. Folk tales originate from an oral tradition of passing down stories from one generation to the next, with each telling reshaping, embellishing, and adapting the narrative; folk tales are added to and enriched by those digesting them. It is interesting to compare such a tradition with accounts of UFO sightings being discussed at UFO conferences or through Internet forums. When new evidence or accounts are offered up, participants add new twists to well-known reports, and new elements gradually become accepted as part of the mythology. A UFO account will be retold and retold, becoming slightly more embellished each time, and external influences, especially thematically relevant ones like science fiction, will provide additional minor details to the narrator, much like traditional folktales.

Linda Dégh was one of several folklorists who applied the idea of ostension to the study of contemporary legends. An ostensive definition conveys meaning of a term or concept by pointing out comparable examples of a thing or using descriptive gestural actions rather than words. With folklore and urban legends, the idea is used to explain the formation of new variations of such myths by reenactment or perceived reenactment of something similar. New folklore can be created or existing myths expanded when real-life happenings seem to parallel events in pre-existing legends. This can involve direct copies or re-enactments of folktales or interpretation of ambiguous actions or events as linked to such legends. For example someone may act out or hoax an activity based on folklore, an individual may draw some detail from legend and claim it to be his or her own experience, or someone may misinterpret and yoke an unrelated event to a local folktale. In this sense any differences between fact and narrative can become interchangeable.

A clear example of ostension is what is sometimes called legend tripping; this involves a purposeful visit to a site, such as a cemetery, cave, tunnel, woods, an abandoned building or some uninhabited area, thought to have been the scene of a tragic or supernatural event. Activity in such places, often at night and often involving trespassing, can lead to local concern about happenings at the sites, and may even fuel rumours of renewed occurrences of the supernatural nature of an area. One example is the frequency of visits made to the Devil's Tramping Ground in North Carolina. Teenage pilgrimage to this site has been responsible for local tales concerning Satanic cults or strange disappearances. More recently the suggestion has been made that the soil in the area is barren because of a UFO landing, and the high level of radiation from the extraterrestrial craft has permanently damaged the ground. Most likely it is just a fun place for the youth to escape their parents and get drunk.

Much folklore is concerned with fear of the unknown, and in particular death, a tradition going back to ideas of the Celtic Otherworld. As a result, figures associated with death often play a key role in what could now be generalized as fairy tales, such as the Ankou, the dullahan, the Cù Sìth, or the Grim Reaper. Fairies, elves, and goblins are often evocative of the returning dead, or of representing a fear of death. Such creatures are commonly described as being green or grey; it is no coincidence that these same colours are the ones most associated with rotting putrid flesh. Grey and green is the colour of the returning dead, and are also the favourite choices of alien skin-tone. Green aliens are common in science fiction. Edgar Rice Burroughs's John Carter books, like *A Princess of Mars* from 1912, describes the green men and women of Mars;

other examples include Marvin the Martian, the Mekon from *Dan Dare*, and the character Yoda from the *Star Wars* movies.

Modern aliens work well as metaphors for the returning dead: they come from the great unknown, another dimension, the future, or possibly the afterlife. They are often described as grey or green, with large black eyes representing both dead, dilated pupils and the bulging of the eye sockets after death caused by internal gas build up. Bald aliens may represent a rotting corpse that gradually loses its hair as an early stage of the decomposition process. It is interesting, too, that the term 'little green men' has one origin in World War II slang used by US Marines to describe camouflaged Japanese soldiers, people seen literally as foreign bringers of death. Survivors of the atomic blast over Hiroshima suffered severe radiation effects, resulting in loss of hair, disfigurements, and clouding of the eyeballs as a result of cataracts; when images of these survivors arrived in the West, the guilt of such destruction may well have also informed some aspects of the American subconscious. In this regard it is interesting to note that Roswell Army Airfield was home to the 509th Operations Group, the bombardment group that dropped the atomic bombs over both Hiroshima and Nagasaki in 1945.

A more recent comparison is the urban legend of the black-eyed children, supposed paranormal creatures who appear as normal young children, paled-skinned, but with solid black eyes. Some have speculated such children to be ghosts, extraterrestrials, or the result of an alien-human hybrid programme. In reality they have their roots in 1990s pop culture and Brian Bethel's online creepypasta postings.

In folklore, the Coblynau, mythical Gnome-like creatures said to haunt the mines and quarries of Wales, are similar to the English Goblin, the Irish Cnoc, the German Kobold, and the American Tommyknocker. Sounds of knocking would attract miners down passageways, just before a cave-in. Such stories may have their roots in old tales of volcanic hills, such as the Cnoc Fírínne in Limerick. Immigrant Welsh miners brought tales of the 'knockers' to Western Pennsylvania during the 1820s, and similar ideas began to spread to other parts of the US. Often described as short, green in colour, and mischievous in nature, they have arguably appeared several times in UFO-related accounts.

One such account now dubbed the Hopkinsville Goblins case occurred in August 1955. Billy Ray Taylor of Pennsylvania was visiting the Sutton family in Hopkinsville, Kentucky. Around 7 p.m., due to the house having no running water, Billy went to the outdoor pump to get something to drink. Outside he observed strange lights in the sky, quickly running back to tell everyone of his flying saucer sighting. Around an hour later strange noises and knocking were heard on the doors and walls. Billy, along with Elmer 'Lucky' Sutton, went out to investigate, only to find a strange creature, about four-feet-tall with large elephant-type ears, huge eyes, and silver clothing. The family then spent several hours fending off creatures from the house before making a run for the local police station. Upon returning, there was no sign of what Billy had described as the Goblins. Many newspaper articles subsequently referred to the creatures as 'little green men'.

Author Stephen King makes the comparison of such creatures with the modern idea of the alien explicit in his 1987 novel *The Tommyknockers*. This describes a mysterious object discovered in a nearby wood, which then turns out to be a long-buried alien spacecraft. The craft soon begins to release gases that transform people into beings similar to those who once populated the ship. Written largely as a meditation on his personal substance addiction, the novel also takes as inspiration the HP Lovecraft story 'The Colour Out of Space' and TV series *Quartermass and the Pit*.

A similar (but much earlier) account is known as the green children of Woolpit. This legend concerns two children, with unusual green skin colour, who appeared in the village of Woolpit, Suffolk, during the late-twelfth century. As described by the writer William of Newburgh, the children were discovered wearing unusual clothes; speaking an unknown language they eventually communicated that they came from a land where the Sun never shone. Similar stories are found in the writings of historian and archdeacon of Brecon, Gerald of Wales. Writer Robert Burton suggested in his 1621 work *The Anatomy of*

Melancholy that the green children had fallen from heaven. A more recent re-appropriation comes from astronomer Duncan Lunan, who proposed in a 1996 article for *Analog* magazine, that the children were transported from their home planet by a matter-transmitter malfunction.

Another folk creature similar to the Coblynau is the Banshee, a female spirit from Irish mythology, often seen as an omen of death and a messenger from another world. She often appears as an old hag, with wild hair and a long green cowl cloak. In American folklore, the Banshee became a Ghoul, and stories of such creatures became popular in the late eighteenth century, particularly in the Irish immigrant communities of North Carolina. A possible explanation for the origin of the Banshee is the screech of the barn owl. In Gaelic mythology, the Cailleach is a supernatural hag, who sometimes manifests as an owl; as the cailleach-oidhche, she is the goddess of winter and a bringer of death. In Welsh mythology, the owl is associated with Blodeuwedd, the Goddess of Betrayal. The sound of an owl call has often been thought to be a bad omen or a forecast of imminent death. Chaucer wrote that the owl brings tidings of death; poets Robert Blair and William Wordsworth would often use the image of the barn owl as a bringer of doom. The custom of nailing an owl to a barn door in order to ward off evil persisted through parts of England until the nineteenth century. Certain indigenous American tribes view the owl as an omen of sickness and death; others believe them to be an earthly manifestation of one of their Gods.

A barn owl was also a likely candidate for the sighting of the Flatwoods monster in West Virginia in 1952, a supposed extraterrestrial creature. There are also further links between the banshee and the Flatwoods apparition; the description of a tall female-like figure with a black body, claws, and a large cowl behind her head matches both the Flatwoods creature and the traditional description of the Banshee. Several other witnesses who claimed to have seen the Flatwoods monster later attributed sicknesses to sightings of the creature. Geographically, too, West Virginia is positioned reasonably between North Carolina and Pennsylvania, an area which would be steeped in a rich tradition of tales like the Banshee and the Tommyknocker going back to the nineteenth century.

Sightings of owls seem to account for a number of strange occurrences, such as the 'owlman' spotted in April 1976 by sisters June and Vicky Melling at Mawnan church in Cornwall, who was again spotted that summer by teenagers Sally Chapman and Barbara Perry. All witnesses were young (9-14 years of age) and probably just not that familiar with seeing owls; their descriptions and drawings essentially described a large barn owl. More recently, Mike Clelland has written an entire book *The Messengers: Owls, Synchronicity and the UFO Abductee*, detailing the vital role that owls play with alien abductions and UFO sightings.

As well as owls, other animals, usually cats or black dogs, feature in accounts of the supernatural and sightings of aliens. They are often labeled as shape-shifters, though it's interesting owls, cats, and black dogs are all omens of death from certain cultures. Black dogs serve as guardians to the underworld in European mythologies, such as the Norse Garmr, or as the ghostly black shuck of British legends. The notion of a black cat as an omen of death or bad luck is common amongst Western culture, and has its roots in traditions and folklore from Germanic superstitions. There are many examples of shape-shifters also from Celtic mythologies, such as Tuan mac Cairill, who has changed many times into creatures such as a stag, eagle, and salmon, or the selkie, creatures that can transform from seals into humans. Judy Carroll, from Australia, believes she has been in contact with an alien race called the Zetas for around 50 years; frequently they visit her in the form of owls or cats.

Omens and the superstitions surrounding them play a key role in the developing history of UFO sightings. Things such as comets or meteors are often seen as omens and bringers of doom. On the eve of the Norman invasion of 1066, Harold II witnessed sight of Halley's comet in the sky, recording it as a bad omen. Such feelings were confounded when William the Conqueror defeated his forces, and Harold himself was killed on the battlefield. The same comet returned during the fourteenth century and was subsequently blamed for bringing the Black Death to England. Michael Baillie has argued in his book *The Celtic Gods: Comets in Irish Mythology* that several myths and recorded imagery of around 540 AD are the result of a passing comet. Often attributed to signs from the Gods, the sighting of such objects remain a fascination.

A flap of UFO sightings were reported between 1995 and 1997 as the Hale-Bopp comet passed over the skies. The UK Ministry of Defence received over 1,000 witness accounts claiming sightings of UFO activity during the duration of Hale-Bopp in the visible night sky. Hale-Bopp, too, had an obvious impact on the Heaven's Gate UFO cult. Claims were made in 2014 that the mission to land a craft on the comet 67P was actually a secret communication between humans and aliens. The comet was seen by several, such as Scott Waring, to be an alien spacecraft. Witnesses can frequently see UFO sightings as an omen. In November 2015, astrologer Louis Turi posted images online of UFO-shaped clouds he had documented over parts of Cape Town, South Africa. He described these cloud formations as 'omens or signs created by the Draconis to prepare humanity for more UFO phenomenon in the near future'. After witnessing four separate UFO events, Turi claims he has had the secrets of the cosmic code downloaded into his mind, and has gone on to regularly make future predictions through various websites.

Certain mythical lights associated with folktales and legends are also seen as omens of death or a sign that a funeral is due to take place in the locality. Fabled lights, such as the Will-O-the-Wisp, also known as ignus fatus, jack-o-lanterns, or foxfire, are mythical ghost lights often seen by travellers at night, and said to draw people away from the safe path and towards swamps or marshes. Will-O-the-Wisps may be the result of fireflies, white owls reflecting the Moon at night, bioluminescence, or more recently car headlights or other forms of distant artificial illuminations. In European folklore, such lights are said to be spirits of the dead, the soul of an unbaptized person, or markers indicating fairy gold. In Welsh mythology, they are known as the Púca, a goblin-like fairy that

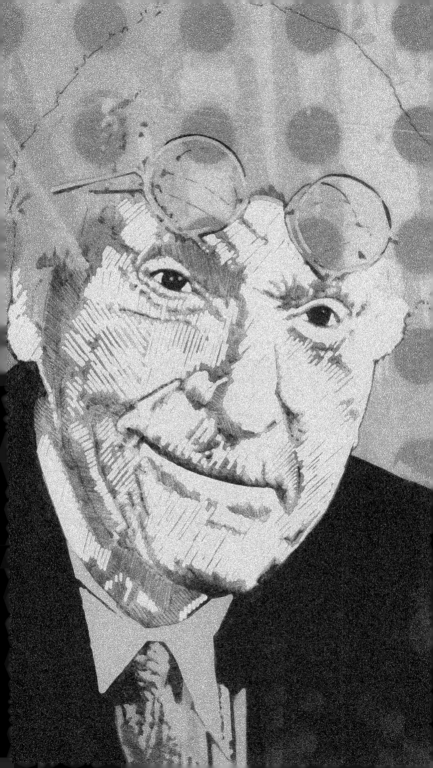

leads lone travellers to danger. Such phenomenon has since become attributed to ghostly orbs or alien spacecraft.

One example includes the local legends concerning lights seen around Brown Mountain in Northern Carolina. A version of this legend involves a woman who disappeared in 1850, most likely taken up the mountain at night and killed by her husband, only to return as a ghostly figure. Another version of the tale involves a plantation owner who got lost while hunting on the mountain; a search party went looking for him with lanterns, and none of them were ever seen again. Accounts likely trace back to misidentifications of train lights made in the area during the early twentieth century, and ever since there have been reports of strange lights spotted on the hills and reports of apparitions, abductions, and strange experiences. Such things have been since attributed to ghosts, fairies, and aliens in equal measure, such as the account by James and Sara Nelson, who claimed they were attacked by a UFO in 2013 while observing the Brown Mountain lights.

Another example are the Marfa lights of West Texas, which have been spotted numerous times and supposedly go back to claims made by cattle ranchers in the 1880s. The lights were actually first reported in 1957 and have been the subject of studies by paranormal investigators, UFO hunters, and physics students. Again, local folklore has attributed them to UFOs, ghosts, or Will-O-the-Wisps, but more likely they are atmospheric reflections of campfires, car headlights, or sightings of nighttime activity at nearby Marfa Army Airfield.

As well as strange lights, dancing fairies also contribute to some UFO sightings and alien encounters. The Irish daoine sídhe are said to be visible to humans at times such as Midsummer, when they dance under the moonlight. Dancing fairies appear in some alien accounts, such as one from Indiana in October 1973, when two creatures dressed in silver were seen dancing in the middle of the road by a couple, Mr and Mrs Donathan. Truck driver Gary Flatter got a look at the creatures about two hours after the Donathans' sighting when he saw them bouncing up and down in a field. He described them as short, having egg-shaped heads, and wearing masks. Considering the time of year, they were more likely kids in Halloween costumes.

In August 1977, policeman David Swift on patrol in East Hull saw three dancing figures who then disappeared suddenly. The story was reported in *The Hull Daily Mail* before being picked up by *MUFON* magazine. Such stories are reminiscent of the Tylwyth Teg, a race of spirits from Welsh folklore who would often be spotted dancing and singing, only to vanish into thin air once approached.

Age-old myths combined with the development of science fiction have created a fertile breeding ground for folklore such as UFO sightings and alien abductions. Accounts of the Sidhe, a clan of Irish fairy, would often involve beings appearing from some hidden place and spiriting people away. Individuals would return after what they thought a few hours, only to find that many years had passed in the world of humans. The story of 'Rip van Winkle' written by Washington Irving and first published in 1819 borrows conventions from such fairy abduction lore, whilst establishing a template for future alien abduction narratives. Here Rip wanders into the Catskill Mountains to escape his nagging wife, when he meets several strange fellows and partakes in consumption of moonshine before passing out, waking several decades later to find the world a very changed place. The story is similar to a number of folk tales from Germany, and also Tír-na-nÓg, the Irish land of the young, a supernatural realm of everlasting youth and abundance.

Examples of people claiming missing time after an alien abduction experience are plentiful. From the two hours of missing time experienced by Betty and Barney Hill to the five days lost by Travis Walton, it is a common ingredient to such claims. Marty Kottmeyer has pointed out that the Betty and Barney Hill encounter also owes a lot to the last segment of the movie *Invaders from Mars*, released eight years prior to the New Hampshire abduction case. There is not only abduction, but also a medical examination featuring needles and a calming optical tranquilizer, and earlier in the movie a star-map is referenced – all details evident in Betty Hill's account. Post-war social concerns, such as the perceived Communist threat, combined with a fascination with space travel produced science fiction products like *Invaders from Mars* and *Invasion of the Body Snatchers*. These same products then informed aspects of emerging folk myths of the day, such as the Betty and Barney Hill abduction case.

Alien abductions relate to many themes evident in fairy tales describing sprites stealing men's wives. Such abductions often involve sexual elements, the harvesting of sperm, gynecological examination, or actual alien impregnation. Rape between employers and employees was common up until Victorian times, with wealthy landowners taking advantage of house servants and farm girls. A returning bride after spending time away with the fairies would often return either bearing a child or after sufficient time to have birthed the infant and returned it to its *real* parent. Nursing mothers are also often popular in fairy folk myth abduction stories, as their rich milk provided better nourishment to infant fairies, while at the same time transferring a soul from mortal mother to fairy child. Up until the nineteenth century it was not uncommon in parts of Europe to hammer nails around a mother's bed and child's cradle, as fairy sprites are often said to have a fear of iron. Issues such as post-natal depression were at one time attributed to fairy enchantment, with the recommended remedy commonly being a good beating. Low infant mortality, infanticide, and harsh cruelty to new mothers were common up until the early twentieth century.

Hillary Porter from Farnborough, Hampshire, claims she has been abducted by UFOs over 100 times, beginning in the early 1970s, and claims she is part of a programme of harvesting human eggs and genetic material for alien breeding purposes. Bridget Nielson and Aluna Verse believe they have witnessed many UFOs and also given birth to thirteen alien-human hybrid babies. Bridget is also a member of the Hybrid Baby Community, a group who believe they have all birthed alien hybrids. Through hybridchildrencommunity.com she acts as a medium for other 'mothers' to converse with their alien offspring; for only $111 a session, such aliens can be contacted through smelling plants and drinking tea. Since 2013, Stephany

Cohen, of Bromley in the UK, has claimed that she has been visited by a variety of aliens for numerous sexual encounters, many of which lead her, she claims, to a heightened state of sexual arousal and hour-long orgasms. More likely these are individuals experiencing some form of Exophilia, a particular fetish involving a desire to be with a non-human extraterrestrial, supernatural, synthetic, or other strange humanoid in a sexual manner.

Other precedents in science fiction provide templates for similar abduction cases. The 1930 *Buck Rogers in the 25th Century* comic book story *Tiger Men of Mars* not only features flying disks but an abduction of a female earthling who is then medically examined before being returned home. Science fiction films from the early 1950s provide strong sources of inspiration for the developing UFO mythologies. *The Man from Planet X,* released in 1951, features aliens from the imaginatively-named Planet X, a dying planet whose inhabitants are looking for a new home to colonize. Their strategy of abductions, leaving strange bits of metal lying around and visiting unpopulated remote corners of America, relates to recurring motifs within many UFO encounters that followed.

The Day the Earth Stood Still, also 1951, was another early and influential sci-fi film. The plot centred on an alien called Klaatu who comes to Earth to warn us of our own self-destruction. A perfect marriage of atomic age paranoia and space age wonder, it was also the first sci-fi film to feature actual flying saucers. Aliens from other worlds with a disproportionate interest in the general welfare of the human race were a common theme in early 'contactee' cases, which gained wider acceptance in the early 1950s after the release of this film. Indeed George Adamski started making his photographs of UFOs the year after *The Day the Earth Stood Still* hit cinemas.

Referencing imagery from science fiction is an ongoing pattern in abduction accounts. Allison Reed claims aliens abducted her for four and a half days, during which time she was shown tanks containing bodies documenting various stages of alien-human hybridization. Her alien hosts were part of a dying race that could not reproduce in sufficient numbers to sustain their species viability. The case was first documented in the 1998 book *The Threat: Revealing the Secret Alien Agenda* by David M. Jacobs. Her account is similar to scenes in both the movie *Alien: Resurrection*, and an episode of *The X-Files* ('The Erlenmeyer Flask') where there are rooms filled with failed alien-human hybrids, both of which were released before her account was made public.

The X-Files was a science fiction drama TV show, which ran for much of the 1990s. The premise of the show centred on the investigations of FBI special agents Fox Mulder and Dana Scully, who would look into unusual and unsolved cases, and often those with paranormal aspects. The show gradually developed its own mythology, involving a complicated, and frequently unresolved plot, concerning the government cover-up of extraterrestrial beings. *The X-Files* takes as inspiration previous shows, such as *The Twilight Zone* and *The Outer Limits*, and in turn influenced a number of imitators, such as *Dark Skies* and *Supernatural*. The popularity of the show influenced many aspects of popular culture too, and it may be one of the key aspects to the growth in interest around government cover-ups, conspiracy theories, and general belief in UFO activity seen through the nineties.

The basic idea that stories breed stories is a well-established one, and the lineage between ancient folktales, literature, cultural trends, and science fiction providing a solid foundation for the development of the UFO phenomenon seems logical. Victorian-era supernatural tales demonstrate a comparable historical template for the development of similar beliefs in popular society. Indeed, contemporary society's fascination with the supernatural, otherworldly, or extraterrestrial has its most obvious roots in the development of Romanticism and Spiritualism through the Georgian and Victorian ages. The continuing industrialization of Britain during the late 18th to early 19th centuries uprooted long-standing traditions, and rapid developments in both science and technology left many confused and discomfited. During the Industrial Revolution, the Victorians devoured tales of the supernatural as a form of escapism from the increasingly mechanized landscape that was fast emerging around them.

Gothic horror developed during the preceding Georgian era, a time of great change, which saw the birth of the Industrial Revolution, the American War of Independence, Darwin's theory of evolution, and an intensification of class division within society. Horace Walpole's *The Castle of Otranto* published in 1764 and Mary Shelley's *Frankenstein* published in 1818 are commonly seen as early and influential examples of the Gothic in literature. Other key Gothic authors such as Ann Radcliffe, Matthew Lewis, Edgar Allen Poe, and Bram Stoker produced works that were essentially products of Romanticism and a reaction against the rational and scientific worldview made prevalent through the Enlightenment. The supernatural became a vehicle from which to critique the modern world, as the Gothic responded to a variety of issues and events including the French Revolution, developments in science, social injustice, and racism.

Romanticism became a reaction to the Industrial Revolution, emphasizing the importance of intense emotion as a form of aesthetic experience, as terror, awe, horror, and apprehension all became subjects in their own right. An emphasis was placed on the sublime, as ancient customs, folklore, and anything in contrast to the rational enlightenment of scientific development was looked upon favourably.

During the Victorian period many writers began work preserving the folk traditions of times past, writers such as Thomas Crofton Crocker, Thomas Keightley, and Andrew Lang re-established the popularity of fairy stories and related folk mythologies. It is the Victorian obsession with such folklore that provides much of the source material for what is now commonly understood to be age-old traditions. Without such British fairy-lore would be largely limited to particular works by Shakespeare or Simeon Steward's writings from the seventeenth century.

The influence of such depictions upon aspects of the popular imagination was clear. Spiritualism thrived during the 1840s to the 1920s, as belief that the spirits of the dead could have the ability to both manifest and potentially communicate with the living captured popular imagination. A significant catalyst for such interest came in March 1848 when sisters Kate and Margret Fox of Hydsville, New York, reported that they had made contact with a spirit. Like the Coblynau, it communicated through a series of knocks and taps. The Fox sisters' account helped move Spiritualism into wider awareness as it was reported through many newspapers of the day. Ironically by 1888 the sisters admitted any such contact was hoaxed, but the movement continued. An account recorded by British folklorist Katharine Briggs from the 1880s describes the sighting of a group of dancing fairies on the Isle of Skye in Scotland. Charles Leadbeater wrote in 1895 that such fairies were inhabitants of a different astral plane, and had the ability to change their shapes. Like other supernatural occurrences, many recordings of fairy sightings often occurred around graveyards, perhaps relating to legend tripping and Linda Dégh's ideas around ostension. Edward Hartland, an anthropological folklorist, wrote in his 1891 book *The Science of Fairy Tales* that no clear cut distinction could be made between ghosts and fairies, since they share the same traits and the same tales.

The popular idea of the fairy as a tiny winged creature comes from the Victorian age. The Victorian fairy is a celebration of magic in an age when prevailing thought sought to rationalize every aspect of nature and being. Depictions of fairy folk in fine art paintings began to emerge through the Victorian period, notably by artists such as Richard Dadd, Joseph Noel Pattern, Richard Doyle, and later Arthur Rackham. They would appear regularly at the Royal Academy exhibitions, increasing their popularity and respectability. Strongly influenced by the Romantic Movement, early works focused on fantasy themes inspired by Shakespeare characters, such as those from *A Midsummer Night's Dream*. Admirers of Victorian-era fairy painting included Charles Dickens, Lewis Carroll, and Queen Victoria.

These winged creatures became so accepted as the image of the fairy that depictions in illustrations began to inform apparent sightings and claims of otherworldly encounters. The infamous case of the Cottingley Fairies involved production of a series of five photographs taken by Elsie Wright and Frances Griffiths in 1917. The pictures were produced by use of cutouts of fairy illustrations taken from *Princess Mary's Gift Book*, and supported in shot by hidden stands and pins. They were later promoted by author and spiritualist Arthur Conan Doyle, and received some press attention during the early 1920s. The women eventually admitted to faking the images in the early 1980s.

Sir Quentin Craufurd and Bernard Sleigh founded the Fairy Investigation Society in Britain in 1927. The society attracted over 100 members at its peak, and kept active in some form up until the early 1990s. The group operated much like the more recent UFOlogy societies, arranging meetings, giving talks, and collecting evidence of fairy life. There is much to the pattern of the Victorian fairy and its acceptance by areas of society that is transferable to the UFO phenomenon.

As trends in culture evolve so, too, do the characteristics of folk characters. The Gothic and the Romantic gave birth to what would now be described as science fiction, and in turn age-old motifs were re-invented for alternative genres. Science fiction keeps pace with general scientific knowledge; as science makes new discoveries or explores new possibilities, so science fiction embraces such ideas within its stories. The French-born novelist Jules Verne is best known for his adventure stories and wide influence on the science fiction genre. A number of his writings may have also had a direct influence on the early development of the UFO phenomenon. *From the Earth to the Moon*, published in 1865, described an attempt by the Baltimore Gun Club to launch a trip to the Moon via space cannon. A year later Verne produced *Robur the Conqueror*, which opens with claims of mysterious objects seen in the sky. The novel features a giant flying machine, and an anti-hero who kidnaps (or abducts) three passengers for a 'round-the-world flight. The ideas in the book took as inspiration the French air balloons of the 1860s and the story became popular in America in the 1890s, just before the outbreak of the mystery airship sightings. Many similar fiction stories appeared, featuring flying machines, flying boats, and flying submarines. The cigar shaped

UFOs of the late 1890s reference not just early airships, but also the flying machines of Jules Verne, with accounts of craft with wings, propellers, and fins.

There is a clear evolution of UFO mythology and UFO witness statements that parallel the technologies and scientific understandings of the time that they originate from. UFO accounts of the 1890s are often concerned with otherworldly airships, but such themes disappear with the invention of conventional aircraft. Early accounts of alien encounters often described extraterrestrial visitors coming from Mars or Venus. When in the 1950s this was discovered impossible, such visitors suddenly came from farther afield. UFOs of the 1960s have exhaust fumes and levers, yet by the 1970s they have embraced digital technologies and warp drives. This is cultural tracking in action.

Things such as literature, art, theatre, and film inform folk narratives, not just the themes and motifs of any tale, but also the physical characteristics of the elements within them. 130 years before *Star Wars*, audiences were just as hungry for special effects-laden spectacle. Theatrical productions became increasingly lavish and spectacular through the Victorian age as stage effects embraced new technologies to enchant audiences, while Romantic themes of legends, fairy tales, and ghost stories became popular on stage.

Phantasmagoria was a rear projection process that used a modified magic lantern to display images such as ghosts or demons into a theatrical stage setting. The effect was pioneered by Paul Philidor and Etienne-Gaspard 'Robertson' Robert in the late eighteenth century. An 1801 production at London's Lyceum Theatre that used the phantasmagoria effect soon became a popular hit and the process became more common. A similar process developed after phantasmagoria was known as Pepper's Ghost, named after its scientist inventor, John Henry Pepper. The effect was first demonstrated in 1862, though its general principle dates back to experiments undertaken in the sixteenth century. An effective stage trick, ghostly objects appear to fade in and out of view by use of controlled lighting and carefully positioned reflective glass. A figure or object in a hidden room is projected (or more accurately reflected) into the visible area, allowing apparitions to appear and disappear. Spirit photography, too, became popular during the same period, as people such as William H. Mumler came across the technique of double-exposure. This again created semi-transparent ethereal figures floating within the natural world.

The special effects industry informs the general population of what a particular spectre is supposed to look like. Ghosts traditionally look floaty and transparent because such an effect was possible to create on stage with techniques such as Pepper's Ghost, or on film through double-exposure. Such things cement the look of a ghost within the popular consciousness. The same is true of more recent developments in science fiction cinema and television.

In film aliens are often humanoid, partly because of the practical issues of using a human in a suit to portray them on camera, as well as limitations resulting from available technology and funding. In the original *Star Trek* TV series, budget limitations and a desire to create alien races viewers could relate to resulted in most extraterrestrials being humanoid, with an added 'alien' extra feature, such as Vulcan ears, green skin, or unusual foreheads.

Star Trek debuted in 1966, and was basically envisioned as a combination of science fiction exploration adventures, with the drama style of TV Westerns. Its creator Gene Roddenberry intended it to have a progressive social and political agenda that reflected the emerging values of the youthful counter-culture movement. The bridge crew of the *USS Enterprise* features a Russian, a Japanese, a strong Black female, and an alien, Mr. Spock, who came complete with elf-like ears. Still, it held a strong patriotic underpinning synonymous with the climate in which it was created. The show featured fairly obvious references to the Cold War, with Earth's Federation staffed principally by Americans and 'alien threat' the Klingons being a rather unflattering interpretation of the Russians. The Starfleet logo, too, essentially looks like a large stylized *A* for America. *Star Trek* became a cult phenomenon, and is noted for its influence upon the real world. Automatic doors, mobile phones, scanning equipment, and 3D printers, now realities, were all imagined previously as science fiction within the world of *Star Trek*. Other concepts such as warp speed and being 'beamed-up' were a neat and cheap way of transferring the story from one location to another.

Such ideas may be responsible for several UFO accounts, too. Marty Kottmeyer has documented a number of UFO and abduction cases relevant to *Star Trek* plot devices. A 1975 account by Sandra Lawson describes removal and replacement of her brain, very much like the process that occurred in the 1968 episode 'Spock's Brain'. Many others include accounts of being beamed aboard craft, or use of dilithium crystals to power craft (a substance invented as a fuel source for the Starship Enterprise). In 1989, John Ford witnessed what he described as a bright light in the night sky, which then made a sudden and dramatic departure above Eastbourne. He described the movement of the UFO being like when the Starship Enterprise engages warp speed, only to disappear in a flash of light. The most successful installment of the *Star Trek* film series *Star Trek IV: The Voyage Home* was released not long before Ford's experience, and the following installment was due in theatres around the time of the sighting. American football quarterback Aaron Rodgers claims to have spotted a UFO in 2005, which he described as flying through the sky 'like when you're watching *Star Trek* and they go warp speed'. More recently, in July 2015, Greg Prescott from El Paso, Texas witnessed a cube-shaped UFO, which he described as 'a sign of the Devil'. Similar cube-shaped UFOs have allegedly been spotted over Los Angeles and in Coacalo de Berriozábal, Mexico, in January 2014. Such cube-shaped UFOs seem to reference the distinctive Borg spacecraft from *Star Trek: The Next Generation*.

The practical realities of producing something for screen impacts the final results. When Steven Spielberg made *Close Encounters of the Third Kind* in 1977, he originally wanted the climactic aliens to be non-humanlike, to glide instead of walk. At one point, dressing an orangutan in a suit fitted with roller-skates would create the desired effect. When this proved both impractical and unsatisfactory the design was modified, using

162

children in rubber costumes, eventually producing the classic bald aliens with thin limbs and large eyes. Carlo Rambaldi designed the aliens with help from Bob Baker and additional effects were provided by Doug Trumbull (especially the dramatic entrance of the alien mother-ship). Rambaldi was also later responsible for the visual effects of *Alien* and *ET: The Extra-Terrestrial*. Creatures from all three films, though superficially different, do share a humanoid appearance: all have thin limbs and oversized heads. Such forms allow for actors or puppeteers to control the creatures; thin limbs are practical for puppetry, and the general figure-like shape allows for a person to at least be partly enclosed within the costume. In the case of the alien from *Alien*, the large head serves a further practical purpose in housing the mechanisms for its protruding mouth pincer. Like Pepper's Ghost, the available special effect techniques informed the ultimate outcome, and the quality of work created genuinely iconic creatures. The typical description of an alien as a bald bug-eyed grey humanoid with a large head and thin limbs became popular in the 1980s after the success of such movies. Aliens look like *aliens* because of things like *Close Encounters of the Third Kind*.

Spielberg's movie re-packages many classic UFO ideas from popular culture: contactees, government knowledge of extraterrestrials, and classic saucer-shaped motherships. He had been attempting to get *Close Encounters* off the ground since 1973, though originally he conceived filming a documentary about people who believed in UFOs. The film was partly inspired by an event from the Director's childhood, when his parents rushed the children into the car without warning and drove them to a remote area were others were gathered in order to watch a meteor shower. The title is derived from J. Allen Hynek's classification system – a third encounter being one in the presence of an animated alien creature. It even features a brief cameo from the UFO veteran himself. Interestingly J. Allen Hynek's son, Joel Hynek, has had a successful career working as a visual effects artist in Hollywood, and has worked on such science fiction movies as *Predator*, *Event Horizon*, and *Jumper*.

Strong visuals such as those found in Hollywood blockbusters have a significant effect on our perception of what certain things should look like, as broad themes and motifs move in and out of fashion over time. Spikes in UFO reports parallel releases of blockbuster Hollywood movies, such as *Star Wars* in 1977 and *ET: The Extra-Terrestrial* in 1982. In the mid-1990s a re-newed interest in aliens and a wave of UFO reports followed the success of *The X-Files*, *Independence Day*, and *Men in Black*, as well as the celebrations around the fiftieth anniversary of the Roswell incident in 1997. For example, in December 1996, a few months after the release of *Independence Day* (a movie that featured huge UFOs hovering over North America), claims of a huge UFO mothership were reported by a number of witnesses over the skies of Yukon, Canada. Satellite expert Ted Molczan later matched the sighting to the re-entry of the second-stage rocket that launched the Cosmos 2335 satellite that same day.

It is interesting to consider the wider media's influence on such things too. The general reporting of UFOs as circular disks, for example, increased dramatically after they started being described as flying saucers in news reports and magazines. Before big budget cinematic spectacles like *Star Wars* and *Close Encounters,* pulp magazines provided much of the template for the blossoming UFO phenomenon. One of the earliest depictions of a circular UFO comes from the October 1929 edition of *Science Wonder Stories*, which featured a very flying saucer-looking spacecraft on its cover, courtesy of artist Frank R. Paul.

The end of World War II saw a renaissance in pulp magazines, as half of the editors, authors, illustrators and even the audience of the pre-war magazines failed to return home from active duty. This, coupled with limitations on circulation and printing stock, led to a re-think of both style and content. A new range of scandal, crime, adventure, fantasy, and smut emerged in cheap print from the aftermath of world conflict.

Truth in pulp magazines has a long tradition of meaning the exact opposite, as such publications understood the appeal of fantastical stories presented as fact rather than fiction. Many contained overly sensationalized news stories; others bothered even less with reality, inventing stories wholesale and then presenting them as factual news. One example, *True Story*, comprised of entirely fictional articles but presented as if they were fact. Other titles, such as *Uncanny Tales* and *Real Mystery*, followed a similar formula.

In 1938 the Ziff-Davis Publishing Company purchased the failing magazine *Amazing Stories*. Owner William B. Ziff, not convinced it was going to be particularly lucrative, decided to take a chance and give editorial control to an emerging science fiction writer, Raymond Palmer. As a child Palmer had suffered severe injuries after he was hit by a truck at the age of seven, the accident left him crippled and dwarfed in stature. He had a challenging and often lonely childhood, becoming isolated due to his physical difficulties. However, he soon found escapism through cheap magazines and science fiction, and quickly began writing his own stories. Before long he was producing fanzines and having several stories published, and by the age of twenty-eight found himself editor of his own magazine. Palmer targeted the revived *Amazing Stories* at the emerging teenage boy market, filling it with non-fiction items and pseudo-science articles, the majority of such features were just written by Palmer himself under various pseudonyms.

In the early 1940s, Palmer came across a letter from Richard Shaver in a rejection pile in another editor's office. The letter revealed Shaver's perceived 'truth' regarding a race of freaks he called the 'Deros' who lived under the surface of the Earth. Palmer took the letter, re-wrote it, and ran it as a feature in his magazine. He subsequently received various letters from readers providing further evidence to support the claims of his story. Palmer quickly realized the lucrative potential of publishing such oddball claims. He encouraged readers to send in such letters, and soon began re-writing more of them. Paranoid fantasies mixed with fabricated truths and the combination was a success. By 1945 *Amazing Stories* was selling 250,000 copies a month. Richard Shaver, as it turned out, was in fact a budding writer, and later produced a number of short stories published in Palmer's magazine, such as 'The Sun-Smiths' and 'Cave City of Hel'.

The September 1946 edition of *Amazing Stories* featured one article describing experiments with circular craft, and another concerning aliens visiting Earth in spaceships to kidnap humans. It was only nine months later that Kenneth Arnold's 'flying saucer' story broke into the news. After the Arnold story, Palmer decided to put out an all-flying-saucer-based issue of *Amazing Stories*. He also produced a new magazine, *Fate*, which featured a re-print of the Arnold story. By 1950, *True* magazine was also embracing the UFO craze, which allowed publishers the chance to recycle old science fiction covers, a cost-saving measure to maximize profit. Palmer kept interest in the theme through the early 1960s by publication of his *Flying Saucers* magazine, as well as promotion of various UFO clubs. Even the phrase UFOlogy emerged from a 1963 edition of *Flying Saucers*.

A number of early Ray Bradbury stories were first published in pulp magazines, such as *Planet Stories*, *Amazing Stories*, and *Super Science Stories*. Aliens display telepathic abilities in a number of his science fiction stories, such as 'Mars is Heaven!' first published in 1948. The collective work *The Martian Chronicles* also features other telepathic aliens in stories such as 'I'll Not Ask For Wine' and 'The Spring Night'. Such abilities have since become an ongoing theme in UFO-related narratives. One believer in the telepathic connection with aliens is Clifford Stone. He suffered a mental breakdown after his son died in accident and his marriage dissolved in the aftermath. Stone then relocated to Roswell and became obsessed with UFOs. He claims he was covertly recruited into an elite UFO retrieval team due to his natural ability to communicate with extraterrestrial beings. One exercise apparently involved the retrieval of an alien from the Kecksburg UFO crash. He maintained this story until he was questioned about specific details of the site, and then changed his account to the claim that his assistance was provided exclusively via remote viewing.

Raymond Palmer was instrumental in inventing and facilitating a whole system of beliefs through his stories concerning flying saucers and visiting aliens, and once such a belief system had been set up it soon became self-perpetuating. A good example is the Bermuda Triangle story, invented for a February 1964 edition of *Argosy*, which was then turned into the 1965 book *Invisible Horizons: Strange Mysteries of the Sea* by Vincent Gaddis. This was then added to by Ivan Sanderson's Devil's Graveyard accounts, written in 1972, before Charles Berlitz cemented the myth with his own book *The Bermuda Triangle* in 1974. By this time the Bermuda Triangle was recognized through a wide enough section of society as an actual thing, that soon further evidence started to appear to support the notion of its existence. There are no doubt examples of individuals who claimed experience of things in the area as a result, and certainly felt genuine fear when passing through on a plane or boat. The fact was it all just had its roots in a trashy 1964 short story, which itself was informed by old tales of sea monsters, themselves based on accounts of tropical storms, sightings of whales, and underwater volcanoes.

Re-writing forgotten pulp stories as fact and unsolved mysteries soon developed into an industry in itself. An early example of the promotional exploitation of folk-myth involves the marketing of a science fiction movie. An actor claiming to be a real FBI agent (known only as McKnight) made claims that the tales of a captured UFO from Roswell were true. It turned out it was a publicity stunt for the movie *The Flying Saucer* released in January 1950. Writer, director, and star of the movie Mikel Conrad was one of the first to cash in on the late-'40s flying saucer flap, making claims that his movie was based on genuine footage of alien spacecraft filmed around Alaska. The opening title cards of the movie thank 'those in authority' for allowing the film to be released. The gimmicky promotional campaign even made it into a number of national papers.

Over twenty-five years later movies like *Star Wars* were employing a more sophisticated version of a similar concept. While no attempt is made to suggest *Star Wars* is anything but fantasy, it explores contemporary obsessions like spaceflight, with a re-invented selection of historical templates, mythological archetypes, and re-imagined folk-tales and fairy stories in order to sell a product. *Star Wars* was not only responsible for an increased fascination with space adventure, but for establishing a trick of re-packaging old adventure stories into modern cultural products. George Lucas repeated the trick a few years later with his *Indiana Jones* movies, taking inspiration again from 1930s adventure serials.

Lucas had in fact tried something similar before *Star Wars*. His *American Graffiti* movie from 1973 owed much to his own nostalgic reflection of his teenage years of the late 1950s and early 1960s. Much was the mood of the time; there was an appetite during the 1970s for a nostalgic reflection of past eras, particularly the 1950s. After the turbulence of the 1970s, the comfortable days of rock n' roll, milkshake bars and good ol' American values presented a dependable blanket of escapism from war and scandal. TV shows like *Happy Days* were popular, as were other '50s-themed movies like *Grease*. Some cultural references were less obvious but still played with the general formula, such as John Carpenter's *Assault on Precinct 13*, essentially a modernized remake of the 1959 *Rio Bravo*.

As with all rose-tinted re-interpretations of past times, trends, fashions or events, the re-imagined version is always different to the past reality. Things become re-shaped, exaggerated, or re-molded in ways that bear little resemblance to the past realities. Similar to the evolution of folktales, nostalgic reflections can create false perceptions and memories of times gone by, as they are gradually added to and embellished through re-telling. Over time such re-imaginings can become mixed with facts, leaving some confused as to what was real and what is fiction.

Such an effective commercial formula did not go un-noticed within the UFO community. Charles Berlitz, who had past success with his Bermuda Triangle writings, was aware of the commercial potential of revisiting old urban myths. Selling people a new take on a pre-existing story or concept is always easier than getting the consumer to buy into something totally new and unknown. When he was approached in the late 1970s by a pair of UFO researchers about a book that would revisit a half-forgotten case from the 1940s he would have been well aware of the lucrative possibilities. *Star Wars* had refashioned something from the 1940s and made it a huge financial hit. For some in the UFO community the successful formula had been duly noted.

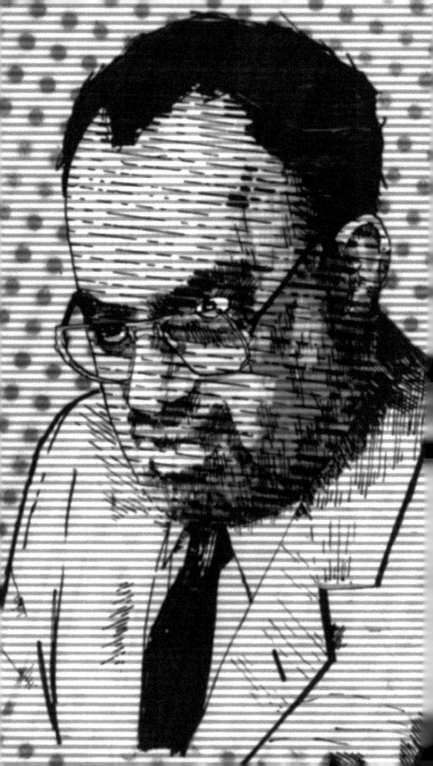

PART SIX
An Alien Industry

The Roswell incident briefly received national and some international coverage in 1947, but over the next thirty years largely faded from public view. It did occasionally receive passing attention, such as a special article on UFOs published in *Look* magazine in 1967. Stanton T. Friedman, a UFO enthusiast and researcher, is often credited with rediscovering Roswell in the late-1970s. Friedman gained an MSc in Physics from the University of Chicago in 1956, and worked for various companies between 1956 and 1970, mostly doing provisional research for engineering projects. Interestingly none of the projects Friedman worked on ever progressed past the original development phase. Friedman became interested in UFOs in 1958 at the age of twenty-four, whilst working for General Electric. It was here that he ordered a copy of *The Report on Unidentified Flying Objects* by Edward J. Ruppelt, supposedly to complete a book order so he could take advantage of free shipping. His interest in UFOs continued and in 1960 he came across a copy of Project Blue Book Special Report 14 at a university library in California. This was to be a pivotal moment as the information in this report formed the backbone for a lot of his 'research data' that he would essentially use to make a living from soon after.

Although Friedman has never claimed to have seen a UFO, his friendship with Dr Robert Wood (they met in the late 1960s while colleagues at the McDonnell Douglas Corporation) may have been a key influence on the relatively young physicist. Wood has maintained a long and increasingly erratic obsession with the subject of UFOs, in later years claiming that both he and Friedman had been hired at one point to reverse engineer UFO technology. In 1967, Friedman was given a copy of the book *Flying Saucers – Serious Business* by acquaintance Frank Edwards. This book soon became a bestseller and the possibility that there could be serious cash involved in UFOs was opened up to Friedman. Edwards was a popular radio broadcaster who by the 1960s had re-invented himself as a writer of supernatural topics. He also had success with the radio show *Stranger Than Fiction* that discussed, amongst other things, UFOs. Edwards died in the summer of 1967, and soon after Friedman started contacting radio talk shows to see if he could promote himself as an expert in the UFO field. After getting a talk at Carnegie Mellon University in Pennsylvania through a friend of a friend, he got his first paid UFO gig, receiving $100 for it. When he later found out other speakers in the same evening were earning around $1200 per talk, Friedman upped his price and left his career in physics engineering behind him. By his own admission the bottom had fallen out of his career in nuclear physics, especially by 1969 when Westinghouse Nuclear laid him off and he realised making a living out of UFO research was suddenly a viable option.

Keen to promote himself as 'The Flying Saucer Physicist', Friedman likes to remind people at every opportunity of his science background. In his book *Top Secret/Majic*, Friedman states that as he gave more lectures, he found he enjoyed speaking and that 'people believed me no matter what I said. After all, I was a nuclear physicist…' Despite his claims, Friedman's science career was fairly mediocre; he moved from temporary contract to temporary contract, including the one at McDonald Douglas that lasted only three months, before finally giving up in his mid-thirties. He has not been professionally involved with physics or indeed any science for the last forty-five years.

Friedman has stated that he doesn't hunt UFOs themselves; he hunts an audience to talk to. In fact, the bigger the crowd, the better. He has now delivered his lecture 'Flying Saucers ARE real' (or variations of it) at over 700 meetings, conferences, and college campuses. Earnings for each talk range between $1,000 and an estimated $2,000 at the height of his popularity. The talk he was giving in the late 1960s is pretty much still the talk he is still giving today. Friedman was one of a number of scientists who provided a written statement to the 1968 US Committee symposium on UFOs. The statement he provided for this symposium (produced only a year after he started lecturing) is almost a word-for-word transcript of the bulk of the lecture he is still giving forty-seven years later. The statement itself is rather brief and slightly lacking in scientific scrutiny. Friedman makes a weird argument about not all women being Brigitte Bardot, but the fact that she does exist means some sightings of UFOs must be extraterrestrial craft. If that doesn't make sense, don't worry; it makes no sense in Friedman's statement either. He also cites his favourite UFO document, Project Blue

Book Special Report 14, which he claims (writing in 1968) had never been made publically available. This isn't accurate, as Friedman himself had come across a copy of it in a library eight years previous and the document had been de-classified since 1955. After a few years, Friedman had clearly seen all the evidence he needed and has stuck to his guns ever since.

At his busiest he was delivering up to twenty-five talks a month (that's a conservative guess of $30,000 for a month's work). The UFO business has certainly been profitable for Friedman; in addition to lectures, he has appeared on many talk shows, in documentaries, and at UFO conferences. He also has a number of books to his name, including *Crash at Corona*, *Top Secret/Majic*, *Captured! The Betty and Barney Hill UFO Experience*, and *Flying Saucers and Science* to name a few. In the early 1990s he established a premium rate phone number, dubbed the UFOLINE, that allowed callers to listen to pre-recorded information on UFOs provided by Friedman, or to leave him a message regarding your own UFO sighting. In 2014 he even appeared on an American TV commercial promoting Bongiovi Pasta Sauce.

Performing and debating are really where Friedman's real strengths lie, and I suspect they are his real passion. He is a charismatic speaker and able to talk confidently around his chosen subject, having a range of quick retorts at his disposal for ongoing debates. He became interested in debating while at Linden High School and joined the Debate Team for a number of years, going on to win a debating championship. By his senior year he also became interested in drama, acting in two plays during his final year at college.

In October 1995, Friedman participated at an Oxford University debate about extraterrestrials visiting Earth. He won, with roughly 60% of the debating house voting he had presented a more compelling argument for the notion than the one presented against it. Debating at the Oxford Union takes two forms: one is competitive debating, where top international debating societies tackle serious and often controversial issues; the other is Chamber debating, where guests are invited to talk to the audience about a chosen topic. It is far less formal than the competitive debates, and topics can range from serious political or ethical discussions to the ridiculous (*Can Beauty Queens save the Planet?* or *Who's better, Oasis or the Beatles?*). Dare I say it might essentially just be a bit of fun? Friedman participated very definitely in the second category of debating. The Oxford Union has hosted important and influential speakers such as US Presidents Richard Nixon and Jimmy Carter, the Dalai Lama and Malcolm X; equally it has hosted more playful speakers, such as Jon Bon Jovi, porn star Ron Jeremy and Kermit the Frog. Winning a debate of this kind at Oxford University probably sounds far more impressive than it really is, and Friedman presents such a triumph as further evidence to the acceptance of UFOs as alien spacecraft. Some students said so; it must be true.

With Friedman arguments are carefully constructed, supporting evidence (no matter if a little tenuous) is highlighted, and contradictory facts are simply ignored. Like many conspiracy theory-style writers, a narrative is created, then fragments of evidence or obscure facts are collated to support such a claim; all are classic debating techniques. Take for example the big deal Friedman often makes about a 1955 press release regarding Project Blue Book presented by then Secretary of the US Air Force Donald Quarles.

In a press statement regarding UFO sightings in relation to Project Blue Book, Quarles declares that 'even the unknown 3% could have been explained as conventional phenomena if more complete observational data had been obtained'. The fact frequently highlighted in lectures by Friedman is that there are charts in the Blue Book report (not released as part of the press statement) that list the Unknown category as 21.5% rather than 3%. This is for Friedman hard proof that the government is lying. In fact, lying about *everything*. The fact of the matter is that this suggests that Friedman has never really progressed past page 20 of the 300 so page report or, if he has, he makes the (probably correct) assumption that few else will have bothered. He never seems to cite anything from the report past the beginning section, most likely as the general thrust of the rest of it suggests there isn't anything much to UFOs. The table that Friedman proudly shows in his lectures to support his claims doesn't actually feature in the report; it is his own interpretation of a number of charts that appear in the Blue Book document. The 21.5% is an accurate quotation, but it is taken out of context. It refers to the total number of unknown occurrences recorded within all reports (things that may not even include flying objects). When this is limited to sightings of actual objects the number goes down to 19.7%, and when the unknowns themselves are analysed as a group (you have to read on to page 78 to get to that) only 12 sightings out of 434 (or 2.7%) are suggested to be genuinely unexplainable. It's fair to say that's about 3%. It is perhaps the difference of phrase between unknown, as in unexplained, or Unknowns, as in the classification grouping used in the report that has led to such confusion.

It is however the work done around the Roswell case that made Freidman's name within the field of UFOlogy, and the thing that has dominated much of his time over the last forty-or-so years. Friedman received his first real Roswell-related tip in 1978 while appearing on a news programme in Baton Rouge. The station manager mentioned that his Ham-radio buddy, a certain Major Jesse Marcell, had once handled wreckage of a flying saucer that crashed near Roswell. Marcell was now retired from the Army and working as a television repairman in Louisiana. After a phone conversation Friedman soon interviewed Marcell, a cool thirty-one years after the events of 1947. Initially Marcell could not accurately recall the month or even the year of the crash, but as the attention lavished upon him grew, so it seems did his ability to remember details. Friedman then used his contacts to set up an interview for Marcell with *National Enquirer* magazine. It seemed likely that Marcell would keep talking so long as someone else was paying for lunch.

Marcell had a tendency to exaggerate things, and a history of trying to write himself into local infamy on the back of his fifteen minutes of fame, handling 'wreckage of a flying saucer'. Marcell went on to make a number of questionable claims, such as being an ace pilot for the military, going so far as to say he test flew alien craft. Records have shown that he did not even hold a pilot's licence and certainly there is no record in his military history of him ever being a pilot. Marcell claimed he studied physics at a number of universities; in reality he only ever attended one university, and there he did not complete his course. If anyone was to catch out Marcell on his bogus claims about a physics background, it should have been 'the Flying Saucer Physicist', but either Friedman didn't ask too many critical questions or just didn't want to know that his star witness might not be all that reliable.

It is interesting to note that the other Army Air Base representative involved in collecting the debris from the Foster Ranch, Captain Sheridan Cavitt, has never really featured much in any later Roswell narratives. Despite being interviewed by several UFOlogists, his account rarely makes it into any books. One suspects this may be because his version of events suggests the debris was not an alien spacecraft. Whenever he is mentioned in the Roswell crash tale he becomes 'the government man' and a sinister cover-up agent.

Friedman soon compared notes with fellow UFO researcher William Moore who had independently conducted some interviews concerning Roswell. William Moore was an active UFO researcher from the mid-70s until the late 1980s. He had also recently co-authored the book *The Philadelphia Experiment – Project Invisibility* with Charles Berlitz. A book concerning the Roswell incident was conceived as a suitable vehicle for Berlitz, despite him having little interest in UFOs. It was to be researched by Friedman, written by Moore, and have Berlitz's name on the cover, a partnership that was purely economic. Due to the involvement of the better-known Berlitz, publishers agreed to an advance of $100,000 for the book (this was before the research was even complete). As stated by Friedman in relation to his Roswell work, 'the book advance and later royalties justified the goal'. With the publication of the best-selling *The Roswell Incident* in 1980, Roswell as a story began to take on new proportions, as did its lucrative potential.

Following this renewed interest in Roswell, the story began to spread. Marcell had gained wide attention for his telling of the story, and soon additional 'witnesses' who claimed association with the events of 1947 began to come forward with their own information. Throughout the 1980s the modern mythology of Roswell developed and began to evolve and expand as other tellings of the same tale began to emerge. This included expanding on the detail of the alien craft, developing multiple crash sites, the recovery of actual aliens, and alleged greater witness intimidation from the military.

Walter Haut, the Roswell Army Base public

information officer responsible for the first 'official' press release was another key witness that many researchers wanted to talk to. Since being kicked out of the Army in 1948, Haut had worked as an assistant for a local insurance firm. After the interest in Roswell started to grow again throughout the 1980s, so too did the same fertile imagination that put out the original 'flying saucer' press release. Haut enthusiastically put himself forward as a central part of the narrative. He also promoted his friends Glen Dennis and Frank Kaufman as witnesses, despite the fact that neither of them had even the slightest connection to the recovery of any crashed debris.

Glen Dennis provided virtually all the details of what now makes up the popular version of the Roswell myth, including recovered alien bodies and UFO craft taken away by the US government. These 'personal recollections' have since been proven to be exaggerated, inaccurate, or outright inventions. Walter Haut and Glen Dennis apparently invented the idea that bodies were recovered from the crash one night over dinner in 1987. Dennis chose the UFO hotline provided at the end of a Roswell-themed episode of *Unsolved Mysteries* aired in 1989 to make his account known to researchers. Although most of the details from Dennis's account actually have some basis in reality, it is not a reality that has any connection to the Roswell crash. Dennis was a mortician, and as a result was exposed to a number of traumatic scenes, such as aftermaths of accidents. His accounts are basically a recollection of the most exciting things he witnessed over his fifteen-year career, condensed into one night in 1947 and embellished with a bit of aliens.

Walter Haut and Glenn Dennis, along with several others, went on to found The International UFO Museum in Roswell in 1991, with Haut presiding as president until 1996. Initially occupying a few disused rooms above a bank, it relocated to an old movie theatre for the fiftieth anniversary of the Roswell incident in 1997 and has stayed there since. The museum is for all intents and purposes a large UFO-themed shop, selling a range of books, posters, toys, bumper stickers, novelty soap, jewelry, and t-shirts, amid some cheap-looking dioramas of plastic aliens and framed copies of newspaper cuttings. Plans for a new purpose-built $25 million building were discussed but eventually scrapped in 2011 after the museum failed to raise the required funds. Despite this the organization attracts an estimated 150,000 visitors a year (three times the actual population size of the town itself) and helps secure part of the annual $57 million in UFO-related trade for the state economy. The City of Roswell, along with the UFO Museum, also now helps support The Roswell UFO Festival, which attracts close to 20,000 visitors a year, generating $1.25 million for the town over the course of the annual four-day event.

Haut changed his own version of the Roswell tale many times before his death in 2005, his account becoming more embellished each time. Just before he passed, he was still adamant about his claims of alien craft; he had heard and told so many UFO stories that he perhaps began to really believe them. Walter Haut's delusional daydreams and sensationalist claims may have had a more direct influence on the modern UFO myth than anyone else.

In his talks, Friedman makes a big claim of his extensive fieldwork, saying that he spoke to about sixty witnesses for his research towards *The Roswell Incident*. The book actually presents only twenty-five witness testimonies, most of which are secondhand retellings of something someone else had seen or heard or may have seen. The majority of such interviews were also done over the phone, and not 'in the field' as Friedman suggests. Only five of these accounts are firsthand claims from people who have allegedly seen or handled any crash debris from Roswell and, out of that number, one of them is now by Friedman's own admission considered false and another clearly does not support the idea that the debris was a flying saucer. So essentially the book is based, as is common with many UFO claims, on just a handful of witness accounts – in this case principally those of Jesse Marcell and Walter Haut.

Stanton Friedman and William Moore were not the only researchers interested in Roswell. Researcher Kevin Randle has written around eighty novels of science fiction and adventure since 1984, and in the early '90s turned his hand to the Roswell case. He has written fiction concerning the incident, such as *Operation Roswell*, but presents several books as 'fact'. Kevin Randle and Donald Schmitt published *UFO crash at Roswell* in 1991. This book expanded the myth principally by the additional information provided by Walter Haut and Glen Dennis. Beside Friedman, Randle is often considered one of the leading researchers into the Roswell story. Kevin Randle originally studied anthropology at the University of Iowa, though he has since claimed to have studied journalism and psychology to both Masters and Doctorate level. These degrees are both from California Coast University, which was not accredited to award any postgraduate qualification until 2010. Prior to this, in 2005, the US General Accounting Office had investigated California Coast over claims it was acting as a 'diploma mill'. Randle gained his 'PhD' in 1999 through an 'off-campus accelerated program of distance learning'. He has also had a military career to some extent, serving as a helicopter pilot and also an Air Force intelligence officer. Randle flaunts his military credentials like Friedman does his physics. In Randle's view, his ability to have once piloted a helicopter has a direct relevance to an ability to accurately cross-examine historical witness testimonies.

Donald Schmitt claimed he was a medical illustrator, with training in criminology, sociology, and theology. He also claimed to hold a bachelor's degree and to have been working towards a doctorate. In reality he has no real qualifications of any note, and had in fact worked as a rural mail carrier with the US postal service since 1974.

Randle and Schmitt's following book *The Truth about the UFO Crash at Roswell* was published in 1994. This actually added little new information but tidied up all of the competing mythologies. A few new witness accounts were added (notably Frank Kaufman), while some old favourites were quietly removed as they no longer quite fit the overall story. Many questions have been raised over Randle and Schmitt's research methodologies as their two books are actually quite contradictory in places, with events, names, and dates changed in support of whatever the main plug of either book is. Randle has made several unverifiable claims with his Roswell research; he also has a habit of rarely recording or even documenting his interviews. The line between documented statements and Randle's own fiction is decidedly blurry.

The Roswell story had expanded into an ever more elaborate tale, and one with increasingly less relevance to the actual events of July 1947. Many more books, TV shows, documentaries, conferences, lectures, debates, and even found footage of an alien autopsy have kept its brand of commercial enterprise going strong. There is even a Roswell debunking industry, most notably headed by Philip J. Klass, who had many public disagreements with Stanton Friedman and also wrote extensively on the subject of disproving UFO claims until his death in 2005. Particular to Roswell, Kal Korff has written a whole book, *The Roswell Crash: What They Don't Want You to Know*, detailing inaccuracies in the majority of the main Roswell literature. Korff has however since begun describing himself as a Colonel in the Israeli Special Secret Services, despite no group of that name existing. Slightly more grounded in reality, Benson Saler and Charles Moore's book *UFO Crash at Roswell: the Genesis of a Modern Myth* provides pretty conclusive evidence of the Project Mogul explanation for the crash, and James McAndrew's *The Roswell Report: Case Closed* is an official follow-up to a near-1,000-page US Air Force report from 1994 which explains in mind-numbing detail every last aspect surrounding the events of the crash.

Stanton Friedman's further expansion of the Roswell tale came after meeting Vern and Jean Maltais at the end of one of his UFO lectures. They told him that their friend Grady 'Barney' Barnett had seen a saucer wreck in New Mexico. They couldn't be any more specific beyond it occurring sometime 'in the 1940s' – but that was enough for Friedman to link it specifically to the Roswell crash of 1947. With no desire to be outdone by any other Roswell researcher, original investigator Stanton Friedman, along with co-author Don Berliner, produced *Crash at Corona: US Military Retrieval and Cover-up of a UFO* in 1992. Written as a third person narrative, this expanded the Roswell myth by inventing a second crash site and making a central issue of the government cover-up aspect. As well as Barney Barnett's account, Friedman had come across an even bigger 'smoking gun' – official government documents that proved the existence of aliens and that the Roswell debris was a crashed flying saucer. This proof, the 'Majestic-12' documents, would blow the whole alien conspiracy wide open; at least, that was the plan.

The Majestic-12 papers had a gradual process of development. In May 1980, Myrna Hansen contacted the New Mexico State Police with a story that she had been abducted by aliens. She was put in contact with Officer Gabriel Valdez, who was known for investigating strange events. Valdez then contacted 'Dr' Paul Bennewitz whom he had met at a meeting concerning cattle mutilations the previous year. Bennewitz was once a PhD candidate in physics, though he never completed his studies. He later worked as an electronics specialist and, in 1979, had begun recording films of strange aircraft activity near Manzano Mountain in New Mexico. He had an interest in UFOs and was an active member of the Aerial Phenomena Research Organiszation (APRO). After talking to Jim Lorenzen, the head of APRO, about Myrna Hansen, both she and Bennewitz were put in touch with Leo Sprinkle.

Dr Leo Sprinkle was from the mid-1960s a pioneering researcher in alien abduction-related hypnotic regression. After becoming interested in the abduction phenomenon he slowly became convinced of the validity of the claims made by abductees. Sprinkle himself even began to believe that he had been abducted as a youth. He claimed to have witnessed two UFOs during the 1950s on separate occasions. He was a professor at the University of Wyoming and in 1980 founded the Rocky Mountain UFO Conference, which ran until he was eventually asked to leave the university in 1989.

Sprinkle agreed to conduct a hypnosis session with Hansen. Perhaps unconventionally, the hypnosis session was performed inside Bennewitz's car, which had been specially 'sealed' with aluminium foil. It is quite possible that Bennewitz had also been actively encouraging UFO-themed ideas in Hansen's head before any hypnosis began. Using such un-biased and scientifically-respected methods, Hansen then claimed under hypnosis that she and her young son saw five UFOs descend into a cow pasture. She claims she was abducted by aliens, witnessed cattle mutilation, and was herself examined before being taken to an underground base where she saw tanks filled with human body parts.

Hansen's account of animal mutilation (a subject of interest to both Bennewitz and Sprinkle) also has a suspicious similarity to some of the issues proposed in Linda Moulton Howe's film *A Strange Harvest*, first broadcast just before the hypnosis session in May 1980. Moulton Howe is an investigative journalist and documentary producer, but best known as a UFO researcher. Her film concludes that some cattle mutilations are caused by 'non-human intelligence and technology'. She claims to have seen secret government documents that prove aliens are mutilating cattle and abducting people. Moulton Howe's film even features Gabriel Valdez and Leo Sprinkle.

A brief side note regarding cattle mutilations and UFOs: since the 1970s the FBI has, on and off, investigated cases of animal mutilations through America. However, other than the odd psychopath, the vast majority of cases can be explained fairly easily by natural causes. Animals in such cases are found with 'bizarre wounds', have missing organs, have 'surgical incisions', have a missing tongue, often suffer an 'anal core', and are drained of blood. After an animal dies, many natural scavengers will quickly take advantage of an easy lunch. Things such as foxes or buzzards will contribute to a number of bite marks over a body and may even dig in deep enough to get a flavoursome organ or two. Insects, mostly flies, will then in turn be attracted to the bite wounds, cleaning them up and chewing around the soft fleshy edges to create a neat surgical appearance. Common targets for all involved are the juicy and easy-to-eat bits like eyes, tongues, genitals, and the anus. A large animal like a cow, when dead and on its side, will also 'lose' blood from its upper body section as gravity drains its liquids into a pool within its lower half, creating the illusion of it being drained of blood. A claim that hemoglobin has been magically extracted from the blood is most likely an indication that an animal was anemic, probably caused by malnutrition or serious loss of blood (both common contributors to animal deaths). In 1979, Sheriff Herb Marshall, who was dealing with cattle mutilation complaints in Arkansas, placed a dead cow in a field and recorded it for forty-eight-hours. After it had been feasted on by a wide variety of creatures, it held all of the typical mutilation wounds.

Like many seemingly strange phenomenon, odd wounds on dead cattle defy easy explanation for casual onlookers with only a limited understanding of the factors. However, it is still a dramatic leap of faith to move from 'I'm not sure how this happened' to 'It must be Aliens'. More likely there is already an ingrained alien hypothesis from people who are actively looking for evidence. The seemingly unusual is often an easy source of such proof, even if any actual connection between dead cows and aliens is pure invention. As a result, animal mutilations appear as evidence in a range of sensational claims, including not just aliens, but also satanic ritual cults, bestiality enthused sexual sadists, secret government programmes, and underground medical experiments.

It was soon after the Hansen hypnosis session that Bennewitz became increasingly edgy. His witness to Hansen's hypnosis clearly had a significant effect upon him. Unknown to Sprinkle, Bennewitz suffered severe delusional paranoia and had been treated in a mental health facility on a number of occasions. Bennewitz soon became convinced that Leo Sprinkle was an undercover CIA agent and broke contact with him. He then started carrying guns with him wherever he went, talking about aliens coming out of the walls, and developed a delusion that extraterrestrials were slowly taking over the US government.

Two months after the Myrna Hansen hypnosis session Jim Lorenzen received an anonymous letter from someone claiming to be an airman at Kirkland Air Force Base (near Manzano Mountain). The letter concerned an account of a 'Craig Weitzel' who had claimed to see a UFO, and that a crashed UFO was kept in part of Kirkland's Manzano storage area. It was suggested that this UFO was the same one as had crashed in Roswell in 1947. Lorenzen in turn sent this letter to UFO researcher William Moore, expert on the Roswell case and co-author of *The Roswell Incident*.

Richard Doty, an agent for the US Air Force Office of Special Investigations (AFOSI) later admitted that he had written the letter as bait for whoever it was in the local UFO community who had been recording secret test flights of craft at Kirkland Air Force Base. As Bennewitz's delusion intensified, it is alleged he had been recording goings on near Manzano Mountain more readily. As an expert in electronics he had the right knowledge and equipment to tap into sensitive communications and projects occurring at Kirkland, or so it was claimed. Doty maintains he had been tasked by the AFOSI to create hoax documents to give to UFO researchers. He made contact with William Moore with the intention of getting to whoever was making such recordings.

It is unclear by this point how much Doty was actually just following orders and how much was his own creative approach to the assignment, or even if such an assignment existed. Doty had met with Moore for lunch on a number of occasions in 1981, where he provided him with several documents as well as a further report on UFOs in 1982. The extent of Doty's hoaxing seems at odds with an AFOSI objective that was essentially to identify and discourage specific individuals from recording the aerial activity around Kirkland.

Doty worked at Kirkland Air Force Base from around 1979 to 1986, when he was asked to leave after he submitted his own fabricated reports to officials, claiming they were from Communist secret agents. He managed to retain work at the air base as a cook in the mess hall. He soon left, becoming a Sergeant for the New Mexico State Police. He did however keep up his active interest in UFOs, appearing in several UFO documentaries and being interviewed on radio talk shows.

By 1982 it was clear in any case that Paul Bennewitz had been the one with a keen interest in Kirkland's aerial testing. Bennewitz had started publically pushing an idea concerning underground bases using his old films of strange aircraft to promote the idea of a secret UFO base at nearby Dulce. He detailed his ideas to those at APRO, who regarded him as a deluded paranoid. As part of his ongoing truth campaign he even went as far as to make contact with Kirkland Air Force Base to ask for a grant to research his theory. It seems likely that the base ultimately humoured him as a local eccentric, but Doty continued his hoaxing campaign regardless. Bennewitz became increasingly paranoid and fearful of alien attack. He wrote a paper called 'Project Beta', detailing how an underground base could be attacked, and by 1987 had a complete mental breakdown.

The term 'MJ-Twelve' made its first appearance in one of the 'secret documents' provided by Richard Doty to William Moore in 1981. In January 1982, Moore approached *National Enquirer* journalist and UFO enthusiast Bob Pratt about collaborating on a UFO-themed novel. Moore's working title for this was *Majik-12*. According to Stanton Friedman, Moore had suggested in 1982 that he wanted to create some Roswell related documents 'to open some doors'. Friedman has since allegedly confided to fellow UFO researcher Brad Sparks

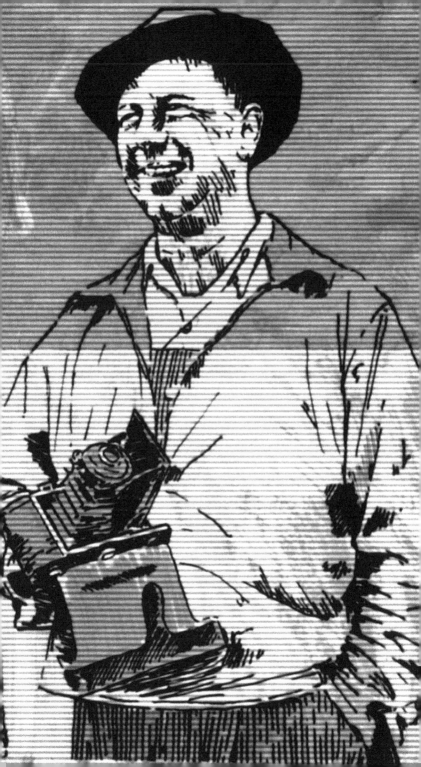

that the hoaxing of such documents was 'a good idea'. So, allegedly, was born the 'majestic twelve'.

In 1984, an anonymous roll of film was sent by post to filmmaker Jamie Shandera, who happened by sheer chance to be an acquaintance of both Moore and Friedman; the trio had made a UFO documentary together in 1980. The anonymous package had a postal address of Albuquerque, New Mexico, hometown of Richard Doty, who it is also alleged was acquainted with both Shandera and Friedman after an introduction from William Moore. Shandera had the film developed and discovered a series of photographed documents which provided evidence of the crash at Roswell, a UFO cover up, and a secret government group – 'the majestic twelve' – tasked to deal with extraterrestrial issues. The documents identified leading government and military figures as being part of the group, including Roscoe Hillenkoetter, Dr Vannevar Bush, James Forrestal, Nathan Twining, Hoyt S. Vandenberg, Dr Detlev Bronk, Dr Jerome Hunsaker, Sidney Souers, Gordon Gray, Dr Donald Menzel, Robert Montague, and Dr Lloyd Berkner.

If any hoaxed documents concerning Roswell were to be produced, William Moore and Stanton Friedman certainly would have been well placed to be aware of the correct details required to create a convincing text. It also seems likely that Friedman would have at least provided the information, either knowingly or unknowingly, for the content of such documents; he has certainly had the most mileage out of them in terms of financial gain, their content seeming to chime all too well with his previous research. What a stroke of luck that these documents supported the very same UFO case that Moore and Friedman had researched and written a book about. How curious, too, that some phantom whistleblower chose a little-known documentary filmmaker to send such a film to, rather than any high profile Washington journalist. Moore and Friedman did later admit to at least altering some of the MJ-12 documents to give the appearance of government censorship.

Not long after the mysterious roll of film was delivered to Shandera, both William Moore and Jamie Shandera also 'discovered' a memo in Box 189 of the National Archives in Washington DC. This memo was from National Security Advisor Robert Cutler to Nathan Twining, Chief of Staff of the US Air Force, and mentioned the 'MJ-12' group. Suspiciously there was no reference to this memo within further archive records and no other document within the archives is recorded as making any reference to 'MJ-12', 'Majestic-12', 'Majik-12' or any other variation of the phrase. The document was not recorded within the official contents of Box 189 and was found stuffed in-between normal archival folders. Further the memo was dated 14th July 1954, a day later found to be during a period when Robert Cutler was out of the country and therefore not able to write an official memo from his office. Bizarrely this fact is claimed by some to be proof that the memo is genuine.

Smuggling a document into a national institution is a not an uncommon act within cases of elaborate fraud. John Myatt and John Drewe made millions out of selling forged paintings 'by' modern masters such as Georges Braque and Le Corbusier, the authenticity of which were supported by documents discovered in the archives of the Victoria and Albert Museum and the Tate in London. John Myatt produced the forged paintings, while John Drewe spent time fabricating authentic looking provenance documents and smuggling them into National Archives, only for them to then be 'discovered'. Often the security of such places is mostly concerned with people taking things out, less so with them taking forgeries in.

Despite initial suggestions that the MJ-12 documents were 'smoking gun' proof of a government cover up regarding knowledge of extraterrestrials, they are almost certainly forgeries. It is unclear exactly who was directly involved with faking such documents, though the most logical finger should point towards William Moore or Richard Doty. Moore has since all but admitted that the majority of his research was made up, going further to suggest that he was an under-cover double agent spreading misinformation on behalf of secret government organisations.

When the general consensus, even amongst the UFO community, later moved towards the view that the documents were in fact fake, Friedman changed his tune suggesting that 'some' of them were not genuine. The false assumption of course is that any remaining documents must be genuine. His thorough research had identified some inconsistencies in font types and sizes, though such scrutiny passed him by when he was actually being paid $16,000 by FUFOR to do just that several years earlier.

The Moore and Friedman relationship soon deteriorated after the MJ-12 episode. The final straw came when Friedman talked TV producers into making him the exclusive UFO consultant for the show *Unsolved Mysteries*, a position that had originally been promised to Moore.

British UFO researcher Timothy Good was an early supporter of the MJ-12 documents. A classically trained violinist, Good worked for a while as a session musician on recordings for Phil Collins, Rod Stewart, and Depeche Mode. He became interested in UFOs after a family member gave him a copy of Donald Keyhoe's book *Flying Saucers are Real* at an impressionable age. Good's own book *Above Top Secret: The Worldwide UFO Cover Up* became a bestseller in 1987. This was one of the first public publications concerning the MJ-12 documents. Through later writings, Good has gone on to claim that US President Eisenhower met with aliens in 1954 and that aliens have influenced the genetic makeover of human beings. He has also suggested that the West has secretly developed advanced weaponry to deal with a possible interstellar threat. He also attempted to revive the accounts of contactee George Adamski through the 1983 book *George Adamski: The Untold Story*, written with Lou Zinsstag.

Good once claimed to have met an alien. His experience amounted to him sitting in a hotel lobby and sending a 'telepathic request for proof that aliens were among us'. Imagine his surprise when soon after, a man sat near him for a while, in a busy New York hotel lobby of all places, didn't say a word, and then soon got up and left. This was sufficient proof of communication for Good, who describes it as a cathartic experience. It perhaps demonstrates the standard of what he considers evidence.

Generous interpretations of certain events provide convenient evidence for the likes of Friedman, Moore, and Good, who revived many UFO stories through the 1980s. Tales of UFOs and alien bodies buried in the deserts of New Mexico that developed around this time may also owe some of their propagation to a dumping of a more familiar extraterrestrial. In 1983 hundreds of thousands of copies of the Atari 2600 game *E.T.: The Extra-Terrestrial* (considered one of the worst commercial failures in video game history) were buried at a restricted dump near Alamogordo, New Mexico. Disposal of this game was denied by Atari for many years, until the site was excavated in 2014 proving the rumours true. Numerous urban legends about buried technologies and extraterrestrials that developed in and around New Mexico through the 1980s and '90s may be a result of re-telling and misinterpretation of such an event. While the Atari example may be a convenient local myth for UFO enthusiasts to adapt, it was unlikely to be an attempt by the software developer to actively fabricate UFO-themed evidence – yet other buried truths are not always so coincidental.

Deliberate hoaxing is a key element of many UFO myths, such as the Majestic-12 papers, and is evident in almost all aspects of the phenomenon. Such hoaxing goes back to the early reports of mystery airships. On 17th April 1897, *The Dallas Morning News* ran a story exposing three boys who had hoaxed a mystery airship sighting by soaking a cotton ball in kerosene and tying it to the leg of a turkey vulture. The hoax was discovered when the bird landed on the roof of the local high school and the burning cotton ball set fire to the building.

In May 1950, Paul Trent, a farmer from McMinnville, Oregon, produced what he claimed were several photographs of a flying saucer. Considered by many, including William K. Hartmann, member of the Condon committee, to be some of the more plausible and persuading images of an alleged UFO. The images were shown initially only to Trent's banker, Frank Wortmann, but were later picked up and promoted by local journalist Bill Powell. The story gathered pace and soon the images were reprinted in *Life* magazine, with Trent maintaining that they were genuine. Researcher Joel Carpenter suggested the image actually displayed a small circular mirror suspended on thin thread from two conveniently placed wires that appear above the object in the top frame of the photograph. Trent's image also seems to have been taken from a low vantage point close to the ground, an old photography trick to give things high up more perspective distance. Other skeptical researchers, such as Robert Sheaffer and David Slater, have spent time analyzing high resolution scans of the photographs, and found strong suggestive evidence of a fixed wire or thread suspending the object.

A similar series of images appeared over a decade later. On 3rd August 1965, Highway maintenance inspector Rex Heflin claimed that he photographed a UFO on the Santa Ana freeway in California. The images were published in September that year, though the original Polaroid photographs were apparently handed over to a member of the North America Air Defence Command (NORAD). The Heflin images, three pictures of a flying disc taken out of the window of his truck and one of a smoke ring, are considered by many to be some of the most convincing photographs taken of a UFO.

Heflin was by all accounts an odd man. He led a lonely life, spending much of his time travelling up and down long stretches of roads examining signs and potholes. He was described as having an offbeat sense of humour, being a known practical joker and enthusiastic model train maker. Edward Ripple, a fellow maintenance worker, recalled seeing the Polaroids taken by Heflin before they were published (though after NORAD had supposedly confiscated them), and further that Heflin was bragging about his joke photographs being considered genuine. The three main images were created using a toy train wheel from one of Heflin's models, suspended on fishing wire, in turn attached to a stick that rested on the roof of his truck. This was then photographed at a number of angles using a low quality Polaroid. Heflin never made these originals available, using only second or third generation reproductions to give to media sources. The story that the originals were given away to the military was pure invention; desperate for attention in 1993, Heflin miraculously came into possession of these originals again in an attempt to revive some attention in his story.

The image of a smoke ring is simply from an entirely

unconnected event. It shows no point of reference and is only associated with the UFO images due to the claims by Heflin. It is likely just a snap of a smoke ring taken at the annual air show held near to where Heflin lived. Heflin never admitted to faking the images; he died in 2005 still claiming they were genuine. UFOlogist Ann Druffel has essentially made a living from promoting the Heflin case. One photograph has been extensively enhanced (or reworked), to highlight an apparent exhaust trail coming from one image of a craft. It really just looks a lot like a conveniently placed cloud with the contrast turned up.

Michael Shermer, editor of *Skeptic* magazine has argued extensively that UFO images are frequently faked. In 2007 he set about proving it by running a workshop for children where they made UFO models out of household materials, glue, and silver paint. The models were then suspended by fishing wire and the children produced photographs of them against the sky. Shermer then presented the photographs to a professional photo-analyst; unaware of the experiment, he judged the images to be genuine. He did not detect the fishing wire and claimed that the photographs appeared to have not been manipulated or tampered with. Soon after, the pictures began to receive attention from UFO believers, and so Shermer released a video documenting the children's workshop. Even when confronted with this evidence a number of UFO enthusiasts refused to acknowledge that the images were fake.

Some hoaxes are substantially more elaborate than simple faking of a photograph. 'S4 Area 51' is a phrase from the Majestic-12 documents, but it was really a KLAS-TV interview between George Knapp and Bob Lazar that brought Area 51 and its link to UFOs to wider attention and helped establish the current mythology around it. Interestingly S4 was also the section of secretariat in the

British Ministry of Defence that investigated UFOs during the 1960s.

The US Air Force Facility commonly known as Area 51 is actually part of Edwards Air Force Base, which itself is part of the Nevada Test and Training Range. The specific area known as Area 51 is actually called Homey Airport, though it was briefly referred to as Area 51 during the Vietnam War. In reality the restricted area used for testing that is close to this site has the memorable name of R-4808North. This site has likely been used as a testing ground for several experimental aircraft and systems. Testing of the Oxcart, Nerva, U2, and later F-117 Stealth Fighter crafts probably account for the vast majority of UFO sightings reported in the area. Highway 375 – now renamed the 'Extraterrestrial Highway'– runs close to Edwards Air Force Base. The small town of Rachel is the closest point of civilization to the restricted testing area. It is a common stop for UFO tourists, where the main attraction is 'The Little A'Le'Inn' (previously 'Rachel Bar and Grill'); it is currently run by Pat Travis, and a stop off here will allow you to buy alien head coffee cups, Area 51 t-shirts, and get a classic Alien Burger.

In 1989, a man named Bob Lazar contacted the Los Angeles TV station KLAS-TV, claiming he had previously worked for the government back-engineering alien spacecraft. Journalist George Knapp took up the story and initially interviewed Lazar, referring to him in interview only as 'Dennis'. Lazar claimed he undertook this work at a base called 'S-4', several miles south of 'Area 51'. He stated that he was employed at this facility near Groom Lake between 1988 and '89, working on a total of nine alien spacecraft, primarily examining their systems of propulsion as well as some technical details. Lazar decided to go public after getting fired for showing some friends late night testing of alien craft.

One of these friends was John Lear, son of aviation pioneer William Lear. Lear, Jr. became interested in UFOs after hearing accounts of the Rendlesham Forest incident in the UK. In 1988, he met Bob Lazar and became involved in his S4-Area 51 story. It was Lear who originally spoke to George Knapp, promoting the Lazar story, and it seems likely Lazar and Lear had developed the supposed events together. The association with John Lear is not usually a benchmark for reliability and accuracy. Lear, Jr. worked for his famous father until he was fired for nearly bankrupting the company. He used his father's money and influence to buy access to every airman's certificate he could get his hands on. Over time Lear has become increasingly interested in conspiracy theories, especially those associated with far right politics. He does not believe man ever landed on the Moon, though he does believe there are bases of the far side of it, and that Bigfoot comes from Mars. He claims that no planes hit the twin towers on 11th September 2001, and that the Cold War was faked so that the US and Russia could concentrate on getting to Mars.

Many of Lear's more recent ideas concerning Moon bases clearly have their origins in the story told in *Alternative 3*. This was a mockumentary TV programme broadcast only once, in the UK, in 1977. It was intended to be shown on April Fools' Day, but was actually broadcast in June. Presented as a news style science report, the programme details an undercover plan to make the Moon and Mars habitable. Clearly Lear never got that this was fake, and has been known to refer to ideas raised in it as evidence.

Bob Lazar was born in Florida in 1959; he studied electronics at Pierce College and also worked at Fairchild Electronics. He married his first wife, Carol, in 1980. In 1985, the couple invested heavily in a local brothel known as Honeysuckle Ranch. A year later he filed for bankruptcy, and left his wife to marry new love Tracy. Carol committed suicide two days after Lazar's second marriage. He worked for a period at Los Alamos National Research Laboratory as a sub-contracted repair technician before becoming a photo-processor. It was during this time that he began creating his Area 51 narrative. He also had his car licence plate personalized to 'MJ-12' and often drove around with an Uzi machine gun in the boot for 'protection'. Lazar claims to have degrees from California Institute of Technology and Massachusetts Institute of Technology, though neither institution has records of him – the government erased them apparently, along with the memory of everyone he ever met during his time there.

A year after going public with his UFO claims he was arrested for pandering individuals into prostitution as part of his association with the Honeysuckle Ranch. Though Lazar claims he only ever set up the computers there, he did however plead guilty to all six charges laid against him. In 1991, he set up the business United Nuclear with his third wife, Joy. His business was raided in 2003 for selling illegal chemicals often used to make fireworks and small explosives. Despite the questionable records of Lazar and Lear, their account of activity at Area 51 helped establish much of the myth now associated with it – and it wasn't long before other similar stories began to emerge.

Phil Schneider claimed to be involved in the construction of underground US military bases, including the base at Dulce, specifically for the study of alien spacecraft technology. He claimed there was once an underground battle with aliens, and he was one of only three human survivors. He also claimed that aliens ran the UN. Schneider's ideas are an obvious mix of those of Paul Bennewitz and Bob Lazar, both of which were deluded and/or con men. Between 1994 and '96, Schneider gave numerous lectures about his claims but was never willing, or able, to prove his allegations. In 1996 he was found dead at his home, an apparent suicide. Schneider had previously claimed there had been eleven attempts on his life, and it has been suggested that his suicide was a staged murder. However, he also suffered from multiple physical illnesses including osteoporosis and had been diagnosed with an aggressive form of cancer. There was no suicide note left by Schneider as such, but someone did leave enough information around to suggest a possible staged murder – most likely engineered by Schneider himself (possibly with the help of his wife, who claims all his UFO lecture materials and evidence then 'went missing') with the aim of securing his legacy in UFO mythology.

It is often part of the thrill of UFO hoaxing to remain stubborn in the insistence of the genuine nature of any evidence. Though even when some people fully admit to the hoaxing, a number of believers are too invested in the illusion to accept such claims.

Crop circles are geometric designs that generally appear in wheat fields, and are most commonly found in the UK, especially Wiltshire. UFO believers often attribute their cause to alien craft, generally because they appear suddenly with no obvious sign of human trampling through the fields around them. Perhaps they are a strange impression caused by alien landing gear, or an intentional attempt at communication through creation of curious markings. UFO enthusiasts claim that such circles display otherworldly properties: wheat that has been superheated, high levels of radiation, plants that emit bursts of energy, magically changed soil, and designs impossible for humans to have created. There is even the 'science' of Cereology, which studies the formation of crop circles. Greg Jefferys, a PhD student studying crop circles at the University of Tasmania, believes such circles are caused by an ionised plasma vortex, a rare form of electromagnetic energy.

A group of crop circle makers emerged in London during the early to mid-1990s. People such as Rod Dickinson, John Lundberg, Doug Bower, Rob Irving, and David Chorley all shared an interest in UFO myths and crop circle designs. Rob Irving views the construction of such circles a form of art, and claims that deception is part of creation, as illusion is part of the artist's trade.

Doug Bower and David Chorley apparently came up with the idea of making crop circles on a walk home from the pub in 1978, and since then have become responsible for the majority of the more elaborate designs, creating over 250 circles over many years. The pair came forward in 1991 to explain that they were responsible for many of the interventions, though some still believe the circles are the result of aliens, and that Bower and Chorley are disinformation agents funded by MI5. The pair did not invent crop circles; indeed such things can be traced back to the late-seventeenth century, though these early reports are more likely descriptions of actual storm damage, mushroom rings, or vandalism. A story from 1678 describes an account from a Hertfordshire farmer who claims a devil mowed a circle in his wheat field – the day after a heated dispute with a farm labourer. The 'devilish' labourer who took out his grievance on the farmers' fields later became a genuine supernatural being when writer Lewis Evans embellished the tale in the late-nineteenth century book *Witchcraft in Hertfordshire*. However, the main inspiration for Bower and Chorley came from a spate of circles created in the town of Tully, Australia, in the 1960s. These were commonly referred to as 'saucer nests' after a farmer, George Pedley, apparently spotted a bright light hovering above a trampled circle of wheat.

Even the most detailed patterns can be produced by fairly rudimentary equipment. Surveyor's tape, stalk stomping boards attached with rope handles, and plastic garden rollers can produce impressive designs. Modern day technologies such as handheld GPS devices and lazer guides make the task even easier. Mysterious properties found in circles by enthusiastic investigators often just demonstrate a naivety of what it is they are looking at. Common background radiation is cited as something uncommon, and bent and elongated nodes in the wheat are a result of phototropism, not alien intervention. To get into the middle of fields without causing damage, circle-makers use the latest in cutting edge technologies – lightweight ladders and wooden planks. Creators of such circles want the most elaborate, most complex pattern to appear in the most impossible place, in the most impractical of timeframes. Like countryside graffiti, using wheat instead of spray paint, such deception is largely the point.

Like crop circles, graffiti is not a twentieth-century invention but has its roots in the inscriptions found on the walls of ancient sepulchers, such as the catacombs of Rome. The earliest example of modern style graffiti is from the ancient Greek city of Ephesus, apparently depicting an advertisement for a prostitute. Graffiti can act as a form of expression, political statement, territorial marking, memento, or decoration. A common aspect of graffiti is the appearance of intricate painted designs in areas that seem impossible to reach and that appear in seemingly impossible periods of time. Such appropriations are often highly planned, sometimes dangerous, and without doubt produced with skill and ingenuity. Many sub-genres of graffiti exist beyond the most widely known use of spray-paint or marker pen. One example is yarn bombing or guerrilla knitting, a type of street art using traditional craft materials and techniques, like crocheted yarn, pioneered by Magda Sayeg and Bill Davenport. Like traditional paint graffiti, a yarn bomb is a complex intervention in a public space, monument, building, or other structure that seemingly appears at random and out of nowhere. The principles are the same, the concept is just adapted for use with different materials. Crop circles are really just another sub-genre of graffiti, transplanting the concept from the urban environment into a wheat field. Indeed it is no real surprise that Rod Dickinson and John Lundberg graduated from the Slade School of Fine Art, and consider what they do in wheat fields, and also the way in which they do it, to be a form of artistic expression.

Creative expression combined with a desire for attention can be powerful motivators for certain hoaxing cases. Ray Santilli is a British musician, record producer, and UFO hoaxer. He started AMP entertainment in 1982 and has helped produce works with a variety of musical artists such as Uriah Heap, Chris de Burg, Noddy Holder, Boy George, and Slipknot. In the mid-1990s, he claimed filmed footage of what appeared to be an alien autopsy came into his possession. The seventeen-minute-long piece of footage was supposedly supplied to him by an anonymous military cameraman. The film was allegedly from 1947 and showed the autopsy of one of the alien bodies recovered from the Roswell crash.

The film was picked up by Fox Television and broadcast in August 1995. The programme based around the footage, *Alien Autopsy: Fact or Fiction*, gained high ratings, and so was re-broadcast twice by the network. *Time* magazine wrote an article on the footage, and apparent experts, such as forensic pathologist Cyril Wecht and cinematographer Allen Daviau, supported its authenticity. Upon filming a follow-up for Fox, director John Jopson became highly suspicious of Santilli. Producers however discouraged Jopson from the pursuit of exposing any hoax in the fear that it would not receive particularly high ratings.

In 2006, just before the release of the British comedy *Alien Autopsy* (based on the production of the Santilli film), a documentary was broadcast featuring Ray Santilli admitting the autopsy footage was not genuine. Santilli claims it was only a reconstruction of a genuine film that he had seen in 1992. The autopsy was actually produced in an empty flat in Camden Town, London. The special effects were provided by artist John Humphreys, who made the alien bodies out of rubber, and stuffed them with chicken entrails, sheep brains, and raspberry jam.

As special effect technologies develop so to do the opportunities and potential for would-be hoaxers. Recent developments in affordable 3D-rendering computer software have also resulted in a rash of UFO films populating the Internet. An early example emerged in 2007, apparently filmed over Haiti and showing close-ups of alien craft. After analysis it was found that every palm tree in the film was identical. The creator of the video, known only as Barzolff81, has since admitted it was faked, and indeed every aspect was created in a computer. He used a programme called *View6Infinite* and created the film for fun and as an exercise in CGI rendering.

Such homemade CGI hoaxes are now in abundance over the Internet. There are even hoaxers who essentially make a living from their production. Thirdphaseofmoon is a website set up in 2010 by brothers Brent and Blake Cousins, with the aim of hosting exclusive UFO videos. Many of the videos are likely fabricated by the brothers themselves, a fact established when it was pointed out numerous videos (from supposed different sources) contained exactly the same sound effects. All seem to be of a similar formula, and amazingly the brothers seem to have a near constant influx of exclusive UFO footage, uploading several new films a week. They have also included videos of interviews of several UFO witnesses and researchers, including Stanton Friedman and Richard Dolan. The Thirdphaseofmoon *YouTube* channel has now uploaded over 1,500 UFO videos, collecting 370,000 subscribers along the way; their most popular video ('UFO Sightings Air force flying Saucer? Enhanced Close Up Video Stills!!!') now has in excess of 6 million views. The video, just a fake photograph of a US Air Force branded UFO, isn't the most viewed UFO video on *YouTube* though. That honour goes to 'Real Alien UFO Caught on Video!', uploaded by yourjudgeandjury in 2011. The 30-second clip mostly consists of some people in a boat pointing at something, and then what looks like a separate bit of footage of two tiny UFOs (they might just be planes or CGI creations – they're so small it's hard to tell). The video has now gained over 21 million views.

The rapid growth of digital technologies means that huge numbers of people now have good quality cameras in their pockets most of the time. The volume of photographs and videos produced and uploaded onto the Internet in recent years is mind-boggling. Around 90% of all photographs ever produced have been created within the last two years. Not only uploaded to the Internet – just in general. Ever. That's a lot of pictures. If there was going to be a time when the elusive high quality image providing strong evidence of alien craft would appear, it should be about now. In fact the number of recorded UFO sightings are lower than they were twenty years ago. Either the aliens are just camera shy and are now keeping clear of snap-happy earthlings, or they were never really there in the first place.

The reason why people hoax UFO experiences, or actively exaggerate claims is varied. Often it seems to be a combination of a prank that has got out of hand, attention seeking, or an attempt to make money. The fact that many UFO hoaxers have not made substantial profits from their endeavors may not be governed by ethics, but just by the limitations of their own business model.

Certain UFOlogy writers, like Stanton Friedman, act like a type of raconteur. They collate and spread stories from modern folklore; archivists of contemporary legends, they disseminate such accounts for popular consumption. In many ways such people should be viewed as entertainers and storytellers. If re-telling of stories, such as the Roswell incident, result in financial gain – so be it – people need to earn a living. Popular modern legends, like Roswell, continue to provide a template for such methods. In 2012, former CIA Official Chase Brandon claimed he had seen a box containing alien-type material from the Roswell crash at the CIA Headquarters. He believed the contents confirmed not only the extraterrestrial origin of the Roswell crash, but also the recovery of alien bodies, and government cover-up and knowledge of the event. Brandon approached press about this story near the sixty-fifth anniversary of the Roswell incident, and also during the promotion of his own science fiction novel *The Cryptos Conundrum*, the plot of which, unsurprisingly, concerns a CIA cover-up around alien knowledge.

The fact that such stories are re-interpreted as evidence of advanced alien beings may only exist in the minds of those who are already firm believers in such things. Of all his years on the lecture circuit, Stanton Friedman claims he has been heckled or challenged only a handful of times. Such talks are generally given to a room full of people already susceptible to the claims being laid before them. They either already believe in UFOs, or are open minded enough about a topic that they are seeking affirmation for their strongly growing belief.

A pre-existing belief in such things is generally required to accept increasingly fantastical claims. A hardened skeptic is not likely to convert to believer overnight without there having been a long and gradual change to that person's belief structure. Someone with a deep belief in ghosts and the supernatural is more likely to attribute an unusual event to a ghostly manifestation than someone who does not. A deeply religious person may believe a similar event to be a sign from a deity; for others, it becomes a UFO. People will rationalize strange occurrences based on their belief structure and the prevailing views of the society in which they live. A devout Catholic is unlikely to experience what they consider a spiritual apparition and attribute it to Buddha. A pre-existing belief in aliens and UFOs is more likely to make even the most mundane sighting of lights in the night sky attributable to visiting spacecraft rather than simply a helicopter.

People of strong faith, especially when such faith is threatened, also strive to preserve consistency in their beliefs by adapting new and potentially contradictory information to suit the accepted system. Such behaviour is evident in large-scale organised religions as well as small closed groups; the status quo is maintained largely by ongoing intolerance of contrary opinion or eventual assimilation of a modified version of such views.

The word hoax is thought to have derived from 'Hocus Pocus', itself a shortened form of the dog-Latin phrase *hax pax max Deus adimax*, a nonsense expression used at one point by stage conjurors. A magician, William Vincent, who went by the stage name Hocus Pocus in the early seventeenth century and the work *Hocus Pocus Junior: The Anatomie of Legerdemain,* published in 1635, may also have contributed to the phrase. It may also owe something to the Norse folklore magician Ochus Bochus. The term has also been suggested by the seventeenth century Archbishop of Canterbury John Tillotson, to be a derivative or corruption of the Latin *Hoc est corpus meum* (this is my body), the phrase traditionally spoken by priests during the Eucharist, the imitation of Christ's last supper. Shamans of all faiths have employed a range of tricks to promote their own particular faith and to encourage conversion. The range of late twentieth-century New Age religions, which were at least partly inspired by the UFO phenomenon, were no different.

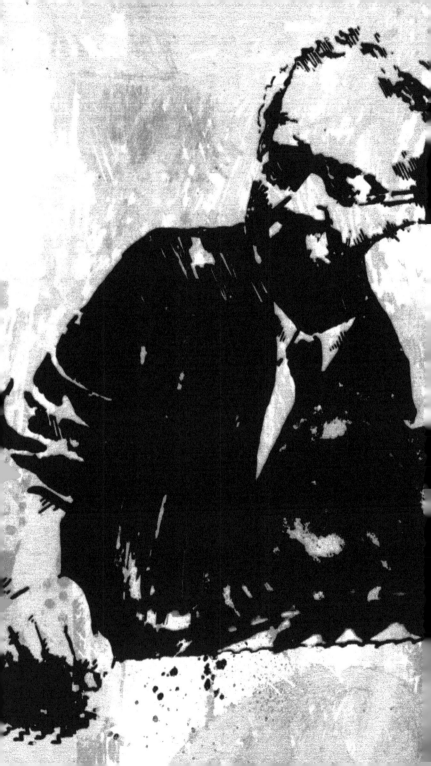

PART SEVEN
Here Comes The Sun

The sky has often held important cultural, symbolic, and religious significance to many cultures all over the world. The Sun, stars, the Moon, comets, and events such as solar eclipses and shooting star showers have led many to gaze in awe at the wonders of the cosmos. Ancient cultures would have looked to put significance and meaning behind such things, which are visible, yet utterly out of any tangible reach. Through the ongoing inquisitive process of trying to assign purpose and understanding to such sights, it is not surprising that many religions have frequently had a number of deities associated with the sky.

Ancient Egyptian society embraced a number of deities through a complex system of polytheistic beliefs. To the Egyptians the Sun represented light, warmth, and growth. Pre-dynasty Egyptian beliefs saw Atum as the Sun God, especially in terms of the evening sun. Ra was later seen as the Egyptian Sun God, especially representing the morning and midday suns. The two later combined to create the powerful Amon-Re, the supreme creator of all things. Horus was seen as the God of the Sky, and many saw the Sun and the Moon as his right eye and left eye respectively. In later Egyptian dynasties the God Ra merged with Horus to become Ra-Horakhty, believed to rule all parts of the created world.

Partly as a political gesture of collaboration, and partly to ease the process of appropriating other cultures into the Empire, the Romans would often create hybrid versions of Gods. Ammon-Zeus became a mix of Egyptian and Greek deities used by the Romans to honour the Sun. This process of appropriation can be seen through the change of the dominant religion of the Empire into Christianity. During the Roman Empire, a festival of birth of the unconquered Sun was celebrated around the Winter solstice, the point at which marks the shortest day and the longest night. This celebration, Sol Invictus, marked the re-birth of the Sun after this point, traditionally held on December 25th of the Julian calendar. Through the Christian domination of the Roman Empire, this date was eventually (but not until the fourth century) appropriated, along with the Roman festival of Saturnalia, itself into the story of the birth of Christ and is still celebrated as the Christmas festival.

Long before the Christian, era the Sun was referred to as the Son of Ormuzd, part of the creator and single God of Zoroastrianism, one of the oldest religions that dates back to the early second-millennium BCE. Dominant for a time in the area now known as Iran, Zoroastrianism is seen by some as a template and key influence for the newer Abrahamic religions of Judaism, Christianity, and Islam. Themes concerning a single, all-powerful God, creation by divine intervention, the afterlife, final judgment before a divine power, resurrection, and a virgin birth certainly emerge as strong parallels.

The concept of sky worship can be seen in a number of religious practices all over the world. Surya is a solar deity of Hinduism, particularly in the Saura tradition often practiced in areas of India such as Gujarat. In medieval Hinduism, Surya also acted as an epithet for Shiva and Vishnu. In the *Rigveda*, a collection of Hindu hymns produced around 1500 BCE, Surya is given particular reverence in relation to the rising Sun, and is symbolic of a great empowering knowledge. In Buddhism, Akasagarbha acts as a Bodhisattva of the Jewel family, and is seen as the Matrix of the Sky. He is associated with wisdom and the dawning of light from the rising Sun.

In the traditional cultures of the Americas there is a rich tradition of sky worship. The Aztecs had numerous sky gods, such as Cipactonal, God of the Daytime, Oxomoco, Goddess of the Nightime, Tonatiuh, God of the Sun, and Coyolxauqui, Goddess of the Moon. The Incans worshipped Virococha, a sky God, who is a God of the Sun and storms as well as creator of the universe. The temple at Machu Picchu was associated with an Incan religious cult dedicated to the worship of the Sun.

In many Native American cultures, such as the Iroquois and Plains Peoples, the Sun is recognized as a life-giving force. The Sun Dance ritual of such cultures represents a renewal of the bond between man and life. Astrological observations informed aspects of such cultures, too. The Papago of Arizona divide their year by positions of an open star cluster in the constellation Taurus. The Oglala Sioux use twenty-eight poles to erect their Sun Dance lodge, in reference to the twenty-eight days of the lunar month. The homes of the Skidi band of the Pawnee have their doors facing east, towards the rising Sun. For many tribes stars can represent past shamans or dead council leaders, and are looked upon for knowledge and wisdom. On the Cardenas Hilltop, to the east of the Grand Canyon, is a site used by the Anasazi around one thousand years ago. Here a series of stone landmarks record celestial dates, such as summer and winter solstice, through defined use of carefully positioned holes, allowing sunlight to denote such events. Important astrological observations were also recorded through paintings by the same tribe.

Sun observation goes back to at least eighth century BCE and the time of the Babylonians. Ancient Greek and Chinese astronomers noticed things such as sunspots. Court astrologers in China, who believed such activity predicted important events, made the first written record of sunspot activity.

In the West, before the scientific enlightenment, astronomical observation has historically been driven by the Christian faith and other spiritual beliefs. An English monk, John of Worcester, is said to have made the first drawing of sunspots in 1128. In the sixteenth century, the early pioneers of astronomical observation – such as Tycho Brahe, who did much to set the foundations for accurate measurements of the positions of the stars – were still keen to attribute any celestial symbolism to astrology and the implications this may have to Earthly activity. Early astronomy was often just as concerned with casting horoscopes and attributing meaning to eclipses of the Moon as it was to challenging preconceived ideas concerning fixed stars. Astrology, alchemy, and medicine were largely intertwined, and men of learning were often supported through the Church, and the beliefs that came as a consequence. In 1578, Pope Gregory XIII had the Tower of the Winds built, one of the oldest astronomical institutions in the world. The observatory was built largely due to the Church's interest in astronomical calendars, by which several holy days, such as Easter, are determined each year. The Vatican observatory, an astronomical research and education institution – again one of the first of its kind – was established in 1774 in Rome.

By 1845, French physicists Leon Foucault and Louis Fizeau were making the first successful photographs of the Sun, initially creating a small daguerreotype image after an exposure of just one-sixtieth of a second. It is fitting too that the first apparent photograph of a UFO was taken whilst observing the Sun. Mexican Astronomer José Banilla took a series of photographs in 1883 whilst studying the Sun, which were first published in an 1886 edition of *L'Astronomie* magazine. From the observatory in Zacatecas, New Mexico, he documented a significant number of dark objects moving across the face of the Sun. While UFOlogists suggest such spots to be a fleet of alien spacecraft others have suggested them to be broken fragments of a comet passing through the shot, or even geese flying past the camera.

During the 1947 UFO flap, the Sun was in the middle of a vigorous period of sunspot activity. In fact the largest ever sunspot was recorded that year. A few weeks before the Ken Arnold and Roswell stories broke, the Pacific Astronomical Society published a report about the great sunspot observed between March and April that year. Writing in the MUFON journal in June 1996, Joseph Ritrovato noted the coloration between periods of high UFO activity in relation to the cycles of the Sun.

Modern day UFO sightings may be at least in part an adapted remnant of long established solar worship: mystical lights in the sky that represent a greater intelligence. It is certainly interesting to note that the most common reported shape of a UFO since the mid-1940s has been a circular disk; often they are reported as metallic and reflective of natural sunlight, or able to emit their own bright luminance. Such circular light sources in the sky draw parallel to the Sun, stars, or the Moon. Carl Jung speculated that circular UFOs were a type of Mandala symbol, a spiritual icon from Indian religions that generally represents the cosmos or universe. The second most common UFO shape, a triangle, seems also to make reference to a pyramid, often synonymous with solar worship, an idea that, even if not always accurate, has been made common belief through spiritualist and New Age reinterpretations.

As well as established religious practice and scientific investigations, the Sun has continued to play an important role in the development of what became known as the New Age movement, which developed through the late nineteenth- and into the twentieth century. Through a revised interpretation of many Eastern religious practices and the influence of spiritualism, ideas such as Theosophy emerged as an alternative to typical Western faith traditions. With Theosophy, the Sun is seen as the Solar Logos, the god of the solar system, and a visible manifestation of the great consciousness. In *The Secret Doctrine*, a key Theosophical text written in 1888 by Helena Blavatsky, the Sun is described as 'the nucleus of mother substance', an entity in its own right, and bringer of life to the world. In a prophecy of sorts, Theosophy describes cycles of humanity that have gone through great waves of development. In such ideas humanity is moving gradually toward enlightenment, and toward the Sun; alleged great events in the past once transferred life from Mars to Earth, and they will again in the future move life on to Venus and then Mercury.

Helena Petrovna Blavatsky came from an aristocratic Russian-German family. Born in Russia in 1831, she eventually moved to New York where, in 1875, she founded the Theosophical Society alongside the lawyer Henry Olcott. This group met with the aim of exploring occultism and the unexplained powers evident within man and nature. She saw people as being divided into 'god-informed men', such as Aryans, and 'less fully-human primitives', like Africans or Tasmanians. Blavatsky saw evolution as a spiritual process and practices like the Jewish faith as harmful to human spirituality. It is no great surprise that such writings went on to influence aspects of Nazism; indeed, Adolf Hitler's book *Mein Kampf* is dedicated to Dietrich Eckart, who claims he introduced Hitler to Blavatsky's works.

Blavatsky claims she travelled widely around the world, especially the Far East and India, where various masters of ancient wisdom taught her how to develop psychic powers. If she travelled much at all is open to some debate. She wrote numerous texts and claimed to be in contact with mahatmas, saintly Asian masters of ancient knowledge, who spoke to her while she was in a trance. Much of her work aimed to bridge the gap between Eastern religions and modern Western science through a filter of occult ideas and Victorian spiritualism. Theosophy borrowed bits from Hinduism, Zoroastrianism, Ancient Egyptian beliefs, and myths like the story of Atlantis. Blavatsky often adapts aspects from a range of beliefs, but frequent motifs involve those that reference light, energy, the development of knowledge, and rebirth – all common in relation to numerous solar deities. The great pyramid at Giza, for example, was, according to Blavatsky, constructed 78,000 years ago by colonists from Atlantis, who used it as a literal path or gateway towards a higher state of consciousness.

Close to a century before *The Secret Doctrine*, Karl von Eckartshausen wrote about enlightened mystics guiding the development of the human race in his late eighteenth-century book *The Cloud upon the Sanctuary*, which provided the blueprint for much of Blavatsky's work. Eckartshausen's writings about secret knowledge influenced not only Theosophy, but also the occult ideas of English magician Aleister Crowley. Theosophy became a key influence on various New Age religious ideas emerging through the twentieth century, as well as a number of fiction writers such as H. P. Lovecraft and Robert E. Howard.

Another key influence on ideas derived from Theosophy is Alice Bailey, an English writer who produced her best-known works in America during the first half of the twentieth century. Bailey very much continued were Helena Blavatsky left off, exploring similar ideas such as the ascended masters, telepathy, astrology, occultism, and external influences on the development of humanity. Bailey spoke of masters who had evolved beyond the human level; like Blavatsky's ideas concerning levels of human evolution, Bailey saw a spiritual hierarchy, with humanity being guided by a group of ascended masters.

The concepts derived from New Age philosophies like Theosophy allowed for the formation of what could be described as a number of UFO religions, which emerged from the mid-twentieth century onwards. There are a number of these, though many share several variations on recurring themes, such as evolution to a higher spiritual level, guidance from ascended masters of ancient wisdom, some form of spiritual significance to a celestial body both real and imagined, an end times prophecy, and salvation for a chosen few. The masters of wisdom in Blavatsky's and Bailey's writings were sometimes referred to as the Great White Brotherhood, becoming a supposed secret society, the influence of which can be seen today in both the concepts of advanced alien intelligences and Illuminati-style organizations. The notion of this Great White Brotherhood was encouraged in the 1934 work *Unveiled*

Mysteries by Guy Ballard, who went on to found the I AM movement.

I AM is often considered the original ascended master religious movement. It borrowed heavily from Theosophy and formed the template for many of the New Age movements to appear during the mid- to late twentieth century. Although it isn't technically a UFO religion of any description, its idea of 'ascended masters of ancient wisdom' is clearly a forerunner to the Contactee phenomenon and the UFO cults that followed. Guy Ballard and his wife Edna founded the movement in the 1930s, after Ballard claimed to have encountered a man who introduced himself as Saint Germain while he was hiking on Mount Shasta. Following this the Ballards claimed to be in contact with various ascended masters. Guy Ballard claimed to have been introduced to all manner of mystical teachings through his contacts, including getting to view the planet Venus via a TV screen. The Ballards began to publish their own books about these meetings and helped to spread their message across America. Their popularity spread, and the group had a reported one million followers by 1938. Though apparently not in it for the money, they did accept 'Love Gifts' from their followers.

One of the earliest groups that could be called a UFO religion was the Church of Scientology, established in 1953 by L. Ron Hubbard. An American author and failed civil engineer, Hubbard became an influential figure and remains the most published writer of all time, with 1,084 works to his name. From a young age Hubbard had an active imagination, and would often 're-invent' his own history. He made claims he was a child prodigy, who could ride a horse before he could walk, and by the age of six be out hunting coyote on the backs of broncos alongside the Native American Blackfeet tribe, who had by this point made him a 'blood brother'. In reality he grew up in a townhouse in Helena, Montana, about one hundred miles from the nearest Native American settlement. He re-invented two vacations to Guam and the Philippines with his parents as a 'great exploration of Eastern philosophy and human suffering'; similar to Helena Blavatsky, he claimed he spent time with Buddhist lamas and Chinese magicians.

During the 1930s, Hubbard began to put this active imagination to practical purpose, becoming a well-known and prolific pulp fiction writer, and had success publishing several short stories and couple of novelettes in magazines. A reaction to a dental procedure produced an overly dramatic response from Hubbard, which he described as a near death experience – however he later claimed this event inspired him to begin work on a manuscript. With the work that resulted, *Excalibur*, Hubbard believed he had created a book 'more important than the Bible' and that his writing would soon 'revolutionize everything'.

That wasn't quite the case, as the work has never been published, but this was the first draft of what would become his theory of Dianetics, and then Scientology. Hubbard failed to sell *Excalibur* to any publishers, later claiming that most who had read it had not been able to mentally cope with its contents, even claiming several editors had committed suicide in response to reading the work.

Hubbard had a short military career during World War II, serving as a junior Lieutenant for the US Naval Reserve. Most of this time was spent ashore performing administrative duties, though Hubbard later claimed he was a decorated war hero. At the end of the war he moved in with Jack Parsons, a rocket propulsion researcher, who would become a key influence on Hubbard. Parsons was also an occultist and Thelemite and avid follower of English magician Aleister Crowley. Parsons and Hubbard soon began following the 'Babalon Working', a sex magic ritual intended to summon an incarnation of Babalon: a Thelemist goddess and the great mother of Abominations. This ritual essential comprised of Hubbard having to watch Parsons masturbate.

Soon after, Hubbard returned to writing. Finding it hard to earn a living, he survived on handouts from his parents until 1948 when he was arrested for petty theft. During a science fiction convention whilst bemoaning his financial situation, Hubbard is reported as saying, 'if a man wants to make a million dollars, the best way would be to start his own religion'.

Reworking aspects of *Excalibur*, Hubbard first introduced his idea of Dianetics in April 1950, in a piece published in the pulp magazine *Astounding Science Fiction*. Dianetics describes how all of a person's problems are actually caused by 'engrams': subconsciously remembered experiences from the past. The core idea was based around the principle that the brain recorded every single experience in a person's life (and past life); bad experiences were stored away and could be triggered in later life, causing emotional problems. By carrying out a process called auditing, and using a device known as an E-meter, a person could become 'clear'. A true clear would be cured of all physical ailments, have an improved IQ, and develop a photographic memory. Dianetics was mostly copied from the writings of Jose Delgado, a Spanish professor of physiology who developed ideas around an invention called a stimoceiver, an EEG monitor that could stimulate emotional responses. Several famous people became involved with Dianetics, including the writers Aldous Huxley and Theodore Sturgeon.

Dianetics morphed from a form of therapy into a religion, and by 1953 Hubbard had founded the Church of Scientology on much the same principles, borrowing its name from a 1907 work by philologist Alan Upward. In 1959, Hubbard moved to the UK and set up headquarters in an old manor in Sussex. By the mid-1960s Hubbard was offering a higher version of auditing, known as Operating Thetan Level III, for a select group of Scientology followers. As auditing is concerned not just with your current life, but also your past life, he developed a narrative that described the evolution of the human race on Earth as descendent from an ancient alien civilization. 75 million years ago, according to Hubbard, the galaxy was ruled by an evil overlord known as Xenu. As a solution to rampant overpopulation on a number of planets Xenu paralyzed billions of people using ethylene glycol, and transported them in interstellar spacecraft to Earth, then known as Teegeack. Here the people were positioned around the edge of several volcanoes, and subsequently killed as Xenu dropped hydrogen bombs into each mountainside. The souls of the dead became the Thetans, which were then gathered by Xenu and forced to watch confusing images until they came to believe themselves God, the Devil, and Christ. Today an invisible cloud made of the souls of these Thetans engulfs people, and the only way to clear yourself is through the Scientology auditing process. In December 1967, Hubbard became the first to reach Level III.

Such ideas of leveling may owe a debt to the work of anthropologist Gregory Bateson, who had previously described the idea around learning levels throughout the 1940s and '50s. In his work, learning level III was described as a level requiring high mental experience; indeed, Bateson warned that even to attempt Level III was dangerous, and many would fail at the attempt, but for those who succeed the mental breakthrough, this level offered a vast personal understanding of cosmic interactions.

The alleged apocalyptic event of Scientology may have already happened seventy-five-million years ago, but the religion still relies on using ancient wisdom to guide the chosen through to a more enlightened level. Scientology is unique within UFO religions as it is both highly secretive and also disguises the alien hypothesis at the heart of its teachings. It is quite possible that current leader David Miscavige sees this as a threat to the commercial growth of the group, and may be working toward brushing such ideas under the carpet. Scientology has attempted to make itself more widely accepted, attracting well-known followers such as the actors Tom Cruise and John Travolta. Despite this, Scientology struggles to distance itself from the UFO phenomenon. In June 2013, several UFOs were spotted by a passenger plane above the Scientology HQ in the UK. It is also alleged by BBC reporter John Sweeny, in his book *Church of Fear: Inside the World of Scientology*, that the group has produced a huge hillside marking in the desert of New Mexico to act as a message for visiting aliens.

Dorothy Martin was a housewife from Chicago who experimented with automatic writing, a supposed psychic ability that allows practitioners to channel messages from a spiritual or supernatural source. She was originally involved with Hubbard's Dianetics movement before branching off on her own. In 1954 Martin claimed she had received a telepathic message from the planet Clarion. She claimed to have received warning from a great intelligence that on 21st December that year, a great flood would destroy the world, though through spiritual awareness, a small group of the chosen few could be saved by a visiting UFO. As a result of her claims a group of believers gave up much of their possessions to begin preparation for departure on the spaceship due to rescue them from Clarion. The date of Martin's apocalypse is also a key part of the lunar calendar, being the winter solstice.

The group was first studied by Leon Festinger in the

1956 book *When Prophecy Fails: A Social and Psychological Study of a Modern Group That Predicted the Destruction of the World*. Festinger was an American social psychologist who introduced the concept of cognitive dissonance in his *When Prophecy Fails* work. Cognitive dissonance is the reaction to mental stress caused by having two or more contradictory beliefs at the same time. Festinger argues that when faced with such a scenario, the human mind moves towards a state of internal consistency. Conflicting beliefs are justified internally, reconfigured, and adapted, and inconvenient facts ignored or assimilated to support the conflicting issue. His first main study of this process was based around observations of Martin's group; specifically, Festinger was interested in observing the especially committed cult members who had to come to terms with the reality that the flood did not happen.

After both the spacecraft and the flood failed to materialize, the group engaged in a steady process of cognitive dissonance. Martin reconfigured the events to suggest that she had actually been sent a message from the God of Earth informing her the planet had been spared destruction. Martin later went on to adapt her beliefs forming the Association of Sananda and Sanat Kumara, another group practicing the channeling of extraterrestrial messages through other UFO contactees. Such ongoing adaptions to a belief structure allows groups to continue even in the face of numerous unfulfilled predictions and prophecies.

In the same year that Dorothy Martin predicted the end of the world, Ernest Norman met Ruth Nields, who would soon become his third wife. The two met at a spiritualist convention and quickly found that they held a very similar and somewhat unique view of the world. Ernest claimed that planet Earth was being watched over by an extraterrestrial brotherhood known as Unarius, and that with a bit of practice anyone could make psychic contact with these 'space brothers'. Later that year in Los Angeles, Ernest Norman founded the Unarius Academy of Science, which aimed to advance a new 'inter-dimensional science of life'. By 1957 it became an officially recognized non-profit organization, the Unarius Educational Foundation.

Ernest was a self-described 'child prodigy genius', a belief that seems to be largely based on the fact that he once helped to build a rabbit hutch at the age of six that was, as far as he was concerned, better than his neighbours'. By the late 1940s he was acting as a philosopher, poet, clairvoyant, scientific researcher and paranormal investigator, or at least his own interpretation of what those things should be. Ernest Norman led the Unarius group until his death in 1971 when, in the words of the group, he transitioned to 'the higher planes of light'. After his passing, Ruth Norman succeeded as leader and 'primary channeler' of the group. Adding her own spin to things, she began calling herself Loshanna and claimed she had spent a past life living in Atlantis.

Like Scientology, Unarius followers believe that the solar system was once inhabited by ancient interplanetary civilizations, and that people living today are the reincarnated souls of such visitors. These distant space brother relatives will eventually return to improve humanity. The central prophecy in Unarius is not apocalyptic, but one of salvation. This prophecy has grown over time out of a collection of unfulfilled predictions and adapted narratives, an ongoing process of cognitive dissonance. In early 1974, Norman predicted that the space brothers' space fleet would soon land on Earth. In preparation, she led the Unarius society to purchase property to serve as a landing site, acquiring an expensive 67-acre plot in Jamul, California. They never came. She blames this error of judgment on a trauma she encountered in a past life.

Norman went on to revise the space brothers' landing date many times.

In other references to Theosophy and Dianetics, the Unarius followers believe in reincarnation, past-life memories, and that the human race will evolve to an advanced state of consciousness. Light and energy is central to their beliefs, and every October the group holds a celebration called the Conclave of Light, which involves releasing doves and having mental conversations with the space brothers.

By 1976 Ruth Norman, who had renamed herself again – to Uriel – was offering psychic group therapy as a form of healing practice and a way of accessing memories of past-lives. Not one to lack confidence, in 1979 she also announced herself 'Lord of the Universe', and subsequently began charging followers $5 a time to attend her meetings. The early 1980s saw the group embrace video production and public access cable TV, allowing them to promote messages across America. Ruth embraced the media and began wearing a variety of attention grabbing brightly coloured and elaborate costumes. The videos became increasingly outlandish and theatrical, often involving garish special effects and images of Uriel offering enlightenment to primitive man.

She became a recognizable figure in El Cajon, California, where she was often spotted driving around in her blue Cadillac, which was decorated in UFOs and with a large metallic flying saucer strapped to the roof. Unarius gained some notoriety as a result of such promotional activity, with Norman appearing on mainstream TV shows such as *Late Night with David Letterman* and *The David Susskind Show*. After breaking her hip in 1988, Ruth Norman's health began to deteriorate and she eventually died in 1993. Followers of Unarius dropped after Ruth's demise, however the group still exists with active members

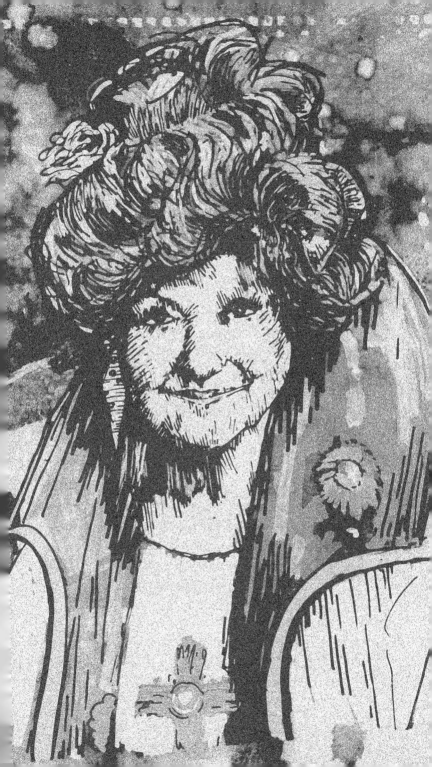

in both America and Europe, where they still wait for the arrival of the space brothers.

Around the same time that Ernest Norman was developing his Unarius movement London taxi driver George King founded the Aetherius Society. The backstory to King's narrative is again a variation on those presented by Hubbard, Martin, and Norman. The Aetherius Society believe an ancient planet called Maldek once existed within the solar system; the planet and all of its inhabitants were destroyed by a powerful hydrogen bomb. The millions of lives lost on Maldek were reincarnated on Earth. Only a chosen few know of this secret and must work with other cosmic masters to stop Earth destroying itself like Maldek did. The group embraces the idea of reincarnation and, like Theosophy, is primarily based on the continual spiritual evolution of humanity. Some cosmic masters still live on Earth; they hide within mountains and volcanoes and are here to help guide human evolution along the right path.

King's mother was a psychic healer who had encouraged her son to explore occult ideas. Later he made claims that his mother had been a passenger on several UFOs, at one time travelling to Mars. King borrowed bits from certain eastern philosophies and religions, and was an active member of some Theosophy-inspired groups operating in London. He was an avid practitioner of yoga, claiming it had helped him to develop psychic powers. The Aetherius Society basically combined King's interest in Yoga with UFOs, and followers of King spent most of their time channeling positive energy into boxes, or Spiritual Entity Batteries, which could then be sent to 'those in need'.

By the mid-1950s, King began conducting 'skywatches' around Avebury with UFO enthusiasts, after having an alleged experience with a Cosmic Master from Venus in his flat in London. Soon after, he claimed to be in contact with an alien intelligence called Aetherius who represented an 'interplanetary parliament'. Through cosmic telepathic transmissions (which he recorded on reel-to-reel tapes), King disseminated Aetherius's wisdom for the benefit of humanity. King began to develop a following when he regularly performed his trance-like communications in London's Caxton Hall in the mid-1950s. Here he made contact with cosmic masters, such as Saint Goo-Ling, allegedly a member of the Great White Brotherhood. It is curious that Aetherius is essentially a portmanteau of the words ethereal and Arthur, as in the legendary king from British medieval myth. George King enjoyed the allusion his own name had to royalty, something that he became increasingly obsessed with as his following grew; he eventually claimed his full title to be His Eminence Sir George King, PhD, Metropolitan Archbishop of the Aetherius Churches. Aetherius, the ethereal-Arthur, the space-king, was clearly a manifestation of one of George King's own ego-driven fantasies, and not an overly subtle one at that.

On 21st May 1959, King appeared on the BBC TV programme *Lifeline* to demonstrate his ability to communicate with beings from other worlds. He managed to channel an extraterrestrial intelligence hailing from 'Mars Sector Six'. The Aetherius Society have since claimed this event was a historic occasion, when the message of Aetherius was shared with millions. Complaints to the BBC suggested general viewers didn't quite share the view of this being a momentous happening, with several questioning why the channel was taking advantage of a confused and deluded individual, or giving airtime to a con-man and hoaxer.

Like Unarius before it, the Aetherius Society has had to adapt its belief structure when certain aspects were brought into question. Cosmic masters, originally from

Venus and Mars, relocated to higher spheres of existence once such planets were proven to be lifeless. Despite King's death in 1997, the Society is still active, believing King himself to have transcended to the level of cosmic master.

Claude Vorilhon founded Raëlism in France in 1974, another UFO group that followed a similar template to Aetherius and Unarius. Vorilhon had some success as a singer at a young age, releasing 'Le miel et la cannelle', which became a minor hit in France. He was later editor of the sports car magazine *Autopop*, and then became a part-time racing car driver.

According to Vorilhon, he was out for a walk in the mountains close to the Clermont-Ferrand region in France when he witnessed a UFO emerge from the Puy de Dôme volcano. Soon after, the UFO landed and an alien disembarked the craft, allowing the two to then begin a conversation. In a later account, Vorilhon claims that the alien's first words to him genuinely were, 'Do you come here often?' He was then invited aboard the spacecraft and given a scented bath by female robots. The alien informed Vorilhon that a race of creatures from the planet Elohim had created the humans from their own DNA around 25,000 years ago. After the event, Vorilhon soon changed his name to Raël, and announced that he had been given a mission to inform the world of humanity's true origins. Then forming the Raëlian movement, he began making preparations for the return of these extraterrestrial ancestors. According to Raëlian belief, the scientific wisdom of Elohim is not supernatural but can allow, through science, abilities such as reincarnation and telepathy. Elohim will return at the age of Apocalypse and allow humanity to progress and to colonize other planets by way of the great scientific wisdom that would be made known by their return.

Since the mid-1970s the Raëlian movement has

targeted members on a global scale, setting up missionary activities in parts of Africa, Japan, and America. The International Raëlian Movement suggests that their influence is spread across ninety countries and has membership in the region of 90,000 followers. However, independent sources claim membership to be closer to a couple of hundred at best.

As well as believing all life was created by extraterrestrials, Raëlians believe in nudity and sexual freedom, regularly enjoying the spiritual benefit of giving each other sensual meditation, a type of erotic massage, through their guilt-free lifestyle of hedonism and sexual experimentation. Raël teaches that the human body is one of the greatest works of art, which should be enjoyed in every way possible. Raël himself has been married three times, most recently to sixteen-year-old Sophie de Niverville. His ex-wife, Marie-Paul Christini, who is no longer associated with the movement, has been highly critical of Vorilhon's motivations. She claims he would brainwash young girls into believing he was a divine messenger for an alien race, only then to involve them in sexual activities. The official Raëlian Corporation website raelsgirls.com specifically targets women working in the sex industry to become part of the cult. Raël has also helped found a number of causes in his pursuit of pleasure, including National Go Topless Day, and the Infidel Club, which promotes the positives of infidelity, primarily involving men cheating on their wives and girlfriends.

The Raëlian movement, like Unarius, the Aetherius society, Scientology and Dorothy Martin's group all have their own emphasis but share basic ideas that can be traced back to Theosophy. In Theosophy, a central premise is that the wisdom of the ascended masters will allow for a spiritual evolution of humanity. The Raëlians believe Elohim will bring greater scientific wisdom, allowing humanity to colonize other planets. Unarius waits for the space brothers to arrive and improve humanity. The Aetherius society expects an alien race to bring wisdom for the benefit of humanity. The spiritual cleansing of auditing will allow followers of Scientology to reach a higher level of existence. Dorothy Martin hoped cosmic travellers would offer salvation. The comparisons are many. In *The Secret Doctrine*, Blavatsky discusses the continent of Lemuria, a fictional landmass with a similar fate to Atlantis. According to Theosophy, Lemuria was destroyed by a number of volcanoes. In Scientology, Xenu used volcanoes as an aid in the destruction of the Thetans. The Aetherius Society believed cosmic masters were hiding in volcanoes, and Claude Vorilhon claimed to have his fist meeting with an alien on the edge of a volcano. In the same book by Blavatsky, Atlantis is described as being destroyed by a great flood. Dorothy Martin predicted the end of the world would come about via a great flood. Ruth Norman believed she lived a past life in Atlantis.

There are numerous other groups that have used variations on such ideas to a greater or lesser extent. Along with spiritual séances, Blavatsky's occult trance communications and writings about the ascended masters also formed much of the template for the UFO contactee movement. George Adamski and Eduard 'Billy' Meier owe as much to Theosophy as Unarius does.

The blurred distinction between a contactee group and a religious cult is often very slight, and there are numerous contactees who went on to establish small religious followings. One example is Allen Noonan, who worked as an artist and pictorial sign painter around California until in 1947 when, he claims, he experienced a cosmic initiation via a direct channel to the Universal Mind. He claimed during this process he was surrounded by a bright gold light and later transported to a Galactic

Mother-ship, where he communicated with the source of the light. Changing his name to Allen Michael, he maintained telepathic contact with this great intelligence. By 1967 he had established a small following, the One World Family Commune, based out of his natural food restaurant in San Francisco. The ambition of Allen Michael to spread the message of his extraterrestrial contact saw him founding the Universal Industrial Church of the New World Comforter in 1973. The growing chain of natural food stores, which reached eight outlets at one point, supported the group, allowing them to host public talks and publish a number of books, such as *UFO-ETI World Master Plan*. With growing ambitions, the group went on to form a political party, the Utopian Synthesis Party, which allowed Allen Michael to run for President, with limited success, in 1980 and 1984.

Another group that embraces aspects of Theosophy, extraterrestrial contact and an obsession with 'ancient wisdom' is the United Nuwaubian Nation of Moors, a religious organization founded by Malachi 'Dwight' York in 1993. The group has its origins in the Black Muslim groups of New York that emerged during the late 1960s. York combined elements of The Nation of Islam, Freemasonary and The Moorish Science Temple of America to create a quasi-Muslim Black Nationalist movement, which was originally known as Ansaar Pure Sufi. In the late 1980s, York began to phase out the Muslim aspect of this group in favour of Theosophy-inspired ideas, and intertwined them with adapted Ancient Egyptian, African, and Native American customs.

In the early 1980s York worked as a music producer and his Nuwaubian teachings had an impact on the New York focused hip-hop movement. Artists such as Jay-Z, Afrika Bambaataa, Outkast, Lisa 'Left-Eye' Lopez, De La Soul, and the Wu Tang Clan have all cited him as an influence. The east coast hip-hop scene in the early 1980s took significant influence from the Afrocentric ideas of the 'five-percent nation', a name referencing the numbers of the general population who understood the righteous teaching that God is an Asiatic Blackman. Artists such as Afrika Bambaataa and his Universal Zulu Nation, and also Ramm:Ell:Zee, borrowed heavily from both Afrocentricism and motifs of traditional African cultures, creating a type of Afrofuturism that re-examined events from the past in a way that combined them with bits borrowed from science fiction and fantasy. The American sociologist Alondra Nelson commented on this Afrofuturism approach, noting that space and aliens frequently appear in such art and music, and by using the idea of black people as being an actual alien race, concepts around slavery and alienation can be subverted into hyperbolic tropes that utilize extraterrestrial imagery as literal metaphors.

A precursor to such ideas can be seen with the jazz musician Herman Poole Blount, who later changed his name to Le Sony'r Ra, and then simply Sun Ra, in reference to the Egyptian God of the Sun. From the mid 1950s Sun Ra and his ensemble The Arkestra, performed experimental 'cosmic' jazz music, often dressed in elaborate costumes inspired by both ancient Egypt and space age themes. Sun Ra went on to frequently talk about a trip he made to Saturn via a method of psychic teleportation in the mid-1930s, however he didn't make such claims public until 1952. He subsequently adapted these claims, suggesting that the alien beings he met had told him to drop out of college and become a musician, and later that he himself was in actual fact an extraterrestrial.

Concepts of racial tension brought about through both the aftermath of years of oppression, and the guilt created by the sins of the father, may relate to an aspect of the UFO phenomenon. The creative expression seen in movements like Afrofuturism is one example of the fall out of racial divides fuelling ideas around space and aliens, but there are other more subtle parallels. In *The Multicultural Imagination: "Race", Color and the Unconscious*, psychoanalyst Michael Vannoy Adams describes the idea that intelligent extraterrestrial civilizations could be able to observe, from a distance, the racial divide of our species, providing them opportunity to invade and conquest. As a result they could inflict (or so the western subconscious would fear) the same amount of exploitation upon western society that had, historically, been inflicted on so many others.

The combination of such themes mixed with York's own teachings and with, selected bits from Islam and Theosophy, and created some strange beliefs. In his view the blacks were originally a green-skinned alien race who have slowly 'rusted' as a result of spending time in Earth's atmosphere. Subliminal clues to this truth have been planted into various Hollywood movies, like the *Star Wars* sequel *Return of the Jedi*, which was, in York's view, created with the sole purpose of educating the masses about these extraterrestrials. York believed white people were created by aliens as a race of killers to serve blacks as a slave army, and further that the Christian term 'rapture' really refers to the returning of the Velociraptors, who will eventually reappear to 'dine on the now ripe white flesh'.

He claimed both himself and the ancient Egyptian pharaoh Ramesses II were extraterrestrials from the planet Rizq. York later went on to claim that he arrived on Earth on a spaceship around 1970, despite the fact that it was well known that he lived in Brooklyn in the 1960s and previous claims that he had spent time in the late 1950s travelling to Egypt to learn ancient wisdoms from Egyptian teachers.

As his group grew he eventually established a large

Egyptian-themed complex to act as a base of operations and church for his Nuwaubian religion. The Tame-Re was built in an area near Eatonton, Georgia, on a 476-acre plot. The complex included several pyramid structures, a sphinx, obelisk, lines of animal-headed statues, as well as a bookstore and nightclub. The group was fined for building on the site without a permit, and ongoing lawsuits with county authorities gave rise to the formation of a paramilitary group to protect the complex, called the Royal Guard of Amen-Ra, which was allegedly funded in part by actor Wesley Snipes. York saw a strong affiliation, too, with the local Yamasee indigenous people, and made claims that their culture was formed from descendants of ancient migrants from Egypt, making dubious links to a 2000-year-old Rock Eagle Effigy mound located close to the site of Tame-Re.

By 2000 the United Nuwaubian Nation of Moors had around 500 followers, though this number declined significantly after 2002 when York was arrested and sentenced to 135 years in prison for hundreds of counts of sexually molesting dozens of children, some as young as four, and transporting a number of others across state lines for the purpose of further sexual exploitation. After York's imprisonment for child abuse, the Tame-Re site was sold and in 2005 the Egyptian-themed structures were demolished.

The embracing of ancient cultures from Egypt, Africa, and indigenous American peoples created a highly selective mix of ideas. Such appropriation also frequently attempts to make conscious links between these cultures and a knowledge of or interaction with alien civilizations. Such a trend is often labeled the ancient astronaut hypothesis, and again has its roots in the Theosophical writings of Blavatsky.

In *The Secret Doctrine*, Blavatsky speculates about

life on other worlds and suggests that many ancient masters of wisdom were aware of these otherworldly entities. As well as this she suggests that such beings visited Earth and may have played a role in the evolution of humanity. Very basically the ancient astronaut idea suggests that the human race has been visited by advanced alien beings, going back to ancient times, and that many grand monuments, such as the pyramids, the Nazca lines, or several Mesopotainian artifacts are evidence of such interaction.

As well as the connection to Blavatsky, the idea has some origins in a mixture of somewhat 'adapted' age-old folklores and fantasy writings from the early twentieth century. Writer Charles Fort produced many books on the occult, fairies, mysterious disappearances, and other unexplained phenomenon (creating the term *Fortean* in the process). Fort was a writer and researcher attracted to bizarre stories like raining frogs and spontaneous human combustion, with a constant mistrust of science and authority. He often did not believe the weird stories he collected, but wanted to present an alternative view to the accepted scientific opinion. One of his ideas concerned a super-Sargasso Sea suspended above the Earth, from which intelligent beings created life, occasionally dropped things, and interacted with earth-bound secret societies via psychic powers and teleportation. In 1919, his work *The Book of Damned* features accounts of early UFO sightings and also objects described as thunderstones. Thunderstones have their roots in Pagan folklore, and were primarily a way of explaining the ancient-looking flint arrowheads and other seemingly manmade tools discovered in areas of disturbed earth. European folklore often attributed them to being 'fairy-shot' or 'elf-arrows'. In North America these flints were objects of veneration for many native tribes. These ancient tools were seen as gifts from the Gods and relate to several origin myths.

Some also believed that the objects fell from the sky. By the sixteenth century, the idea that these were implements of early man began to take hold, and the popular folklore diminished but was not forgotten.

Harold T. Wilkins was essentially a successor to Charles Fort; in his 1954 book *Flying Saucers from the Moon*, he discusses the (slightly racist) concept of 'White Gods', which may well be a reference to the Great White Brotherhood of Theosophy. This is an idea that relates in some ways to the thunderstones, and essentially suggests that Caucasian races visited 'primitive' cultures in ancient times; they passed on their wisdom and were worshiped as gods. Wilkins goes on to suggest that these White Gods occupied the whole of South America at one point. He also suggests that the Mesoamerican deity Quetzalcoatl was from Atlantis. Italian writer Peter Kolosimo takes this one step further, claiming the White Gods were actually extraterrestrials. Details of accounts in Kolosimo's writing can be traced to fictional stories published in pulp magazines like *Adventure*. Walter Raymond Drake was another follower of Fort and Harold Wilkins. He published nine books on the ancient astronaut theme, starting with *Gods or Spacemen?* in 1964. These books included 'proof' that ancient civilizations were colonies of extraterrestrials.

The folktales associated with thunderstones and other similar myths provided inspiration for a number of fiction writers, notably H. P. Lovecraft's 'The Call of Cthulhu' from 1926. This short story uses the idea of a cult of 'Great old ones' who existed before man, and who have left many artifacts through history. Ancient Gods are turned into alien beings, and clues of their presence are left in stones and ancient monuments. Jason Colavito wrote the 2005 book *The Cult of Alien Gods: H. P. Lovecraft and Extraterrestrial Pop Culture*, were he argues that the idea of ancient aliens originated with such writings from the mid-

1920s. Lovecraft was inspired by H. G. Wells, the Gothic horror of Edgar Allan Poe, and works by William Scott-Elliots such as *The Story of Atlantis* and the Alfred Tennyson sonnet 'The Kraken'. Many of Lovecraft's stories were not published until after his death, but his writings gained a steady following through reproduction in magazines such as *Weird Tales* during the 1940s and '50s and the French magazine *Planete* during the 1960s.

Planete was founded in 1961 by Louis Pauwels and Jacques Bergier and ran until 1972. The magazine explored a type of fantastical realism, which blurred the lines between fact and fiction. The pair also produced a book *The Morning of the Magicians;* released in France in 1960, it became a bestseller and was later translated into English and released as *The Dawn of Magic* in 1963. The book deals with various conspiracy theories, as well as ancient prophecies and accounts of a race of giants that once ruled the Earth. Such claims run very close to the fiction of H. P. Lovecraft, especially his *Cthulu* and *In The Mouth of Madness* works.

The Morning of the Magicians proved to be an influence on Erich Von Daniken, a controversial Swiss author who wrote *Chariots of the Gods? Unsolved Mysteries of the Past* in 1968, a work supporting the ancient astronaut hypothesis, in 1968. The book went on to be a bestseller, perhaps in part by popular interest around similar themes caused by the success of Stanley Kubrick's film *2001: A Space Odyssey*. Released around the same time, *2001* explores the evolution of man by influence of some unknown extraterrestrial other. In its opening section, pre-human apes explore an ancient black monolith, its age and origin unknown; as the Sun symbolically rises in the back of the scene, a simple but effective juxtaposition between a basic tool and a spacecraft acts as visual shorthand for 250,000 years of technological development. A similar black monolith found buried on the Moon results in a sequence of events that send a crew towards Jupiter, only for Dr David Bowman to discover a third monolith and possibly be guided towards the next evolutionary level.

Chariots of the Gods? made its author one of the best-known proponents of the ancient astronaut idea. The book borrows wholesale from other writers, mostly Jacques Bergier and Louis Pauwels, as well as Peter Kolosimo; Von Daniken largely regurgitated their ideas, though he denied this following the success of his own writing. Von Daniken makes many claims in his writings, mostly based on misunderstandings of ancient cultures and their religions. He describes the Nazca lines in Peru as some sort of UFO airport, while animal mummifications and hieroglyphs of animal-human deities become evidence of genetic engineering by aliens. The offensive logic evident in most of his ideas is that cultures such as the Nazca people or ancient Egyptians were too stupid, too *primitive* to create any impressive structures themselves. Therefore, it must be aliens. Such ancient feats have been thoroughly researched by historians and the traditions, beliefs, and construction techniques of the Nazca, Mayan, ancient Egyptians and others is now understood, at least well enough, to give rational explanations for any respective achievements. The Egyptian pyramids, as an example, were constructed over a period of around thirty years, using a large workforce of highly skilled labourers (not slaves) who moved large granite and limestone blocks from quarries far south of Giza using the flooding waters of the Nile as a transportation system. Stones were carved using copper tools and dolerite stones before being positioned using sledges moved over a system of ramps and a friction-reducing technique using wet sand. As with a lot of modern Fortean literature, Von Daniken assumes ignorance on the part of the reader.

In 1974 he admitted (in an article published in

Playboy), that he had forged and fabricated some of his ancient astronaut 'evidence' in an attempt to enrich his writing. He also produced photographs of pottery depicting UFO-type craft, which he claimed were found during an archaeological dig and dated to Biblical times. These were later proven fakes when TV documentary investigators found the still living potter who had produced them.

This was not the first time his actions have been somewhat morally questionable. After being convicted of theft at nineteen, Von Daniken went on to be a hotelier, here he was fired for stealing money, before going on to prison for embezzlement and fraud for falsifying documents in order to obtain loans. While on trial, a court psychologist described him as a 'pathological liar'. He was again prosecuted for tax evasion following the success of his books.

None of this has put him off. Von Daniken has gone on to become a prolific writer of fantasy and science fiction, producing a number of additional books adding further 'evidence' to the ancient astronaut idea. He even designed an ancient astronaut theme park, *Mystery Park*, which opened in Switzerland in 2003. It has been in regular financial difficulty, closing and re-opening on a number of occasions. The US TV show *Ancient Aliens* that is largely based around Von Daniken's ideas is now in its seventh series and is regularly watched by 2 million people.

Often referenced as supportive evidence for the ancient astronaut idea are the comparative accounts of World War II-era cargo cults. During the Second World War, and for a period after, a number of cults emerged in areas such as the Melanesian Islands of the South Pacific. During the campaign, large amounts of military equipment and supplies were airdropped into the area due to a number of bases operating close to the islands. When the war stopped, so, too, did the airdrops. Accounts emerged of charismatic individuals who developed cult followings amongst remote populations, as they promised further deliveries from the sky of food and materials.

The John Frum cult formed on the Island of Tanna in the Vanuatu region of the South Pacific. Here cult members worshiped several Americans going by the name of John Frum, who identified themselves as spiritual entities, and who claimed they would provide further cargo to the group in the future. Ancient astronaut theories suggest such instinctual human behaviour illustrates what could have easily happened if, for example, the ancient Egyptians encountered an advanced society in the past.

John Frum was not an individual, and the name was likely a corrupted saying based upon phrases like 'John from Kansas' or 'John from Washington', with John simply being a common Western name. It was assumed at one point that such cults developed due to native tribes not being able to comprehend Western technologies like cargo planes or automatic rifles, thus believing such things to be magical or supernatural. Further studies have shown cult members actually had a primary focus on the development of new social relationships with foreign cultures. The idea that the fascination was based upon manufactured goods comes from Western assumptions regarding commodity fetishism.

The emergence of concepts such as advanced alien races visiting Earth in flying saucers largely developed through the cultures of America. The current population of the United States is a huge melting pot of international influences, from European settlers to South American and African communities, Asian populations, and of course indigenous peoples. Appropriated customs, practices, and traditions from cultures different to the dominant white-focused Capitalist West can often be seen as inspiration and source material for a range of ideas related to the

UFO phenomenon. As an example, a number of ideas, beliefs, and practices of indigenous American peoples have been borrowed and assimilated into aspects of the New Age movement and, in turn, UFO beliefs. It should be remembered that the idea of advanced extraterrestrial intelligences, which manifest from the sky in a UFO, developed in a country that is home to cultures such as the Zia. Such peoples regard the Sun as a scared symbol and hold a belief in spirits called Kachinas who live amongst the sky and visit the ground to share knowledge. Parallels can perhaps be seen in the belief that advanced alien technologies recovered from crashed UFOs originate from extraterrestrial races that reside somewhere up in the sky. It is probably no real coincidence that the modern day Zia Pueblo Reservation, just north of Albuquerque, is only around two hours from the site of the Roswell crash.

It has also been argued by people such as historian Michael Sturma that tales of UFO abductions are just an updating of tales of American Indians capturing white women in the Wild West. In his 2003 book *Aliens and Indians: A Comparison of Abduction and Captivity Narratives*, Sturma suggests that the nineteenth-century American obsession with such stories represented a preservation of the noble and superior white society against the dark and savage *others* from beyond the frontier. Transplanting the same narrative to that of alien abduction suggests a preservation of this historical identity against a confusing and technologically dehumanizing future.

A direct assimilation of such cultures into the UFO phenomenon can be seen with the Star Knowledge UFO Conference, which began in June 1996, and gathered for the first time at the Yankton Sioux Reservation in South Dakota. The conference attracted several apparent spiritual leaders such as Laurance Zephier, who also goes by the name Standing Elk, and claims he is a member of the

Lakota tribe, as well as some apparent spokespeople from the Hopi, Iroquois, and Choctaw tribes. In attendance, too, were the likes of Whitley Strieber, Leo Sprinkle, and Richard Boylan.

An ex-Catholic-priest-turned-ex-psychologist, Boylan started working with people he identifies as 'experiencers' in 1989. The California Board of Psychology revoked Boylan's licence to work in 1995 over allegations of improper sexual interaction with some of his patients. He had used a hot tub as a form of 'hydro-therapy', which involved both him and various female patients getting into the tub together, before Boylan would broach the topic of sexual favours in lieu of payment. As a psychologist, he often worked with patients claiming to have had UFO abduction experiences. One of his patients is Wendi Powers, who was diagnosed as having dissociative identity disorder whilst at college. After spending time with Boylan she now believes she is a star seed, and her multiple personality disorder is down to her Earth body being a vessel for a 3,000 year old alien called Asheoma.

Boylan has appeared at the Star Knowledge conference a number of times, often alongside Wendi Powers. The Star Nations Council, a group formed from the conference, apparently represents 1,438 extraterrestrial races currently in contact with Earth, with the aim of providing spiritual and cultural advancement for life within the star systems. In 2005, Star Nations appointed Richard Boylan Councilor for Earth, tasking him with upholding the laws of the cosmos, most of which seem to have been written by Boylan himself and are available to view on his website.

The Star Nations have, according to Boylan, apparently been well known to the indigenous population of America for some time, as the history of such alien contact goes back millions of years. Suspiciously mimicking the template of Theosophy, Star Nations sees the God of the Universe as a 'transcendent matrix of consciousness' that manifests as an 'overwhelmingly intense light'. Such interaction with advanced races is, apparently, allowing humanity to engage in an accelerated process of evolution, a process that in fact began when modern Homo sapiens were created via fusion of alien and primate DNA.

In a similar way, astrological observations by certain other 'primitive' societies act as apparent evidence of extraterrestrial intervention. Robert Temple, born in 1945, is an American author and part-time TV presenter, who is best known for his book *The Sirius Mystery*. First published in 1976, though he claims he began work on it in 1967, the book suggests that the Dogon people from Mali, West Africa, honour age-old traditions and practices relating to contact with aliens from the Sirius star system. These extraterrestrials apparently taught the basics of civilization to humans, and such interaction is also evident in the cultures of the ancient Egyptians, Greeks, and in the *Epic of Gilgamesh*.

The 'mystery' of the book concerns the Dogons' apparent knowledge of the stars Sirius-B and Sirius-C, neither of which is visible to the naked eye. It is more likely that such information was acquired through contact with European explorers in the nineteenth century. The Dogon were not an isolated tribe; they frequently interacted with neighbouring cultures and independently explored territories abroad of their own settlements. The details of such knowledge has also been misunderstood by Temple and other researchers like French anthropologist Marcel Griaule. A lot of the evidence in support of Temple's idea comes from Griaule's accounts of his time with the Dogon in the 1930s. The Sirius mystery may mostly be a result of Griaule misrepresenting their knowledge of astronomy; Walter Van Beek, another anthropologist who spent a decade with the Dogon found no evidence of any folklore related to Sirius.

Another key contributor to the ancient astronaut hypothesis, and someone who makes the link between such ideas and those of the religious aspects of Theosophy even more apparent, is Zecharia Sitchin. Born in 1920, Sitchin was a soviet-born American author who produced a number of books revising widely accepted historic theory. He studied economics at the University of London and worked as a journalist in Israel before moving to New York in 1952. Here he developed an interest in ancient history and began to teach himself Sumerian cuneiform.

Sitchin developed a hypothesis that suggests some form of extraterrestrials contributed to key developments in human history. In his 1976 book *The 12th Planet*, and on through its various sequels, he argued that the ancient Sumerian culture was largely the bi-product of the actions of a race called the Anunnaki, an alien species from the planet Nibiru. These aliens genetically engineered humans as slave workers by mixing their own DNA with that of female apes. The human slaves were then put to work mining gold as well as producing a range of buildings and aesthetically pleasing objects for their masters.

Such ideas have been thoroughly discredited as pseudo-history by academics, who point to numerous inaccurate translations, exaggerations, misunderstandings, flat out lies, and unsubstantiated conclusions from Sitchin. Most frequently, Sitchin is unable to separate myth from factual events, as he fails (either intentionally or through pure ignorance) to recognise myths as parables or folktales. Rather, he sees accounts of interactions with various gods as hard scientific evidence of alien contact.

With the final book in his Nibiru series, *The End Days: Armageddon and Prophecies of the Return*, Sitchin makes predictions about the return of the Annunaki and the end of the world. Keeping his options open, in 2007 he suggested a range of dates for such an event, including 2012, 2087, 2240 – with the likeliest, apparently, not being until the year 2900. Sitchin makes reference to various end of days prophecies from numerous religions and cultures, he discusses the days of judgment as described in the *Book of Joel* and also *Revelation*, and makes links between the 'Moon turning to blood' and the Blood Moon effect caused by certain lunar eclipses that makes the Moon appear a deep rusty orange colour. The Blood Moon prophecy has become a popular modern apocalyptic belief promoted by Christian ministers such as John Hagee and Mark Biltz, who believe a series of lunar eclipses will signal the coming of the antichrist and the end of days. Hagee believes there are many signs indicating we are moving towards end times, such as satellite television and increased levels of education.

In *UFO: End-Time Delusion*, David Allen Lewis suggests that the UFO phenomenon is a sign of the end of days, seeing an increase in sightings and abductions as an assault on humanity. Lewis argues further that such events are occurring to prepare us for the coming of the antichrist, suggesting that Betty and Barney Hill were abducted by demons as part of a plot to put the antichrist in power. Jeffery Wingo, author of *Alien Antichrist: The Terrifying Truth about UFOs and Aliens, Antichrist, and the End of Days*, argues that UFOs are part of a great deception and represent the coming of judgment and rapture as described in the *Book of Revelation*. In his view, the antichrist is actually a fallen alien king who ruled the Earth during the time of Noah, and is soon to return with his Satanic Empire.

UFOs have frequently become associated with the occult. Much UFO literature will reference ideas relating to mysticism, such as mental telepathy, automatic writing, sudden materialization and dematerialization of objects and beings, abduction, and possession. French astronomer and UFO supporter Pierre Guerin has argued that modern UFO manifestations seem to be only minor variations of age-old demons. As a result of this common ground, such combinations of the UFO phenomenon with religious prophecies and demonology have been embraced by some Evangelical Christians.

John Weldon converted to Evangelical Christianity in the late 1980s, claiming to be a Doctor of Comparative Religion and Apologetics. His qualifications likely came from a fundamentalist Protestant group based in Australia, who goes by the name the Pacific College of Graduate Studies. The college has no campus, and indeed only one member of staff who distributes various degrees obtained by 'distance education' via a fax machine. In the early 1990s, Weldon began working as a researcher for *The John Ankerberg Show*, a weekly half-hour American Christian televangelist programme. John Weldon and John Ankerberg have since written extensively on all manner of fundamentalist Christian views, such as *Heaven: What Will it be Like?*, *The Creation Hypothesis: Scientific Evidence for Intelligent Design*, and *The Facts on UFOs and Other Supernatural Phenomena*. Ankerberg warns that UFOs represent a type of new religion that does not have our best interests at heart. A large amount of Ankerberg's work focuses upon denouncing cults for the good of all Christians, or combating nonsense like evolution. He seems to have a genuine concern about UFOs, one of his main issues being that such reported alien visitors are not devout followers of Jesus, and so might encourage people to leave his cult to join another. He argues that such phenomena represent demonic entities who visit Earth with the aim of social manipulation.

The general consensus among strict orthodox

Christians is that the UFO phenomenon is closely related to the occult and is therefore Satanic in nature, with a tendency to steer people away from belief in Christian doctrine. Monsignor Corrado Balducci, a Roman Catholic theologian of the Vatican Curia and a demonologist, openly declared (before his death in 2008) that extraterrestrial intelligences are a real phenomenon. He stressed that such alien encounters are demonic and in countenance to God's will. Balducci made many TV appearances during his life, often complaining about satanic messages in rock music and talking about his time as an exorcist.

In the 2014 book *Religions and Extraterrestrial Life*, David Weintraub explores how different religions may respond to the realization that alien life exists. He argues Evangelical Christians, who have a very human-centric and Earth-focused approach to God's purpose, may find such a revelation hard to accept. Those who approach the Bible in a far more literal sense may however, Weintraub argues, be more flexible in their acceptance of alien life. Practitioners of Mormonism, Seventh-Day Adventism, and Jehovah's Witnesses often have a stronger belief in extraterrestrial life than other Christian denominations.

The combination of Christian end days, New Age influences, and the wider UFO phenomenon have resulted in some extreme examples of deluded belief, evident within a number of UFO groups through the last quarter of the twentieth century. One example is the Solar Temple, formed in Switzerland in the 1980s. Joseph Di Mambro was a confidence trickster who claimed he had a background in psychology. Luc Jouret was a homeopath with a strong interest in ancient wisdoms. The pair met around 1980 through the Golden Way Foundation, an occult group started up by Di Mambro. By 1984 the pair had formed the International Chivalric Organization Solar Tradition. They soon began giving talks on medicine and conscience, as well as performing several rituals. The duo became obsessed with ideas of eastern mysticism of the type promoted by Helena Blavatsky, as well as mythologies around UFOs. Di Mambro and Jouret believed they were reincarnations of the Knights Templar, twelfth-century warrior-monks dedicated to protecting pilgrims within the Promised Land.

By 1986 the group had grown more ambitious, soon to rename themselves the Order of the Solar Temple. Their aim was to assist humanity through a great transition and make preparations for the second coming of Christ, who would return as a solar-god king. They began to spread their predictions about the end of the world, encouraging followers to join their group. Only through the practice of certain rituals could such apocalyptic events be prevented, though mostly these ceremonies consisted of members giving money to Di Mambro and Jouret or, in the case of women, offering themselves for sex. Events were enriched by projected images of spiritual beings from hidden electronic equipment, leading followers to believe Di Mambro was summoning spiritual entities.

The group soon became unstable as members began to question the claims of Di Mambro and Jouret. One member, Tony Dutoit, discovered Di Mambro was using the group's funds for personal gains. In response, Di Mambro declared Dutoit's infant son Emmanuel to be the Antichrist. In October 1994, selected members from Di Mambro's 'golden circle' stabbed Tony Dutoit, his wife Nicky, and their young son to death. Emmanuel was left with a wooden stake in his chest and wrapped in black plastic. Less than a day later, firemen discovered a burning chalet in a remote Swiss village. Within the basement they found a mirrored chapel containing the bodies of nine men, twelve women and a twelve-year-old boy. The bodies were arranged in a circle with their feet pointing inward, some were hooded with plastic bags, and a large number had been shot in the head. Another farmhouse was found several hours later, again on fire, inside this one was a further twenty-five bodies, dead via the intravenous injection of drugs. Amongst the bodies were Jospeh Di Mambro and Luc Jouret. Writings discovered after these events revealed the ambition to depart through death to the dimension of truth, to the Grand White Lodge of Sirius. An interest in UFOs was only an aspect of the Solar Temple group, and voluntary suicide as a method to reaching the ascended masters in Sirius was perhaps performed by only a handful. Ritualistic murder seemed to be the more common process performed by the group. Certainly, death by eight gunshot wounds to the head, as was the case with one individual, seems unlikely to have been self-inflicted.

As the name suggests, the Order of the Solar Temple saw symbolism and significance in celestial objects. Their obsession with the star Sirius makes links to not only aspects of the ancient astronaut hypothesis, but a broader parallel to the worship of sky gods going back to age old religious practice. Quite how much of this the likes of Di Mambro and Jouret actually believed, and how much of it was a convoluted scam aimed at exploiting others for money and sex is open to debate. Their legacy clearly had an impact as a number of Solar Temple lodges operated over the world, including in Australia and Canada. In December 1995, another group of fifteen followers of the cult killed themselves in a similar fashion in France and again, in March 1997, a further five also committed suicide, this time in Quebec. The Solar Temple group claimed to believe that an environmental catastrophe would soon bring about the end of the world and that members needed to leave Earth and transit to a better world. Such beliefs parallel another group, who again took as inspiration Theosophy, ancient religions, and aspects of the UFO phenomenon – and again these beliefs ultimately resulted in the death in a significant number of followers. The name of this other group was Heaven's Gate, and their story begins in America in the early 1970s.

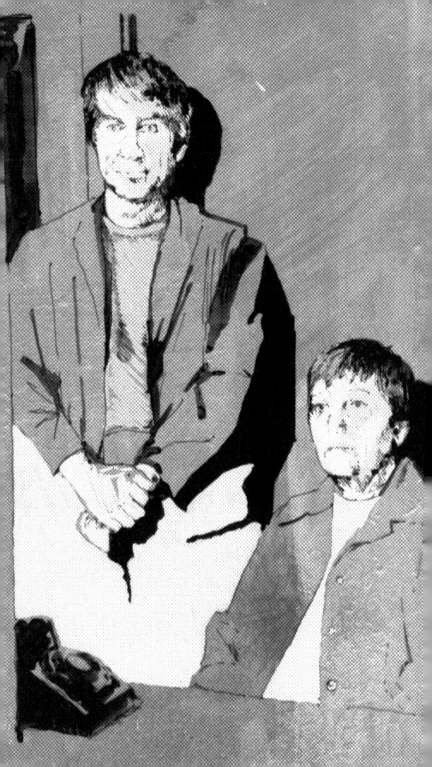

PART EIGHT
The Path to Heaven's Gate

Perhaps the most notorious of the UFO cults was Heaven's Gate. Like the Solar Temple, this group was based around the beliefs created by two individuals – and equally like the Solar Temple, the beliefs promoted by the two resulted in tragedy for a large number of people. Thirty-nine members of the Heaven's Gate group committed suicide in the belief that they would be transported to a spaceship, likely trailing the comet Hale-Bopp, in March 1997; to this day it remains the largest mass-suicide on American soil. It has been argued by some, such as psychiatrist Marc Galanter, that the two leaders of Heaven's Gate, Marshall Applewhite and Bonnie Nettles, shared, like Jospeh Di Mambro and Luc Jouret, a joint psychosis that was infectious, and collectively encouraged others to follow them. Such a shared belief system is sometimes described as the Lasègue-Falret syndrome, named after French psychiatrists Charles Lasègue and Jean-Pierre Falret. Also known as *folie à deux*, the madness of two, it is a syndrome in which delusional belief is consistently reinforced and transferred between two parties.

The term was first used in description of a married couple who had developed a psychosis concerning unseen intruders who, according to the couple, continued to enter their home. Their evidence to this was the spread of dust around the house and soles of their shoes wearing thin. A more recent case from 2008 involves Swedish sisters Ursula and Sabina Eriksson, who were removed from a public bus on the M6 motorway in England after a complication with their luggage. After the police attended the scene, Ursula ran into moving traffic and was hit by a passing lorry that crushed her legs. Within moments Sabina did the same thing, again being hit by passing traffic. The pair then resisted medical attention, claiming medics were trying to steal their organs. After attacking a police officer, Sabina was briefly detained in prison. On her release she went on to stab a man to death whilst trying to track down her sister who was still in hospital. Later at her trial, it was argued that the pair were suffering from the rare psychiatric disorder. Socially isolated pairs are common in cases of *folie à deux*, and gradual changes in belief are reinforced in an ongoing feedback loop between the two individuals.

Marshall Herff Applewhite was born in Spur, Texas, in 1931. Son of a Presbyterian minister, he became highly religious at a very young age. During the 1950s he spent time at the Union Presbyterian Seminary, with the view to following his father and becoming a minister. Though he originally studied philosophy and theology, he ultimately pursued a career in music, a move that was actually encouraged by Applewhite Senior. He soon married Anne Pearce and, after a spell of military service, earned a Master's degree in music focusing on musical theatre. He then attempted to launch a singing career in New York, but it failed to amount to much. It was around this time that the couple had two children, and later Applewhite gained some teaching work at St. Thomas University in Houston, but was soon fired for having sex with a male student. He became frustrated by his homosexual desires. His wife later learned of various affairs with other men and separated from him, eventually divorcing him in 1968. He continued to teach at other schools throughout Texas, having several more experiences with male students along the way.

In 1971, shunned by many former friends and colleagues, he attempted to re-invent himself, moving to New Mexico and opening a delicatessen. Applewhite ran the Sunshine Company deli and its nearby bar in the town of Taos for about a year. Bar manager Dennis Robbins worked with Applewhite, though did not hold him in high regard, later describing him as a scam artist. Taos, located in northern New Mexico on the edge of the Carson National Forest, was known as a centre for New Age-style businesses, and today still has a high number of practicing psychics, acupuncturists, New Age bookstores, and crystal healing centres. It is also home to the Taos Pueblo, one of the oldest continuously inhabited communities in the United States. The Tiwa-speaking tribe of the Puebloan people combine their indigenous religious traditions with Roman Catholicism, a belief system that involves deities appearing as visionary beings. Whether such local cultures played a part in Applewhite trying to set up business in the area, or indeed if it became a source of influence on some of his subsequent ideas, is not known.

In any case the new business did not succeed; confused and unfulfilled professionally and personally, and with mounting debts, Applewhite allegedly began to suffer from depression. The last straw came with the death of his father that same year. Applewhite later checked himself into a psychiatric clinic after he began to hear voices in his head. He suffered from anxiety and severe headaches and may have had other health issues; some have speculated that Applewhite was actually suffering from a form of schizophrenia, though scant evidence has ever materialized to support this notion. Many years later, Applewhite would claim his 'father' came from the evolutionary level above human, though if this patriarchal entity had any relation to his physical birth father is unclear. In his own words, Applewhite would not describe such a spirit as having any connection to his Earthly parent, yet it is tempting to consider such links after what was clearly an emotional trauma. In 1972 he suffered heart problems and was again hospitalized following a heart attack. This near-death experience was to Applewhite both a sign and a catalyst to re-focus his life. He was sure a clear guide would soon appear to him.

Bonnie Lu Trusdale married John Nettles in 1949. Born and raised into a strict Baptist family she became a registered nurse, and had four children with her husband. By the early 1970s their relationship began to suffer, and Bonnie Nettles developed a belief that she was in communication with a nineteenth-century monk who went by the name of Brother Francis. Bonnie was soon in contact with a number of mediums and she began conducting séances in her home to make contact with other spirits. She was also an occasional member of the Theosophic society, part of several meditation groups, and held a strong interest in both astrology and mysticism. Bonnie Nettles also frequented fortunetellers, one of whom told her that she would soon meet a mysterious man with a fair complexion.

In 1972 Bonnie Nettles met Marshall Applewhite – not at Houston Hospital where she worked (as is frequently reported), but most likely at a theatre where

Bonnie's daughter Terri worked and Applewhite was giving drama and music lessons. One of Bonnie's sons had also been a student at a drama class and they likely met via this connection. Directly after their first meeting Nettles offered to give Applewhite an astrological reading, telling him that he had a divine purpose. They both soon decided that there was a clear alignment between their stars and that they had been brought together for a purpose. Later that same year the pair formed the Christian Arts Centre in Houston, essential a bookshop that also organised lectures on mysticism and astrology, and where Nettles would offer psychic readings. The business failed, but it was around this time that they began to believe they were on a divine mission, and likely were the same figures mentioned in the *Book of Revelation* ('*I will grant my authority to my two witnesses…*', *Revelation* 11:3). On New Year's Day 1973, the pair abandoned their lives and families and left together to pursue their great spiritual purpose.

They believed being on such a divine mission granted them spiritual importance above simplistic human laws. They regularly left motels and restaurants without paying and in 1974, after using a card owned by one of their followers, they were arrested in Texas for credit card fraud. The card holder's husband had reported it as stolen, though he later dropped such charges. Around this time Applewhite was caught stealing a car, a rental he had neglected to return in Kansas. Missouri prosecutor Tim Braun later commented that Applewhite's statement claimed that 'a force beyond the earth has made me keep this car'. As a consequence, he was sentenced to six months in prison but used the time productively, developing his manifesto based on his and Nettles's shared beliefs. It is here that the idea that the pair were alien life forms developed. They had, apparently, come from the Heavenly Kingdom into the wombs of women as space fetuses. Applewhite also claimed this mind had come to Earth previously, some 2,000 years earlier into the vessel now referred to as Jesus Christ, and further that he had known Nettles in a past life.

After his release from prison, the pair became avid readers of Helena Blavatsky's *The Secret Doctrine*. They also spent time at the Krotona Institute of Theosophy in Ojai, California. The centre was one of a number of Theosophy colonies and was influenced much by the teachings of Jiddu Krishnamurti. As an adolescent, Krishnamurti was taught by the Theosophists Charles Leadbeater and Annie Besant, who saw him as a 'vehicle' for a New World teacher. Years later, the notion of the body as a 'vehicle' would have a profound resonance with both Applewhite and Nettles. This idea of a physical vehicle encouraged a revision of the pair's origin story; Applewhite later claimed the great mind controlling his earthly body (or 'vehicle') only appeared in the early 1970s, suggesting something more like a type of spiritual possession than any claimed birth rite. Krishnamurti had given public talks in Ojai since the mid-1940s, and lived in the area until his death in 1986. Before his death, Krishnamurti had spoken of a supreme intelligence operating his body, an intelligence that others could get close to so long as they 'lived the teachings'. During this period the pair embraced Theosophical ideas about spiritual evolution and it is highly likely a key influence on the pair's beliefs of ascending to the next level above human.

In the same year, they also consulted with a Filipino occultist who encourage their special mission, and who also gave them new names: Shakti Devi and Shri Pranavah. Although they didn't continue to use such names, the concept of a new identity through a new name provided a useful symbolic method of reinvention and a fresh break from their old selves. From the mid-1970s they started calling themselves 'The Two', 'Guinea' and 'Pig', then 'Bo' and 'Peep', as well as other pseudonyms like Vicky and Seymour Morgenstern, and then finally 'Ti' and 'Do'. The practice of taking on a new name as a marker to illustrate a break from a previous life to a new one in tune with different spiritual values was a custom not just embraced by Applewhite and Nettles, but something that also came to be expected of their followers, later giving them names such as Qstody, Tddody and Jnnody.

Soon after, in June 1974, they visited the International UFO Bureau in Oklahoma City. Here they met the head of the Bureau, Hayden Hewes, and attempted to convince him that they were not beings of earthly origin. Applewhite told Hewes he would be able to telepathically contact him if needed; in later accounts Hewes has suggested such a psychic link did occur. Hewes was obviously taken by the meeting. Two years later he had produced possibly the first writing on Applewhite and Nettles with the book *UFO Missionaries Extraordinary* with the writer Brad Steiger. In the same year Steiger produced the book *Gods of Aquarius: UFOs and the Transformation of Man*, where he introduced the concept of star people. Here he suggests that certain people originated as extraterrestrials and then subsequently arrived on Earth, either at birth or as a walk-in to an existing human body. Such star people can, according to Steiger, experience dramatic awakenings of consciousness as they realize their true origins and purpose. Hewes later suggested that many months after meeting the pair, he attempted a psychic link through use of a thought-code sequence, and soon after received a message from a young man claiming to be one of Applewhite's followers.

In 1975, Applewhite and Nettles founded their group, initially called the Human Individual Metamorphosis (HIM). On 13th August that year, the pair made their first public appearance at Stanford University. Here they told their audiences that they would soon be collected by a UFO and taken to an otherworldly utopia where their bodies would be transformed via a literal metamorphosis to a higher evolutionary level. According to Applewhite and Nettles, in such a process their bodies would be completely changed physically, chemically, and biologically.

Gradually attracting around a dozen members, their numbers grew after they targeted like-minded groups in Los Angeles, such as pupils of Clarence Klug's metaphysical teachings. Even Klug himself joined the group for a brief period. Over the next year, the pair held around 130 public meetings through the United States and Canada. Through such talks and meetings, the group's numbers briefly swelled to around 200 at one point as they gradually recruited members from California, Colorado, Denver, Chicago, New Mexico, and Oregon.

Jacques Vallée's book *Messengers of Deception: UFO Contacts and Cults* details the account of one talk organised by Applewhite and Nettles at the University of San Francisco in August 1975. Vallée noted with interest the distinct difference between the claims of Applewhite, Nettles, and a number of their followers with the standard claims put forward by UFO contactees. During the talk members of the group described the process of metamorphosis, where bodies will be completely changed, so as they could transcend to a new life on board a spacecraft.

In September that year, at the Bay Shore Inn in Waldport, Oregon, the pair gave a talk to around 300 people, describing how chosen followers could enter the next evolutionary level via a spaceship. After the meeting around a dozen people went missing; apparently they had followed Applewhite and Nettles, going to stay at a camp in Colorado. Such disappearances attracted press attention, mostly in response to concerns relatives had about cult activity. The two were soon interviewed by *National Enquirer* magazine and later received a write up in *The New York Times*, all of which raised the profile of the group further.

Following growing public interest, much of which was negative, their prophecy steadily began to take on new forms. Inspired again by the *Book of Revelation* the two believed they would be slayed by *'a beast that ascendeth out of the bottomless pit'*. They claimed they would be publically vilified or possibly assassinated, only to rise, and lead the group to heaven in a spaceship. Such an event they dubbed the 'demonstration', borrowing again from the Christian concepts, specifically that of the resurrection. As followers began to grow, the pair began to make claims that the UFO would soon land in Waldport to collect them. However, when such extraterrestrial visitors did not arrive, a number in the group became disenfranchised and followers began to leave.

One such member was Joan Culpepper, who had been part of the group for two months in 1975 before becoming highly skeptical of the ideas being presented. She later organised a halfway house for former members of the group in Topanga Canyon, California, to aid the process of any departure from the cult. Culpepper would subsequently follow Applewhite and Nettles around the country, posing awkward questions at meetings and picking holes in their teachings. Though no stranger to New Age ideas herself, Joan later believed she could receive information from the fifth dimension, gaining the ability to listen to a group of trans-dimensional entities she called the Higher Selves.

Between 1976 and 1979, the group set up camp in an area of Wyoming, living in tents or camper vans.

The camp was to be used for training to prepare for a life in space. Living in communes, members lived a detached lifestyle in ready anticipation of their ascension to the next level. Applewhite and Nettles began to insist on strict rules: uniforms were introduced and some members patrolled the camp as guards. Communication had to be kept to a minimum. Members of the group were expected to give up their names and possessions, as well as becoming celibate. People were made to follow unusual diets aimed at detoxing the body and maintaining a healthy mind, and periods of existing on fruit and wheatgrass juice would last several weeks at a time. Procedures governed exactly how daily chores such as cooking and laundry were carried out, and specific shifts were designated to allow for sleep. It was here that the two began to preach more readily that Earth was about to be 're-cycled' or 'refurbished', so as life could start over, and that those who wanted to live on needed to join the 'evolutionary level above human'. According to Ti and Do (as they liked to be called by this point), the only method of salvation was to leave planet Earth with the group onboard a spacecraft before the human race was destroyed. Such prophecy borrows from Theosophical ideas about cycles of humanity, a process that allows for supposed great developments in mankind after transitions resulting from catastrophic events, and indeed the movement of inhabited life through the solar system.

Culturally, the early 1970s was also a key point for the developing environmental movement, such as with the first Earth Day in April 1970, the beginning of the Environmental Protection Agency in America that same year, and the formation of Greenpeace the year after. Pessimistic statements released from the first Earth Day talks, by people such as environmental advocate Denis Hayes, made claims that it was already too late for the planet to avoid mass starvation and that there were perhaps only twenty-five years before 80% of all living species became extinct. Such ecological end-days may have added further evidence to the ideas of Applewhite and Nettles; an advert for one of their mid-1970s talks in California warned of changing weather, volcanic activity, and the spread of famine as proof of their prophecies.

The writings of Hal Lindsey offer several more thematic links to the cultural interest in end-times prevalent at the end of the 1960s and start of the 1970s that were likely influential to groups like HIM. Starting with *The Late, Great Planet Earth*, first published in 1970, Lindsey explores various end-time prophecies making comparisons with current events and environmental predictions in a bid to predict future happenings, such as the rapture and the second coming of Christ. In these writings much is made of the idea that such things would begin playing out through the 1980s, with a focus on the approaching turn of the millennium as a pivotal moment for God's Kingdom of Earth. The book was later adapted into a 1976 movie of the same name, featuring a voiceover by Orson Welles. Several sequels to the book were also produced including *Satan is Alive and Well on Planet Earth* in 1972 and *The 1980s: Countdown to Armageddon*.

As well as reference to end-days prophecies and the growing environmental movement, the notion of planetary recycling also draws an amusing parallel to the opening plot device of Douglas Adams's *Hitchhiker's Guide to the Galaxy*, first broadcast as a radio comedy in March 1978. Here planet Earth is due to be destroyed to make way for an intergalactic by-pass, and only Englishman Arthur Dent and his friend Ford Prefect are saved by hitching a ride on a passing spacecraft. There are a number of other thematic links between the pair's developing prophecies, such as human evolution through alien influence or superhuman metamorphosis, with examples of science fiction of a similar era.

Applewhite was a fan of science fiction, and would read works by authors such as Robert A. Heinlein and Arthur C. Clarke. Many of the followers of the pair were also keen fans of science fiction. In the 1953 novel *Childhood's End*, Arthur C. Clarke introduces the concept of a generation of human children who are transitioning into a next stage of human evolution. Stanley Kubrick's 1968 movie *2001: A Space Odyssey*, based on the writings of Clarke, deals with the concept of human evolution to the next level, as influenced by an extraterrestrial entity. Comic book artist Jack Kirby had touched on similar themes back in 1958 with his story *The Great Moon Mystery*, which sees astronauts discovering an ancient alien structure on the Moon, only then to undertake a journey through alien worlds. A number of Kirby's stories proved influential to aspects of the UFO phenomenon, including his *New Gods* work published a year before Applewhite and Nettles met. Kirby himself was openly influenced by the UFO topic; of particular fascination was the 1947 Roswell crash and the subsequent conspiracy theories that grew from the claim. Such associations were obviously noticed; according to Kirby's daughter, a UFO group arrived at the family home in the late 1970s in a bid to get the artist to join their collective.

Themes of human evolution influenced by extraterrestrial encounters appear in several of Kirby's writings. In Kirby's *The Fantastic Four* comics, which debuted in 1961, a leap in human ability comes about when four individuals develop superpowers after exposure to cosmic radiation following a scientific mission to outer space. There are other aspects in Kirby's work that provide conceptual foreshadowing for the beliefs of what would become the Heaven's Gate group. Issue 48 of *Fantastic*

Four introduced the character Silver Surfer, an intergalactic traveller with cosmic powers given to him by Galactus, an entity created by the sentience of the universe who consumes planets for energy. Silver Surfer acts as a herald for Galactus, arriving in the sky in a comet-esque streak before a world is consumed. Co-creators of the issue, Jack Kirby and Stan Lee, again explored the idea of humans who represented the next stage in evolution in their series *The X-Men*, which also made its first appearance in the 1960s.

The British television series *Doctor Who* provides another comparison. It was first broadcast in the UK in 1963, and later sold to stations in the United States in 1972, the year that Applewhite and Nettles met. The series details the adventures of a time-travelling alien, known as the Doctor, along with his companions, as they explore various locations in time and space. As part of a convenient plot device to allow different actors to play the title role, the Doctor will undergo a transformation into a new physical form, allowing transition from one incarnation of the character to another. Here an apparent death is followed by regeneration, and a metamorphosis into a new body, often with changes to personality. Such a process is very similar to the one being described by Applewhite and Nettles as documented by Jacques Vallée in 1975.

A further comparative idea of death leading to an extraterrestrial-inspired rebirth can be seen in Michael DeGaetano's 1974 movie, *UFO: Target Earth*. Here electronics expert Alan Grimes traces an alien signal, only to discover a formless entity trapped under a lake. The alien tells Alan that he is the source of an energy that the entity needs to return home. To help the alien intelligence escape Earth, Alan must sacrifice himself; in death he joins the only other three humans who have managed such ascension, namely Enoch, Elijah, and Jesus.

Mysterious knowledge represents a last salvation for mankind during the end of days in Jack Vance's *The Dying Earth*, a collection of short stories first published in 1950. Here the remnants of human civilization are living in a future were the Sun is nearing the end of its life. Characters learn of ancient wisdom through interaction with otherworldly realms as a way of surviving on the doomed planet. The stories also feature the idea of humanoid bodies being seen as vessels, created in vats with intelligence later invested into such artificial bodies. Applewhite would later describe the soul as a type of hard drive that could be reprogrammed.

The Last Days of Man on Earth, a science fiction movie from 1973, explores some similar ideas around human vessels and metamorphosis. The film includes self-replicating human beings, and also an idea about combining two individuals into one form via solar radiation. Here the new single entity emerges from the process to reveal itself as a messiah and bringer of the end of the age. In the 1977 movie *End of the World*, aliens who have infiltrated a convent attempt to destroy the world through a series of natural disasters. The alien leader, played by Christopher Lee, describes humanity as a hotbed of disease that cannot continue to pollute the galaxy, with the only solution being an ecological re-start.

What impact these cultural sources had on the formation of Ti and Do's prophecies is unclear, they may not even have been aware of some of them, yet the fact that such things existed in advance of their claims being made is interesting to note. According to some surviving members of the group, two movies that were mentioned as points of interest to both Applewhite and Nettles were *The Questor Tapes* and *The Lathe of Heaven*. Written by *Star Trek* creator Gene Roddenberry, *The Questor Tapes* is a 1974 TV movie about an android who gradually becomes sentient. As he searches for his creator and his true purpose, he learns that he is the last of a series of human-androids going back to the dawn of the world, left on Earth by otherworldly 'Masters' to serve and protect mankind. The idea of a benevolent extraterrestrial force assisting human development appears several times in Roddenberry's works, including the last episode in the first series of *Star Trek*, broadcast in 1968. *The Lathe of Heaven* is an adaption of the 1971 novel of the same name written by Ursula Le Guin. The plot centres on the protagonist George Orr, who makes claims that his dreams have the power to change reality. Considered initially delusional or schizophrenic, several doctors soon come to realize that Orr is telling the truth. The story features realities that include the destruction of Earth, as well as an alien invasion.

Interestingly the film cited by Applewhite and Nettles as the most relevant to the truth of their mission was not a science fiction work at all, but rather Robert Wise's 1965 musical drama *The Sound of Music*. The film is set during 1938, when Maria, a young Austrian woman studying to become a nun, is sent to act as governess to the seven children of retired naval officer Captain Georg von Trapp. Through her kindness and love of music Maria wins over not just the children, but also eventually the heart of Captain von Trapp. When Nazi Germany begins the process of annexation of Austria into the Third Reich, the von Trapp family use a music festival in Salzburg as cover to escape across the border to Switzerland. A fan and student of musical theatre, Applewhite was likely well-versed in *The Sound of Music*; its first opening as a stage musical was at the Lunt-Fontanne Theatre in New York in 1959, during which time he had recently graduated as a musical theatre student and was looking to launch his own career in the Big Apple. At university, Applewhite played the lead roles in productions of both *South Pacific* and *Oklahoma*, the experience of being a charismatic lead obviously appealing. Though not initially obvious there are parallel themes between the pair's mission and the plot of Wise's musical. The guiding of a group of children, or a class, into a greater sense of emotional and spiritual awareness, and the potential persecution and eventual escape from one reality to another, do mimic the broad structure of Applewhite's mission. Ultimately it was not Switzerland he aimed to escape to, but the next evolutionary level on a craft in outer space.

The very basic theme of a protagonist learning of a great secret, discovering their true self, or becoming more enlightened, only then to be transported to a new world, realm or reality, and in turn face a threat that must be overcome, is essentially an archetypal narrative. At a basic level this is the narrative that drives the story of Heaven's Gate. Such a structure is commonplace, and can be seen in a diverse range of writings and movies, from *Alice's Adventures in Wonderland* (1865), and *The Wonderful Wizard of Oz* (1900), to *Brazil* (1985), and *Total Recall* (1990), and more recently in *The Matrix* (1999), *Spirited Away* (2001), *Pan's Labyrinth* (2006), and *Avatar* (2009).

The pair provided inspiration for some science fiction themselves. Filmed in 1979, but not released until 1982, writer and director Gary Sherman produced the made-for-TV movie *Mysterious Two*, loosely based on the activity of Applewhite and Nettles. The movie depicts two aliens who visit Earth with the aim of enlisting followers to travel the universe with them. Applewhite acted as an un-credited technical advisor to the film, with actors John Forsythe and Priscilla Pointer portraying the two group leaders. Sherman is perhaps best known for the horror sequel *Poltergeist III* and the cult zombie movie *Dead & Buried*. *Mysterious Two* was actually a failed pilot for a series that was never commissioned, and had the ominous working title of *Follow Me If You Dare*.

By the early 1980s, the pair discovered an issue that put into question their combined spiritual journey to the next level: Bonnie Nettles was diagnosed with brain cancer. In 1983 she had an operation to remove an eye to stop the cancer spreading. Becoming increasingly weak, the cancer spread to her liver, and she quickly deteriorated over the next two years. Her subsequent death in 1985 did not fit into the group's plan of spiritual ascension; she was the one to guide others to the next level, not die of an earthly disease. Applewhite did not take her death well. It raised difficult questions about their mission, and robbed him of his soul mate. In the wake of Nettles's death, Applewhite became increasingly confused and paranoid, he began to insist that most humans had been brainwashed by Lucifer, and that the same evil 'Luciferians' were attempting to stop his mission. In his view, such Luciferians were actually another type of space alien who travelled the nearby heavens looking for bodies to inhabit. Much of this paranoia was further fueled by his increasing obsession regarding stories of alien abductions and alleged government cover-ups of UFO crashes, popular in some press during the 1980s.

In many ways it was Nettles who was the dominant force leading the group. Applewhite saw her as his elder, his guide, even seeing her as being on a higher spiritual level than himself. He considered her his father, not a version of his own deceased Presbyterian minister father, but God the father. The death of Nettles had changed Applewhite's game plan. He began to reconfigure his belief system, embracing a good dose of cognitive dissonance to fit recent events into the bigger plan. After the death of Nettles many of the more explicit New Age ideas began to fade into the background, replaced by Applewhite's more evangelical Protestant concerns. A revision of the group's mission statement was made in the late 1980s, and various bits of information were sent out to a number of New Age centres, health food stores, UFOlogists, and monasteries. By 1988 Applewhite had begun claiming that group members had already been part of the next level and had exited their original bodies during several UFO crashes during the 1940s, presumably such as the one claimed to have happened near Roswell. Government scientists had, apparently, recovered these original bodies, so their spirits were forced to temporarily occupy human vehicles. In this sense group members became pre-determined extraterrestrial entities, rather than simply spiritually aware humans. After the death of Nettles, Applewhite had lost the second half of his *folie à deux*. He sought to replace her, not with a single individual, but with an entire group. Perhaps in this sense a *folie à deux* became a *folie à plusieurs*, a madness of many.

It was decided Nettles had shed her vehicle, or body, to join the next level. Already ascended, Nettles would be able to guide the rest of the group from aboard the spaceship. It cemented an idea for Applewhite that had been gradually developing for some time: to reach the next level required not just spiritual enlightenment, but shedding of the human body. A spiritual metamorphosis was now not enough; death itself was the only way to ascend.

In May 1993, revived and re-named as Total Overcomers Anonymous, the group ran a full-page advert in *USA Today*. The advert claimed again that Earth was due to be recycled, and appealed to potential members with a final offer to join the group so as they could be saved. In early 1994, the group was sure a UFO would soon arrive to collect them from the tip of the Santa Monica pier in

Los Angeles. When this did not happen the group set up base in rural New Mexico; here they began constructing a compound out of tires and lumber, referred to as the 'Earth Ship'.

The compound was an ambitious project. Built around a 4,000-square-foot area, it was to contain living quarters, an infirmary, offices, workshop, a bakery, and a nursery. The idea came from the writings of Michael Reynolds in the book *Earthship: How to Build Your Own*. Reynolds describes a concept for a self-build eco-home that provides for its own power, sewage, food, and water needs. Earth Ship was based near the Manzano Mountains, about an hour northwest of the site of the Roswell crash. During this period Applewhite also briefly encouraged the collection of firearms to prepare for battle against the Luciferians, perhaps anticipating a siege similar to that at Waco in April 1993 that put an end to David Koresh's Branch Davidians group. However, he soon changed his mind and with a number of the group in poor health and with an approaching winter, Applewhite abandoned the compound.

Initially moving to Phoenix, in the autumn of 1995 the group then rented a two-story house in Rancho Santa Fe, San Diego. Around this same time many members had a lot to do with computers, embracing the Internet at an early stage in its public development. They saw it as a good way to spread the word of their group, and also a potential source of income. A company, Higher Source Contract Enterprises, was founded in July 1996, which generally designed web pages, mostly for entertainment businesses, and became a viable way of funding their residence. Over the eight months in which the company operated, it generated around $80,000 in website design and computer services sales.

By 1996 the group had settled on their latest name,

Heaven's Gate. Applewhite continued talking about harvesting and how Earth was soon to be recycled, and made claims he was in touch again with Nettles, telling followers that she was piloting a spaceship that would soon arrive to collect them. That summer, forest fires near the part of California where the group lived created a deep red sky from smoke pollution. The setting sun spoke to Applewhite, appearing bright red in the sky; he believed it signaled that the end times were near and they just needed to wait for the right sign.

Toward the autumn of that year, the group began making more substantial preparations for their coming departure. Applewhite looked to move towards a greater level of physical purity and, as complete abstinence from sexual gratification was difficult for a number of men, he along with six other members of the group went to Mexico to voluntarily undergo a castration procedure as a way of further commitment to their ascetic lifestyle. After the procedure, Applewhite began to suffer from a number of complications. He also developed a problem with his back caused by a pinched nerve, and began to suspect that he was developing cancer like Nettles. Such issues likely increased his desire to move toward the final act. Ascension to a spacecraft was clearly seen as a looming reality by many in the group. In October, the Heaven's Gate group members purchased alien abduction insurance through the firm Goodfellow Rebecca Ingrams Pearson. At an annual cost of $1,000 a year for the group, the insurance firm would pay out $1 million to each member's beneficiaries should they be abducted, impregnated, or killed by aliens.

For various reasons the mid-1990s was a high point in public interest with regard to UFOs and aliens, and the desires and beliefs of the Heaven's Gate group would have been exacerbated by the trends of the time. Pop culture had rediscovered ideas around aliens and government cover-ups through the popularity of TV shows like *The X-Files*, which originally ran from 1993 until 2002, with the show's ratings peaking between 1996 and '97. Around the same time, George Lucas began work on a new trilogy of *Star Wars* films, drafting the outline to his latest installment in 1994; by 1996 anticipation was running high in advance of filming due to begin summer 1997. Other successful movies of the time included *Star Trek: First Contact*, *Independence Day*, and *Mars Attacks!* in 1996 and *Alien: Resurrection*, *Men in Black*, and *Starship Troopers* in 1997. The story of the Roswell crash would be fifty-years-old in 1997, and a spate of press interest, TV documentaries (such as 1995s *Alien Autopsy: Fact or Fiction* and *The Roswell Incident*), and other related merchandise also increased public awareness of such themes in the run up to this anniversary.

Heaven's Gate members were fans of science fiction like *Star Trek*, *Star Wars*, and *The X-Files*; they were also obsessed with pretty much anything to do with UFOs, aliens, and much else. They would often spend several hours a day watching movies like *Cocoon* and *Close Encounters of the Third Kind,* though equally they would just as readily watch *The Price is Right* or *Murder, She Wrote*. Beyond the regimented tasks and procedure-driven chores there was little space for escapism within the group, and the watching of television likely provided enjoyable relief; in the words of the group such escapism was to calm the brain while resting from studies. There was, however, an approval list for what could be watched within the house, and only approved programmes were shown on the house television. Individual members were designated specific seats for watching of films and television, and Cheryl Butcher, a member of the group since 1976, was assigned as controller of what could be watched and when. A number of films must have been suggested by group members and consequentially rejected, as they were specified on a list of prohibited movies; these included *Multiplicity* starting Michael Keaton and the Marlon Brando vehicle *The Island of Dr Moreau*. In a reference to a wider acceptance of conspiracy theories, a copy of a NASA documentary about the US space programme, which was amongst approved titles, was annotated with the note 'this might prove to be a few laughs'.

The group were also avid listeners of the Art Bell hosted radio show *Coast to Coast AM*. Here Bell would often discuss offbeat topics, such as the paranormal, the occult, UFOs, and conspiracy theories, and by 1997 was the highest rated late-night talk show host in America. He has often referred to his *Coast to Coast AM* show as 'absolute entertainment' and has clearly stated that he does not accept every guest or caller's claims; he just provided a forum for them to voice their thoughts. His guests have included John Lear, Bob Lazar, Nick Pope, Linda Moulton Howe, Timothy Good, Steven Greer, Whitley Strieber, Stanton Friedman, and many others. *Coast to Coast AM* was most likely the source of Applewhite's certainty that the long-anticipated spacecraft destined for the Kingdom of Heaven was following the comet Hale-Bopp.

Some, such as skeptic James Randi, have accused Bell of being responsible for the events that soon followed associated with the Heaven's Gate cult members. This is perhaps a bit harsh; he may have promoted far-fetched stories about Hale-Bopp knowing they were likely nonsense, albeit nonsense good for ratings, but Bell promoted a wide range of wacky ideas on his show. Applewhite, too, had also seen symbolism in other natural events; years earlier, for example, he was sure that the volcanic eruption at Mount St. Helens was a sign forecasting the imminent arrival of the fabled UFO. Other things, such as shooting stars, were also seen as evidence of UFO activity by members of the group. Nevertheless, Hale-Bopp had the potency suitable to stand out as the signifier to finally convince Applewhite that the time had come. A powerful omen, the comet had likely fascinated viewers on its last visit past Earth, around 4,200 years ago. Here it may have been spotted in ancient Egypt, during the reign of Pharaoh Pepi I, as certain hieroglyphs in the pyramid at Saqqara may make reference to the comet.

After Alan Hale and Thomas Bopp first discovered Hale-Bopp in July 1995, there were numerous rumours concerning strange signals coming from the comet, as well as suggestions that it seemed able to change direction. In November 1996, Art Bell began discussing ideas about a strange object following Hale-Bopp. The idea that there was an actual craft following it came from amateur astronomer Chuck Shramek, who initially contacted Bell claiming that a UFO the size of Saturn was following the comet. The claim was soon supported by Courtney Brown, Director of the Farsight Institute, who agreed that there was an alien spacecraft following Hale-Bopp. Brown was a big promoter of remote viewing, a practice that allows participants to view activities in different parts of the world, or indeed the universe. He has spent much of his time promoting it as a genuine science and has written various books on the topic, such as *Cosmic Voyage: A Scientific Discovery of Extraterrestrials Visiting Earth*. Brown himself claims to have used remote viewing to speak to both Jesus Christ and Buddha, who it turns out are both inter-dimensional aliens. Through the actions of Brown, several remote viewers backed up Shramek's claims about a mystery object trailing the comet, going on to describe it as a massive metal sphere filled with aliens. Encouraged, Brown then sent Bell a photograph of this object as hard proof. After the image was posted on the Art Bell website, professors from the University of Hawaii proved it was just a doctored copy of a recent photograph of the comet. As the fraud became more apparent, Bell began to quickly distance himself from the claims. Members of Heaven's Gate clearly questioned the validity of a craft following the comet; sources suggest that the group largely debunked the notion by February 1997. However, the Heaven's Gate website still states that whether or not Hale-Bopp had a companion was 'irrelevant', as the comet's arrival was still a 'joyously very significant' event. The website also contains (to this day) links to both Chuck Shramek's Hale-Bopp companion site and Art Bell's webpage.

Another individual to promote stories regarding the comet was Lee Shargel, who at one point claimed to be a NASA scientist before admitting to just being a budding science fiction writer. He made claims that he had received radio communications from the craft following Hale-Bopp, and that the alleged UFO was being piloted by Dolphinoid aliens. These aliens were apparently sending communications to Earth before preparing to destroy the planet via a burst of energy. After the Heaven's Gate suicides, he also appeared on ABC TV's show *This Week*, claiming that he had met with Applewhite, even going as far to claim that Applewhite granted him stewardship of the remaining members of the cult. Shargel has later admitted it was all a publicity stunt to boost sales of his book *Voice in the Mirror*.

Nancy Lieder, an alleged contactee who claims to be in communication with aliens from the Zeta Reticuli system via a brain implant, believed Hale-Bopp was a fiction, designed to distract the majority of the population from the arrival of Nibiru, the fabled planet from Zecharia Sitchin's writings. Lieder began promoting her ideas in 1995, just after Hale-Bopp was first discovered, through her website ZetaTalk.com, though she had been claiming to be a contactee a few years earlier. She appeared on *Coast to Coast AM* before going on to provide a Live Chat service through another conspiracy forum, where she advised people to prepare for the coming of Nibiru by stockpiling canned food and killing their pets.

Another UFO-related event to gain significant media attention around this time was the Phoenix lights incident. This was an alleged UFO sighting which occurred over Phoenix, Arizona, on 13th March 1997 and might, too, have acted as a sign to Applewhite and his followers. According to UFOlogists, lights of various descriptions were witnessed by thousands of people in the sky as two distinct events, a triangular formation and a series of stationary lights. Reports described a massive triangular-shaped UFO slowly moving over the city skyline at around 8 p.m., only to be seen again later that same evening.

An alleged prime witness to the event was Dr Lynne Kitei, who later appeared on several TV shows such as *Dateline* and *NBC News* describing her experience. In a nod to Theosophy, she claimed the lights she saw were 'amber orbs in a pyramid formation' that were 'magical and intelligent'. Dr Kitei later wrote a book, *The Phoenix Lights: A Skeptic's Discovery That We Are Not Alone*, and also produced a documentary concerning the Phoenix lights incident. These lights were not however the first UFO she had claimed to witness; in 1995 she allegedly saw several large orbs near her home and claimed this experience encouraged her to feel a 'real time and long term transformation of consciousness'. Dr Kitei has since quit the medical profession, concentrating instead on promoting her UFO material and becoming part of the Disclosure movement. She is also interested in 'exoconsciousness' which 'explores the extraterrestrial dimensions of human consciousness that link us directly to the cosmos and its inhabitants'.

Fife Symington, the Arizona State governor at the time of the Phoenix lights incident, also claimed to witness such sightings. Originally skeptical of any extraterrestrial explanation, he went about publically ridiculing such claims, including one press conference where he appeared alongside a colleague dressed as a green alien. As time has passed, however, he has later admitted to having witnessed other UFOs and claiming that on reflection the lights he saw that night over Phoenix were 'otherworldly'. Symington's change of heart came after the end of his political career, which ended abruptly in late 1997 when he was convicted of bank fraud charges stemming from a bankrupt real estate empire. He has featured in a number of UFO documentaries recalling the Phoenix lights event; he changed his story when he realized that such documentaries pay, and that career prospects for a corrupt and bankrupt politician are minimal.

The Phoenix lights were really two very distinct and different events, the first of which not many people witnessed, but enough people had heard about it for a good number to witness the second incident. Claims that 'thousands' witnessed the event are gross exaggerations fueled by UFOlogists and the media. According to MUFON, the actual number of reported witnesses was sixty-five. The first event, which was a roughly triangular light formation, was spotted by Mitch Stanley. He was able to observe it with his own 10″ telescope and easily identified that the lights were just high altitude planes. Despite informing local press of this after they had run a news flash regarding passing UFOs, his report was largely ignored. News of the strange lights travelled fast, and a relatively large number of people (though certainly not thousands) were outside watching the sky when a second, unrelated, event occurred at around 10pm. A string of lights appeared in the sky and slowly sank until they disappeared behind the

Estrella Mountain range. These lights were later shown to be a string of flares dropped by the Maryland Air National Guard over the North Tac military range. The two different reports were later conflated by a mixture of different witnesses and news stories. As a result a single explanation failed to satisfy many of the witnesses: those seeing planes were not convinced they had seen 'flares', and those that had seen flares were sure what they had observed were not aircraft. This has allowed the 'unexplained' story to develop over time, with the Phoenix lights often being cited as a classic example of a mass UFO sighting.

The Phoenix lights UFO sighting occurred less than two weeks before the Heaven's Gate suicides. Exactly what impact this event had on the group is unclear but, considering the timing, it likely would only have strengthened the idea that there was extraterrestrial activity in the skies. The Hale-Bopp companion story may have been the final trigger sign for Applewhite, but in a year filled with UFO stories, chances are if not that, then it would have just been something else. Hale-Bopp had its closest approach to Earth on 22nd March, the day that the Heaven's Gate group began committing suicide. Comets have often been seen as great omens, as bringers of doom, enlightenment, or change, and such symbolism was maybe too strong for Applewhite and his followers to resist.

The Heaven's Gate group believed in astrology, tarot cards, psychic channeling, telepathy, resurrection, and reincarnation. They embraced ideas from Theosophy, as well as adapted extracts from Christianity, and saw evolution as a spiritual process; concerned for an impending apocalypse, their only salvation was to be found through devotion to ancient masters of ascended wisdom. There was an interest throughout the group with certain conspiracy theories, in particular those concerning

NASA, government cover-ups, UFO sightings, and alien abductions. Though no members of Heaven's Gate were part of any UFOlogy group, they would actively communicate with such organizations, sending them information, mission statements, and tapes, in particular from 1985 through to 1997. Avid science fiction fans, they embraced much within popular culture that had a thematic resonance with their beliefs. Applewhite insisted that the great extraterrestrial intelligence guiding him had attempted to save humanity before in the form of Jesus Christ, but had found the human race unready for the next evolutionary level. Now it had returned, with its chosen crew, who were ready to enter the next level. Exactly what it was that he considered as his guide to this next stage of evolution is down to his own personal belief, but whether it was a spiritual entity, an actual extraterrestrial being, a combination of the two, or something even beyond normal human comprehension will remain unclear to anyone other than Applewhite himself.

Such an ethereal presence is certainly some form of sky god, much in the tradition of cultures like the ancient Egyptians or Aztecs; the aliens allegedly following Hale-Bopp act as a type of celestial deity, with their promise of re-birth into the next evolutionary level above human. There is a tradition of sacrifice to gods of the sky in ancient cultures of the Americas, which draws links to the final moments of the Heaven's Gate group. In certain aspects of the Aztec culture the People of the Sun offered human sacrifice through providing fresh human hearts as nourishment to Huitzilopochtli, god of the Sun. There is a stronger parallel perhaps with the Skidi band of the Pawnee, who practiced ritual human sacrifice as part of the Morning Star ceremony. The ritual was performed in spring, when Mars acted as the morning star. The sacrifice was not held annually, only when a man had dreamed that Morning Star commanded him to do so, and then only if the man awoke to find the Morning Star rising. The Heaven's Gate suicides were ritualistic and, like the Skidi Morning Star ceremony, took place over several days. If Applewhite was aware of such practice is not known, however he once used the name Morgenstern; translating from the German as Morningstar, it is unlikely the name was chosen at random. Marshall Applewhite certainly had a dream that a supreme being would take him to the next level beyond human, and the comet Hale-Bopp became his personal morning star.

The Heaven's Gate suicides became a supreme sacrifice to higher beings, and an act of total devotion and belief. It is poignant, too, that the group chose springtime for such an act. Beginning on 22nd March, and lasting for three days, the suicides occurred between the spring equinox, 21st March, and the celebration of Easter, that year held on 30th March, a time in many cultures to celebrate fertility, rebirth, and new life.

Symbolism and ritual was rife in the suicides. Clothing was clearly important. The group wore identical black jumpsuits; such black outfits link to death, like those generally worn at a funeral, or also relate to a Catholic cassock, the traditional clerical garment often worn by priests. Members would often reference life at the 'monastery', their uniformed haircuts evoking something similar to the practice of tonsure, where a monk would shave their scalp as a sign of humility and devotion. The Heaven's Gate group arguably viewed their own bodies as a type of outfit, a vehicle, to be changed for something new when they entered the next level. The group all wore matching Nike Decade trainers, black, with a large white Nike logo on the side. The consistency of footwear suggests a consideration to meaning behind such a choice: the Nike swoosh, a reference to the wings of the Greek

Goddess of victory, may also resemble a passing comet. The choice of footwear may have also just been practical: it was the model of shoe that the relevant store manager could get thirty-nine pairs of in the required sizes. Sources have suggested the choice was also informed by the fact that the Nike Decades happened to be on sale, the group collecting the shoes on 1st March, paying just over $14 for each pair. The Nike tag line *Just Do It* acted as a darkly humourous motivational statement for their coming departure, a fact not lost on numerous Internet memes that appeared not long after. The line also related to an inside joke; Applewhite would sometimes wear a black woolen cap, with the Nike logo and phrase on it, and would quip 'Just *Do-h* It'.

In their matching uniforms they resembled a crew from *Star Trek* – an 'Away Team', ready to be beamed up to the passing ship. The 'Heaven's Gate Away Team' badges embroidered onto each jumpsuit were pyramid-like triangles edged in golden thread. In the writings of Theosophy, the interior of the pyramid at Giza was supposedly constructed as a literal path to spiritual enlightenment and a higher state of consciousness; it is the horizon of heaven, a heaven's gate. All members also had money in their pockets, a practice that was common with the group. For some time group members were encouraged to take a five-dollar bill and three quarters in change with them whenever they went out, this was to cover certain vagrancy laws and allow for calling back to the house if needed. Such a custom, part of a dispatching procedure to leave their home (or craft as they called it), was standard practice since the mid-1970s. Leaving Earth to beam up to the passing UFO was the group's final departure.

The inclusion of this money on their persons during the process of suicide was a symbolic reference to them having gone on a journey, and in their view leaving the planet permanently. It acted again, like the Nike shoes, as another inside joke to those in the know. Perhaps, too, it could be seen in reference to other traditions, like the passing of a fare to the boatman to cover journey to the afterlife. In the customs of the ancient Greeks and Romans, and in the associated myths of Charon's obol, coins are placed in and on the mouth of a dead person before burial. Some surviving members of the group may reject such connections, yet the symbolism, intentional or not, does suggest a religious connotation. The Catholic practice of viaticum involves a similar administering of provisions for a journey. Often this is in the form of last rites, consumption of bread and wine as part of the Eucharist, or more traditionally the provision of money necessary to make a great journey to God's kingdom.

Purple shrouds placed over the heads of deceased group members also relate to religious symbolism, mimicking the colour of the cloth placed over a cross during Lent, called a Pall, and also the shroud placed over a coffin when a priest officiates at a funeral. Such was common practice in the Presbyterian churches that Applewhite would have grown up with. In this context, purple signifies repentance, and according to David Taylor, a sociologist who studied the group, it was also Bonnie Nettles's favourite colour.

The method of suicide, a ritual in itself, involved the consumption of food – pudding or applesauce – washed down with vodka, all of which contained phenobarbital. This chosen method again evokes reference to the viaticum; it is not a crude process of suicide like a self-inflicted gunshot, but a methodical and civilized ritual. The group had all been out to a local restaurant, a branch of the Marie Callender's chain, on 21st March, the spring solstice, for their own version of a last supper, which for each member was chicken pie with cheesecake dessert.

Unlike the consumption of powdered fruit drink laced with cyanide, the chosen suicide method for Jim Jones's group, there was no sign of cohesion for the Heaven's Gate members. Jim Jones ensured mass consumption of the deadly cocktail by persuasion of armed guard; Marshall Applewhite seemed to just ask if members wanted to join him on the journey.

A Californian businessman, Nick Matzorkis, who employed Rio DiAngelo, a former member of the cult, became aware the group were about to commit, or may have already committed, suicide. DiAngelo had received a package from Heaven's Gate the day before, containing two videos and a note from the group that detailed their intentions. Members of Heaven's Gate had also sent Matzorkis an e-mail in follow-up to having done some freelance web design work for him some months previously. The somewhat cryptic message detailed being at 'critical crossroads' and of having a 'greater purpose'. The pair drove over to the mansion, and after discovering the bodies inside the house, placed an anonymous 911 call. Wearing a perfume-soaked cloth around his face DiAngelo filmed the contents of the house as a way of preserving the scene; his video was not released to the police until 2002. It was the first job of the day for Deputy Robert Brunk, and one that was initially treated with skepticism; the account of a mass suicide based around belief of a passing UFO seemed too ridiculous to be real.

The ages of the dead ranged from twenty-six to seventy-two. They died in separate groups, sixteen on the first day, fourteen on the second, and the remaining nine on the third day. Beginning on the afternoon of Saturday 22nd March, instruction was given to dress in their graduation uniforms, with members of the group assisting the first batch to depart. Beginning in one section of an upper bedroom individuals were assisted through the process,

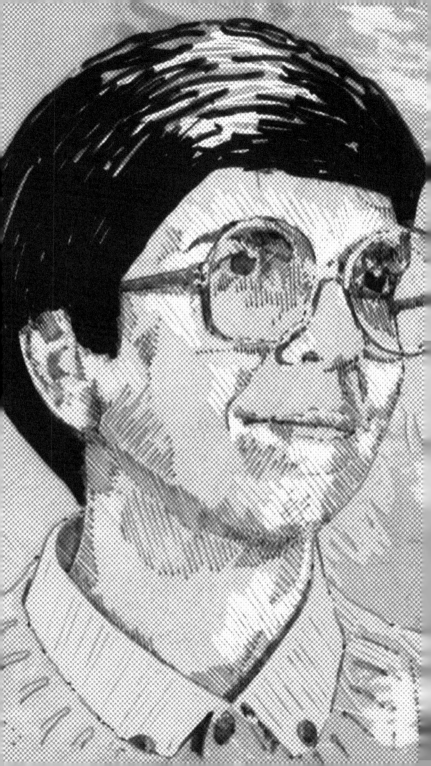

helping them to climb into bunk beds, and then positioning plastic bags to aid asphyxiation. An order was assigned for graduation; exactly the reasoning behind the order died along with the members of the group. Nevertheless, Susan Elizabeth Nora Paup, who had joined in 1975, was the first to ascend. The others who went through the process on the first day included Norma Jeanne Nelson, Ladonna Brugato, Margaret Richter, Darwin Lee Johnson, Joel Peter McCormick, Margaret Bull, Michael Howard Carrier, John Craig, Gail Maeder, Yvonne McCurdy-Hill, Lucy Eva Pesho, Thomas Nichols, Joyce Skalla, Nancy Diane Nelson, and Betty Eldrie Deal. Two groups of four used bunks in separate sections of a bedroom, done in such a way so as bunks could be filled and the room divided off into two parts, partly as a way of maintaining privacy for the departed, and partly as a way of containing the smell. Another two groups of four performed the same ritual in a second upstairs bedroom. At the end of the day the two rooms were closed off, and remaining members ate before going to bed.

The following day saw a similar process, with fourteen members of the group departing. These included Brian Alan Schaaf, Gary Jordan St Louis, Lawrence Jackson Gale, Steven Terry McCarter, Thomas Gordon Welch, Jacqueline Leonard, Lindley Ayerhart Pease, Suzanne Cooke, Judith Rowland, Erika Ernst, Dana Tracey Abreo, David Van Sinderen, and Alphonzo Foster. Last to go on Sunday was Marshall Applewhite, who was propped up on his own in the master bedroom.

Monday 24th March was slightly different. Several members of the group spent a large part of the day running errands. Cars were driven to airport parking facilities, so as they could be picked up at a later date by associates not directly part of the group. Other outstanding practicalities were resolved, such as a $2.50 library fine, before a final trip to a FedEx office to post shipments for specific individuals, such as the package sent to Rio DiAngelo. The packages were date-stamped for 4 p.m. 24th March, after which point group members returned home and continued the last stage of the departure mission. The first seven of the final members to go included David Moore, Cheryl Butcher, Raymond Alan Bowers, Robert Arancio, Jeffrey Howard Lewis, Michael Barr Sandoe, and Denise J. Thurman. Julie LaMontagne and Susan Strom assisted these remaining members, before finally committing suicide themselves; they were the only members to be found without the purple shroud. The house and the bodies inside sat still on the next day, until mid-afternoon on Wednesday 26th March when the discovery was made.

The thirty-nine members of the group had, in their belief, gone to join Bonnie Nettles in the next level. In his book *Heaven's Gate: America's UFO Religion*, Benjamin Zeller suggests that the members of the group ultimately formed a type of dualistic view of their world. Here he argues that these individuals embraced a type of dualism with the rest of society, seeing themselves as the good and wholesome saved members of a corrupt and damaged outside world, and at the same time with themselves they separated the physical body from the true self, the mind, or the spirit. Such dualism perhaps made the decision to separate oneself further from both society, and indeed the physical body, that bit easier. Many members likely did not view their final act as suicide; to them it was not death, but a transition, a graduation as they referred to it. Their belief that there was a new and better life in space offered hope beyond what they saw as a doomed planet under control of Luciferian forces.

The accounts of the Heaven's Gate suicides spread like wildfire across international news networks, with CNN initially dominating the story. Beginning the afternoon of 26th March the story rapidly grew, quickly becoming headline news across the world over the next couple of days. Journalists and reporters poured over the video testimonies left by the group, and quickly began to piece together the history of Applewhite and his followers. The day after the bodies were found, the San Diego Sheriff's Department delivered their largest ever news conference in an auditorium on the Del Mar Fairgrounds. In follow-up to the overwhelming press interest, the Sheriff's Department released a ninety-second video shot inside the mansion house. Detective Rick Scully acted as lead investigator to the Heaven's Gate incident and assessed the event as a mass suicide fairly quickly.

Marshall Applewhite appeared on the cover of *Time* magazine in April 1997, and documentaries such as the BBC-produced *Inside Story: The Cult* promptly appeared in August of that year. Brad Steiger alongside Hayden Hewes rushed a follow-up to their previous work on the group, publishing *Inside Heaven's Gate: The UFO Cult Leaders Tell Their Story in Their Own Words* in May 1997. Other books, like Rodney Perkins's *Cosmic Suicide: The Tragedy and Transcendence of Heaven's Gate* appeared as early as July. The mansion in Rancho Santa Fe was demolished several years later, and even the street name was changed. An auction of items seized from the house, held in 1999, revealed a range of contents belonging to past members, such as books including Peter Brooksmith's *UFO: the complete sightings encyclopedia*, Linda Moulton Howe's *An Alien Harvest*, and John Keel's *Disneyland of the Gods*. During the same auction a number of the metal bunk beds, which previously had been used by the group members during their final moments, were purchased by the Hollywood Museum of Death. Heaven's Gate continued to fascinate the morbid curiosity of some, and the need for answers by others. People were perplexed by what could drive so many to believe in such clearly irrational ideas.

In the first week of July 1997, barely three months after the Heaven's Gate suicides, a weeklong celebration was held in the town of Roswell to mark fifty years since the alleged UFO crash. 50000 people visited the town during the course of the anniversary festival. TV station MSNBC provided all-day live coverage from the town on 4th July, and regional and national news media focused on people dressed in alien suits and other eccentrics. In-depth UFO documentaries played frequently on both the History Channel and the Discovery Channel. *Men in Black* was released in cinemas. Articles on Roswell were featured in *Time* magazine and *Popular Mechanics*, and various books such as *Beyond Roswell* and *The Day After Roswell* were released to mark the occasion. UFOlogy groups, like MUFON, released editions of their news journals focusing on Roswell. In the town itself, lectures were given by Linda Moulton Howe, Budd Hopkins, and Stanton Friedman. The talks sold out and over 650 paying customers at a time filled the hall at the Roswell UFO conference to hear the talks. Many more stood in the aisles to get a view. They listened to the truth about Roswell, government cover-ups, alien abductions, cattle mutilation, and UFOs. They listened in silence, watching the slides click over, then applauded, and went away, a little bit wiser.

EPILOGUE
UFOs in the Age of the Internet

On the corner of Zhonghe Street, in Xinzhuang District, part of New Taipei City in Taiwan, amongst the bustle of scooters, noodle bars, and drugs stores, is a shop-front displaying an American flag upon which is a waving bespectacled cartoon figure. To the right of the flag in red letters is the sign 'Scott's English Center'. This is the school owned by Scott C. Waring, an American now living in Taiwan. It used to be called 'Scott's English School', and has at some point since 2005 been rebranded, perhaps because it's not an officially registered school at all, rather somewhere that offers a short term prep class for English language learners. Waring claims to hold a Master's degree in Counseling Education, and although this is something he mentions often in web forums, he never divulges where or when he studied. Nevertheless, the school has, according to Waring, received forty-five national awards and his students have collectively won 35% of the awards for the National English exam. I'm not quite sure what that means, but it all sounds impressive, and with credentials like that you would expect at least some documentation of the organization to exist online – but beside one very outdated website, there is nothing.

Such a lack of online promotion is surprising, as Waring does not generally seem to be a man to shy away from the potentials of digital communication. He is also the creator and owner of UFOsightingsdaily.com and its affiliated YouTube channels. The website has now gathered over 33.5 million page views, and his main YouTube channel has, since 2007, collected 17,000 subscribers with his videos being viewed over 14 million times. He also seems to operate a number of secondary YouTube accounts, such as UFOteamTNT. Waring principally scours pictures from Google Earth and the NASA database, searching for weird anomalies, glitches, blemishes or visual quirks, and in turn takes Richard Hoagland's style of pareidolia-type discoveries to bizarre extremes. Upon the surface of Mars, he claims to have discovered evidence of iguanas, polar bears, a statue of Buddha, alien crabs, squirrels and dinosaurs. He also claims the Sun is a hollow alien spaceship and that the missing Malaysian airlines flight MH370 was a result of a mass alien abduction. As well as his own content, Waring will happily recycle and re-post any UFO-related thread or video he can get away with. His activity has earned him a fair bit of press attention, especially for some reason with the British tabloid newspapers. Jon Austin is an online science reporter for the UK tabloid the *Daily Express* who seems particularly taken by Waring, often citing sensational claims made on UFOsightingsdaily as if they were news.

Waring became interested in UFOs sometime around the late 1980s. He claimed to have witnessed a UFO in 1989 over Ellsworth Air Force base in South Dakota, where he worked briefly as a contractor. Since this sighting, Waring has made claims that thousands must have witnessed the UFO over Ellsworth, though no one else has yet come forward to verify his sighting. Unperturbed by this, he has made further suggestions that there is likely an underground alien base at nearby Rapid City. The claims do however seem quite similar to an old account produced by hoaxer Richard Doty back in 1977.

In addition to his promotion of UFOs, Waring has branched into other areas of online commerce. He is involved with the site fossils.collectorchest.com, where he seems to be selling fake-looking dinosaur fossils. More recently he has established a financial retirement and savings site, key2saving.blogspot, where he suggests various life hacks to save you money – including such enticing links as 'Life saving tips for saving money on dairy products', 'tips to save money while losing weight', and 'how to make your own ultimate mosquito repellent'. He has also written several books, including *UFO sightings of 2006-2009,* and *Dragons of Asgard*, a science fiction/fantasy novel based on a UFO incident from 2008, but with added dragons.

Scott Waring's model is not unique. Blake and Brent Cousins are based in Hawaii and started making movies as teenagers, even wining an award for their amateur slasher movie short *Slaughter Day* in 1999. In 2001 the pair released *The Night Marchers*, a found-footage-style horror movie based on a local Hawaii legend. The box office success of the film (if very specific local interest in a brief showing at one theatre can be classed as box office success) has been highly exaggerated by the pair. In 2006, they produced the sequel *Night Marchers II: Return of the Ka'Ai* and a year later released the zombie-themed *Rising Dead* on DVD. Their output falls very much into the shot-on-video enthusiastic amateur category, their movies are mostly written, filmed, directed, and produced by themselves, and feature themselves and their friends in prominent roles. Such films have never received any wide attention; the quality of these early horror movies is as low as you can imagine.

In 2008, the pair made a seven-minute *Star Wars* fan film, *Chronicles of a Young Skywalker*, which went on to win a Golden Droid Award for Best Action Hero award (in 2010) and was one of twenty other films shortlisted for prizes: a collaboration between YouTube and the Guggenheim museum to support amateur film making. It was around spring 2008 that the pair created the YouTube channel thirdphaseofmoon, principally as a showcase for a number of *Star Wars* fan films they had made.

Soon after the pair began uploading a series of bottle collecting videos. Their YouTube series *Bottle Hunters of Hawaii* was originally made as a spoof version of the *UFO Hunters* TV show. Many glass bottles from the early twentieth century are frequently found in old abandoned settlement sites over Hawaii. The area around Kalaupapa, near the forest reserve on the island of Moloka'i, was used as a leprosy colony from around 1866. Glass bottles are ubiquitous in this area, and large percentages of archeological artifacts recovered in digs have been late nineteenth- to early twentieth-century glass bottles. Though most are just old beer and soda bottles, some rare bottles can sell for several hundred dollars. From the 1970s onwards, bottle collectors have been known to damage archeological sites, upturning structures, walls, and even burial sites in search of rare and valuable bottles. Various videos show Brent and Blake happily pummeling through forest reserve and settlement sites with a mechanical digger to recover bottle hoards. The videos depict dramatic leaps into deep pits, trekking through jungles, and a very *Indiana Jones* style of archeology. Having posted their digs, they were promoted by bottle collecting enthusiast and writer

Mike Polak. For a while they maintained a side business working as antique bottle collectors, seemingly affiliated with the site antiquetrader.com. They have claimed to unearth around 3,000 collectable bottles around Hawaii in a space of only two years.

Around 2009 thirdphaseofmoon began adding more otherworldly content to their channel. This was initially a combination of concepts (and content) previously made for both their horror movies and bottle collecting videos. Their history of exploiting urban myths and legends, such as local stories of the Night Marchers, or legends around buried remains at past leprosy colonies, soon expanded to include mysterious relics, ghosts, and then UFOs. Early videos of this type are clearly fabricated, and often just repackaged clips from their *Night Marchers* movies or *Bottle Hunters* videos. Artifacts discovered through bottle hunting slowly change into strange relics of the past, before being attempted to be passed off as alien artifacts.

Their UFO-themed videos started appearing in February 2010 and, following their success (at least in terms of viewing figures), they have since rebranded thirdphaseofmoon as a UFO channel. The pair has even started selling DVDs of their collected UFO footage, such as the supposed documentary *UFOs Over Hawaii*. Their strategy for self-produced hoaxed videos has been previously discussed in Part Six. Through thirdphase, the Cousins brothers have uploaded over 1,450 videos, gained 370,000 subscribers and amassed a total of 200 million views. Over thirty of their videos have exceeded a million views each. Often riddled with adverts, they are probably making several thousand dollars a month through the monetization of their YouTube videos.

YouTube operates a monetization option for its users through an advertising partner programme; this is a scheme aimed at regular uploaders with consistently large viewing numbers. Content creators earn money based on a combination of views and clicks to linked advertising sites. YouTube takes a cut, but the majority goes to the video uploader. The money earned can vary hugely, and the vast majority of users will not generate any great income through the scheme. Money from a popular video can bring in anything from a few dollars, to tens of thousands of dollars for massively popular viral videos. Chances of earning this much is similar to winning the lottery, but for some it has become a viable source of money-making.

The YouTube channel Secureteam10 was created by Tyler Glockner, from Ohio, in May 2011. Like UFOsightingsdaily and thirdphaseofmoon it is another popular UFO-themed channel with high viewing figures and a track record of low quality hoaxed video content. The majority of the videos are based around still images of badly Photoshopped UFOs or other anomalies pasted into images. Glockner has admitted to posting videos featuring voices of alleged experts and witnesses, later exposed to be that of himself using a voice pitch modulator effect. Has also used friends to pose as eyewitnesses. The channel currently has 540,000 subscribers, with total video views now over 118 million. Some of their most popular videos have excess of 3 million views each, and like Scott Waring's channel, Jon Austin of the *Daily Express* is also a fan.

Austin it seems is responsible for a large number of UFO videos going viral across the globe. Such UFO stories that treat obviously homemade hoaxes uploaded to YouTube and other sites as actual news are popular with a number of the British press – not just through Jon Austin and the *Daily Express*, but also the *Daily Mirror*, *Daily Star*, *Daily Mail* and others. Such click-bait style promotion can make these videos 700-times more popular than those that do not receive such support.

The term click-bait describes content that is aimed

at generating online advertising revenue, generally at the expense of quality or accuracy. Instead it creates attention-grabbing sensationalist headlines and imagery to attract a web hit. As is common with click-bait, the quality of any content is secondary to the promise teased in the headline or lead image. Page views generate income through associated advertisement charges; such things are particularly prevalent through social media sites, frequently creeping into personal Facebook or Twitter streams. In such a model, quantity always beats quality.

The *Daily Express* aggressively targets click-bait stories, particularly online, as a method of attracting higher volumes of traffic. Several UFO-related stories appear on the *Express* website each week, with headlines like 'Are Aliens draining our Solar system?', 'UFO Mothership caught hiding in clouds could have caused Italian earthquake', and 'Dinosaur skull found on Red planet'. It is not just UFO-related stories, but fantasy weather predictions like polar vortex storms and extremes of temperature, pseudo-science articles about miracle cancer cures and various conspiracy theories most often about the death of Princess Diana and the disappearance of Madeleine McCann. Most of these are based on dubious sources, like Positive Weather Solutions, a company proven to produce fictitious and sensational climate data, speculative accusations targeting the parents of Madeleine McCann (claims that resulted in the paper being sued for libel), and of course UFO content creators like Scott Waring and Tyler Glockner.

Such techniques can be very successful commercially, but people become wise to new scams, marketing strategies and attention-seeking campaigns. The Internet provides a platform for those making wild claims but for every thirdphaseofmoon, UFOsightingsdaily, or secureteam10, there are dozens of similar content creators that get minimal exposure. People can be temporaily sucked in by outrageous claims but, with access to online information, they can also easily double-check the facts.

People such as British historian Ben Macintyre have suggested that as a result of the easy exchange of information online, and the ability to cross-reference claims and ideas, the Internet has chased off a number of fringe ideas, such as belief in UFOs. Claims that the Internet essentially killed off the UFO phenomenon circulated in the early years of the new millennium, as various websites revealed the deception evident within classic sightings. This growth of reasoned rationality in the age of the Internet is supported by Allen Downey, a computer scientist at Olin College of Engineering in Massachusetts, who suggested after a study of data that the use of the web is also resulting in a drop in religious belief. Downey also found higher levels of education and a general reduction in religious influence in childhood had also contributed to the trend. Though interestingly UFOs and religious belief do not always go hand in hand. Research has shown that strong religious belief often goes in countenance to a belief in extraterrestrial life, with atheists statistically more likely to report such a belief compared to those who practice a religion.

Professor Steven Reiss, a psychologist at Ohio State University, has argued that strong belief, such as belief in God, is driven by a set of basic human desires, such as curiosity, idealism, social contact, acceptance, status, and tranquility. If the Internet age is indeed damaging faith in mainstream traditional religious beliefs, then perhaps there is a vacuum of human desire that many will seek to refill. As more question the old traditional beliefs, perhaps in turn they will seek to fill the void with some other new belief.

UFO belief since the turn of the century has been one of peaks and troughs, though the general trend, and in particular any narrative concerning a government cover-up, is broadly on the rise. A 2001 study regarding belief in UFOs by American adults estimated 33% of them were open to such ideas. By 2005 this number had dropped to 24%, though by 2015 this number had then increased to 45%. Since 2012 there have been, on average, 6,500 UFO reports collected by MUFON each year, up from an average of 4,500 in 2008. According to MUFON the total number of reported sightings of UFOs again increased 35% in 2015 from the previous year. During the first years of the twenty-first century, the Internet it seems did not kill off the UFO – rather just recalibrated it during a phase when such things were less in fashion.

The Internet has the capacity to paradoxically explain and debunk fringe ideas while exposing people to wilder ideas (and apparent supporting evidence) to a far greater extent than they had ever previously imagined. Establishing what is real, what is fiction, and what is exaggeration in the multitude of available options can be difficult. Similar to ideas found within pareidolia, Gestalt theory approaches the mind's ability to create meaningful patterns within apparent chaos. Taking its name from the German name for shape, it builds on the theory of Holism, which suggests natural systems (such as biological ones) should be viewed as a whole, rather than as individual parts. Gestalt psychology tries to understand our ability to acquire and maintain meaningful perceptions within disorder. These perceptions are the resulting sum of the various parts of complex interactions amongst different stimuli. The Gestalt effect concerns our ability to generate whole forms when presented with a collection of unrelated elements. When applied to imagery, for example, such an effect can be observed when the mind joins unconnected lines to complete a shape or recognizable image, like a face. The idea can be translated into an understanding of unrelated concepts, ideas, or observations to produce a whole theory, such as when a belief in a UFO claim is formed online by a collective amount of found 'evidence', when random unconnected pieces of information form to create a unified vision. The mind gets to work filling in the blanks.

The American writer on technology and culture Nicholas Carr has written about the impact Internet use has had on the neurological structure of our brains. In his book *The Shallows: What the Internet is doing to our Brains*, Carr argues that frequent exposure to the Internet as a feed for information can have a detrimental effect on cognition, and can potentially diminish the capacity for concentration and contemplation. He argues that through the Internet, information is not scrutinized but rather just explored rapidly, and often out of context. How and what is consumed is governed more by what is popular, rather than what is accurate. This encourages information-seeking in two main ways: firstly, a process of confirmation bias, when information is sought to support an existing belief or view, and second, a search with no preconceived idea, when a person becomes strongly influenced by whatever information reaches them first.

Through a cognitive bias, people can easily filter out conflicting ideas and the Internet can make easier such processes, or indeed exaggerate the method even further. The Internet-based political activist Eli Pariser describes the idea of a filter bubble, a result of a personalized online search that is governed through the selective algorithms of a person's search history. Search engines, such as Google, and selective newsfeeds through social media like Facebook, or video recommendations on YouTube, display information of a particular type to match the habits of the user; they guess what you are interested in and prioritize more of the same. An increase in searches for one particular topic or idea can then begin to separate a user from information that conflicts with their regular interests. So is created the filter bubble, and the further toward an area of interest a user searches, such as evidence for UFOs, the more they will be surrounded by information that supports such ideas. The bubble becomes stronger – and becomes harder to burst.

Pariser is also concerned that greater exposure to a filter bubble scenario may make people more susceptible and vulnerable to propaganda and manipulation. As well as video sites like YouTube, many Internet discussion forums deal with fringe ideas, such as UFOs. One of the most popular for such topics is abovetopsecret.com, which appeared around 1999. Established by Simon Gray, the site has gradually become one of the most popular discussion boards online for conspiracy theories, truth movement topics and UFO accounts, with over 9.5 million posts filling its pages. Abovetopsecret may also have been partially responsible for encouraging one of its members to commit mass murder.

Jared Lee Loughner killed six people in January 2011, during a constituent meeting in Tuscon, Arizona. Just after 10 a.m., Loughner had unloaded his newly purchased Glock pistol at close range into the crowd. Among the dead were Chief US District Court Judge John Roll and a nine-year-old bystander. He severely injured US Representative Gabrielle Giffords (with whom he had a particular obsession), as well as thirteen other people. Loughner had joined the Abovetopsecret forum site in early 2009, going by the username Erad3. He became an avid poster, and sought a replacement online community after becoming increasingly distant from his off-line friends and family. His friend Zach Osler had noted that after Loughner began spending more time posting and reading content on Abovetopsecret, he became increasingly obsessed with conspiracy theories, which went on to have a profound effect on his wider perception of society. He had also become an avid poster on both YouTube and his MySpace account, venting about the US government, with Giffords, the local representative of such an organization, developing into a specific target. Loughner gradually came to believe a range of strange ideas: that the space shuttles and the International Space Station were flying empty, that NASA was faking its Mars Rover missions, and that the US Government was engaged in a process of mass mind control through its manipulation of grammar. To help contemplate such ideas, Loughner had erected an occult altar with a mock human skull in a tent in his backyard. He is now in a prison for inmates with specialized mental health issues, where he will stay for the rest of his life, having been sentenced to 140 years without parole.

Sites such as Abovetopsecret act as an echo chamber, an enclosed system of discussion, where information, ideas or beliefs are amplified or re-enforced by transmission or repetition. Participants in online communities may often find their own opinions constantly echoed back at them, which then cements their own belief system. Those with different or competing views may be censored, under-represented, labeled trolls, or barred from accessing a particular discussion group in the first place.

The Internet has also created a playing field where any and every conspiracy theory is fighting for attention, and UFOlogy is but one of many competing paradigms. This has created a situation where everything is up for grabs, and cross-pollination of theories is rampant. Mind control through water contamination mixes with the hoaxed Moon landings mixes with theories of a flat Earth and anti-vaccination groups mix with UFO enthusiasts and those in fear of the Illuminati. This process embraces the type of social bricolage that Claude Lévi-Strauss was describing in his 1962 work *The Savage Mind*. Here Strauss discusses society's method of creating solutions to social issues, or indeed creating such issues, by the combination of resources, ideas and attitudes already existing, but perhaps re-appropriated from their original context.

During the first decades of the twenty-first century, the first truly digital age, through the Internet and online forums, social media groups, video chats and the near-infinite information on websites, what is real and what is fiction blends to such an extent that it can be difficult to know which is which. Such concepts relate to the idea of hyper-reality, as proposed by the likes of Jean Baudrillard and Umberto Eco, which describes the inability to distinguish reality from a simulation of reality. An immersive video game or virtual reality experience is one such example, but more persuasive to someone's beliefs may be frequent exposure to an online community of contacts exploring their own wayward takes on reality.

In the realm of hyper-reality, the UFO phenomenon is valid, in so much as some people believe in such things, report them and investigate them, yet many of the claims made around the phenomenon are clearly fictional; it is simultaneously real and unreal, fact intertwined with fantasy. Writer and blogger Robbie Graham, who has discussed aspects of the interplay between UFOs and Hollywood, explores further the idea of UFOs and hyper-reality through his book *Silver Screen Saucers: Sorting Fact from Fantasy in Hollywood's UFO Movies*. Here he argues that accounts of UFOs feed pop culture just as much, if not more, than pop culture influencing accounts of UFOs. Examples include many mainstream movies that take as their influence supposedly real UFO experiences, such as *Earth Vs The Flying Saucers*, which was based on a number of allegedly factual encounters recorded in the writings of Donald Keyhoe. But it is not the passive act of watching film that has allowed ideas of the hyper-real to engulf belief; it may have blossomed during the glory years of cinema, but really it is the interactive power of the Internet that has borne the fruits of hyper-reality.

For some, belief in UFOs is a reality, or certainly a more exciting one that they would prefer, as opposed to the one where UFOs do not exist. A choice to surround one's self in supporting ideas can make such a hyper-reality come to life: these things exist if you want them to. The Internet is alive with evidence of UFOs through witness statements, accusations of cover-ups, amazing videos, talks, discussion forums, and photographs. You just need to look in the right place.

Members of the Heaven's Gate group were avid users of the Internet, however such practice came relatively late in the history of the cult. No doubt they would have greater used the resources available online had their collective formed after the Internet boom of the 1990s. Despite the ongoing presence of their website, and their history of making a living through web design, it is not accurate to describe them as an Internet cult. Other conspiracy theories that have blossomed through the first decades of the twenty-first century, most notably the 9/11 truth movement, could however be more appropriately described as cults born through the Internet, but all of that is indeed another story.

The desire to look into content that supports the notion of extraterrestrial UFOs is not something that has confined itself to the twentieth century, nor is the creation of such contemporary folk-myths something that has run its course. In the right circles, the UFO phenomenon is alive and well. John Witness recorded a UFO over Devon in January 2016, describing it as a black object in the shape of a classic flying saucer. Around a week later, an 'alien' hum was recorded around Bristol. A month later, around the same area, Fiona Powell spotted a strange flying object near Bristol's port. That same month Glen Richardson, a Hartlepool-based UFO researcher, reported sights such as a silent rocket, a white glowing object, and even sighting of a teleporting man. In April, flashing lights were seen above the skies of Liverpool; residents such as Stephen Carrison reported the sightings over northern parts of the city around Bootle and Anfield. August saw emergence of a video of a UFO around part of rural Lincolnshire, filmed only a week after the release online of a UFO documentary by Richard D. Hall suggesting the recent disappearance of 1,500 sheep in the area was the result of alien abduction.

In America, the summer of 2016 seemed to be a time of particular activity for UFO spotters too. In July, footage of a flying object was recorded above Charlottesville, Virginia. The video recorded three bright lights in a triangle formation, with a central flashing orange light. The following month, in Cold Spring, New York, a resident reported seeing two objects moving high up in the sky above the Hudson River. A few days later, fifty-miles upstate in Saugerties, a circular object was spotted that appeared out of nowhere in the Eastern sky before travelling south. Over in St Louis, Missouri, surveillance footage recorded at Malcolm W. Martin Memorial Park picked up a strange light hovering above the gateway arch. Chase Rhoads, who said he had seen something strange in the sky and felt the need to record it, also took further footage, apparently of the same light. Another UFO was seen over the small town of Abilene, Kansas, when a witness on a walk in a local park saw an odd light in the sky and recorded the object for about a minute. The video is now being promoted on Scott Waring's UFOsightingsdaily website, along with his recent discovery of a giant worm on Mars and some UFOs spotted passing the International Space Station.

The belief in the fantastical will always be there

to tempt the mind into coming up with solutions for things we don't truly understand. In many ways it is part of human nature, and just a response to the culture and society in which people live, the ideas they absorb, and the possibilities they consider. The 1961 novel *Solaris*, by Polish writer Stanisław Lem, explores the futile attempts of communication between humans and a very alien life form from a distant ocean planet. Studies of this far-away ocean reveal it to be a large all-encompassing organism, that seems to have the ability to expose the observational scientists aboard the orbiting *Solaris Station* to their own personal, and most painful, repressed thoughts and feelings. On board *Solaris*, Dr Kris Kelvin is confronted by a materialization of his dead ex-wife, and is forced to deal with feelings of guilt around her suicide. This physical simulacrum is the alien creature's attempt to communicate, and despite Kelvin's attempts to rid himself of the visitor, the manifestation keeps returning in repeatedly tormenting ways.

The book becomes a meditation on the nature of human memory and a philosophical exploration of man's anthropomorphic limitations. The alien ocean in *Solaris* is open enough for interpretation for it to act as a successful metaphor for many things. A massive alien brain, it may be a reflection of our human consciousness, or perhaps faith, or indeed just belief itself. One thing it probably wasn't a metaphor of, but could work well for retrospectively, is the Internet, and in particular the dissemination of illogical ideas like UFO belief through such a system. Although the foundation for much of what we understand today as the Internet and the World Wide Web developed in the early 1980s, much of the groundwork emerged from the growth in electronic computers through the 1950s and '60s when Lem was writing *Solaris*. The potential of digital communication was still in its infancy when Lem wrote his novel, but it became something he certainly considered as time went by. In his later life Lem became critical of modern technology, and in particular was not a fan of the Internet. He was concerned the Internet could be used as a tool to spread misinformation, and as a new opportunity for wrongdoing. Similar to the ocean's intelligence, the Internet communicates through amassing information and distributing certain parts of it to those who make searches of personal interest. In this alien cyberspace our darkest desires and most repressed fears and wonderings can be accessed and explored through a few simple clicks. In a further interesting metaphor, the only version of *Solaris* currently in print in English language is a version translated from Polish into French and then into English, resulting in places in a few misspellings and loss or change of meaning to certain sentences. The Internet's ability to present things slightly askew of their original context, and through numerous filters and re-tellings can result in similar changes in meaning and context, allowing fringe ideas to develop and make themselves aware to those who search for such things. Like Kelvin's dead wife, UFOs, and conspiracy theories in general, are a type of simulacrum for the repressed concerns, paranoia and wonderings of the end of the twentieth century, and the beginning of the twenty-first, that keep returning, again and again into current times, refreshed, reimagined and considered anew in the mind of the believer.

List of Illustrations

All images contained within this book were produced during 2015 - 2017. The full series of works that form the *And They Witness Light Across The Sky* portfoilio is reproduced in the hardback art edition of this book (ISBN: 978-0-9894462-2-8)

The sample of works included in this edition have been formatted for black and white reproduction.

1. *Karl-Gosta Bartoll*
Originally produced with acrylic, ink and emulsion on ceramic tile and acetate. (2016) 26 x 20cm
This edition, black and white manipulation (2017)
[p 6]

2. *Betty & Barney Hill*
Originally produced with acrylic, ink and emulsion on ceramic tile and acetate. (2016) 20 x 16cm
This edition, black and white manipulation (2017)
[p 33]

3. *James E McDonald*
Originally produced with acrylic, ink and emulsion on ceramic tile and acetate. (2016) 20 x 24cm
This edition, black and white manipulation (2017)
[p 38]

4. *Lonnie Zamora*
Originally produced with acrylic, ink and emulsion on ceramic tile and acetate. (2016) 22 x 25cm
This edition, black and white manipulation (2017)
[p 57]

5. *Gray Barker*
Originally produced with acrylic, ink and emulsion on ceramic tile and vellum. (2016) 22 x 15cm
This edition, black and white manipulation (2017)
[p 70]

310

6. John Podesta
Originally produced with acrylic, ink and emulsion on ceramic tile and acetate. (2017) 21 x 26cm
This edition, black and white manipulation (2017)
[p 89]

7. Yuri Gagarin
Originally produced with acrylic, ink and emulsion on ceramic tile and acetate. (2016) 26 x 20cm
This edition, black and white manipulation (2017)
[p 102]

8. Enrico Fermi
Originally produced with acrylic, ink and emulsion on ceramic tile and acetate. (2016) 21 x 24cm
This edition, black and white manipulation (2017)
[p 130]

9. George Lucas
Originally produced with acrylic, ink and emulsion on ceramic tile and acetate. (2016) 21 x 24cm
This edition, black and white manipulation (2017)
[p 136]

10. Carl Jung
Originally produced with acrylic, ink and emulsion on ceramic tile and acetate. (2015) 26 x 21cm
This edition, black and white manipulation (2017)
[p 151]

11. Stanton T Friedman
Originally produced with acrylic, ink and emulsion on ceramic tile and acetate. (2017) 25 x 21cm
This edition, black and white manipulation (2017)
[p 170]

12. *Paul Trent*
Originally produced with acrylic, ink and emulsion on ceramic tile and acetate. (2017) 22 x 19cm
This edition, black and white manipulation (2017)
[p 189]

13. *Charles Fort*
Originally produced with acrylic, ink and emulsion on ceramic tile and acetate. (2017) 24 x 19cm
This edition, black and white manipulation (2017)
[p 210]

14. *Ruth Norman*
Originally produced with acrylic, ink and emulsion on ceramic tile and acetate. (2017) 26 x 22cm
This edition, black and white manipulation (2017)
[p 227]

15. *Marshall Applewhite & Bonnie Nettles*
Originally produced with acrylic, ink and emulsion on ceramic tile and acetate. (2016) 21 x 16cm
This edition, black and white manipulation (2017)
[p 254]

16. *Susan Elizabeth Nora Paup*
Originally produced with acrylic, ink and emulsion on ceramic tile and acetate. (2016) 21 x 24cm
This edition, black and white manipulation (2017)
[p 287]

About The Author

Kevin Storrar is an artist and researcher based in the UK. He studied Fine Art at the University of Wales, Aberystwyth, and at Lancaster University. He has worked professionally in the arts for over ten years, including work within the Museum and Gallery sector. He has produced imagery and cover work for a number of books. *And They Witness Light Across the Sky* is his first own full length text.

Further information, writing, and images are available via the artists website:
www.kevinstorrar.com

Index

Lightning Source UK Ltd.
Milton Keynes UK
UKHW020630270519
343383UK00012B/1311/P